Behavioural Treatment of Children with Problems

A PRACTICE MANUAL

D1057583

The title of this revised and updated version of the 1981 manual *Behavioural Treatment of Problem Children* incorporates a minor change so as to provide a more elegant description of its subject matter: *children with problems*

Dr Martin Herbert is Professor of Clinical Psychology and Head of the Psychology Department, at the University of Leicester. He has wide experience in child guidance and was a Clinical Psychologist at the Institute of Psychiatry at the Maudsley Hospital. More recently he has acted as Consultant Psychologist to a Paediatric Assessment Centre.

As Director of the Centre for Behavioural Work with Families, University of Leicester, the author, with his colleagues, has been evolving ideas and methods based upon developmental, clinical and behavioural theory for the assessment and treatment of children in the clinic, but more particularly in the natural environment of the home and classroom. Dr Herbert has long practice in teaching these methods to students and professionals engaged in the study of child psychopathology and behaviour modification.

Behavioural Treatment of Children with Problems

A PRACTICE MANUAL

Martin Herbert

Psychology Department
University Of Leicester, England

1987

ACADEMIC PRESS
Harcourt Brace Jovanovich, Publishers
London · Orlando · San Diego · New York
Austin · Boston · Sydney · Tokyo · Toronto

ACADEMIC PRESS INC. (LONDON) LTD.
24/28 Oval Road.
London NW1 7DX

United States Edition published by
ACADEMIC PRESS, INC.
Orlando, Florida 32887

British Library Cataloguing in Publication Data

Herbert, Martin
  Behavioural treatment of children with
  problems: a practice manual. – 2nd ed.
  1. Problem children   2. Behaviour therapy
  I. Title   II. Herbert, Martin. Behavioural
  treatment of problem children
  618.9′289142   RJ506.P63

  ISBN 0-12-341470-9 casebound
  ISBN 0-12-341471-7 paperback

Phototypeset by
Dobbie Typesetting Service, Plymouth, Devon

Printed in Great Britain by
St Edmundsbury Press, Bury St Edmunds, Suffolk

Preface

This revised and updated manual (previously entitled *Behavioural Treatment of Problem Children*), is a practical guide to the behavioural assessment and treatment of emotional and conduct problems of childhood. And it is a guide only! The style of manual writing may well convey an unintended impression of dogmatic inflexibility. There is no one way of carrying out assessments and behavioural programmes. There is nothing preordained about the ordering of the steps suggested.

The practice ideas in this manual are based upon theoretical and conceptual themes developed in more detail (and taking due account of the evidence) in two books by the author: *Emotional Problems of Development in Children* and *Conduct Disorders of Childhood and Adolescence: A Social Learning Perspective*. A problem-solving model informs many of the ideas to be found in the following pages; this is in keeping with my basic attitude to most problems of childhood. Senn (1959) expresses it more succinctly than I can:

> The problem child is invariably trying to solve a problem rather than be one. His methods are crude and his conception of his problem may be faulty, but until the physician has patiently sought, and in a sympathetic fashion found, what the child was trying to do . . . he is in no position to offer advice.

The text is written with various student and professional groups in mind: psychologists, psychiatrists, probation officers, social workers, teachers and school counsellors. It is also intended for care and teaching staff in residential establishments such as community homes, assessment centres and schools for the maladjusted. Although there is a bias (for reasons that are given) towards work in the natural environment of the child, the manual should prove helpful to the clinic-based therapist.

Given the constraints of being concise and practical I have attempted to provide only the briefest account of the basic assumptions about children's problems and the theories that inform the practice of behaviour modification (and therapy). The emphasis is very much on the 'nuts and bolts' of assessment and of designing and implementing treatment programmes for children. Illustrations of the methods in practice are provided in brief case analyses. A manual can only give a *general* set of guidelines: specific problems (such as bowel or bladder incontinence, animal phobias, school refusal and the like) require specific refinements and elaborations of the *basic* approach.

The book is organized into six sections which follow the stages of a problem-solving exercise. After all, as was suggested, the child is usually trying to solve a problem, and so are parents and teachers in trying to cope with the ensuing crisis. Our task then is to use problem-solving methods to identify the areas of difficulty (and they are not always necessarily his alone), and to find practical solutions to them.

The first section examines the basic assumptions underlying the concept of 'problem behaviour' in childhood, and goes on to list the major implications of a behavioural approach to such problems.

The second section is concerned with the initial screening (Steps 1 to 6) and the early definition and specification of the particular problem/s in the individual case.

The third section (Steps 7 to 13) deals with the collection of data and information which will allow you to help the clients (with their active participation) to solve a child's (or, indeed, it may really be the family's) problems. It contains an extended consideration of the factors which influence the therapist's decision to intervene — extended because it can be such a complex technical *and* ethical issue. This section is also concerned with the formulation of hypotheses to explain the clients' predicament and the planning of strategies to undo the harm and misery being generated in the child and/or his family.

The fourth section (Steps 14 to 18) deals with the therapeutic intervention and the evaluation and verification of the choices made (i.e. the testing of the clinical hypotheses upon which the programme is based). This section also explains how to fade out and terminate the problem solving exercise.

An account of the salient issues in parent training is given in Section 5, it is illustrated by three detailed case studies.

The sixth section is concerned with the choice of alternative procedures, the theories of human behaviour and learning that lie behind them, and how to put them into effect.

Martin Herbert

Acknowledgements

It is impossible to acknowledge by name all those to whom I am indebted for ideas, research findings and case material which appear in this manual.

However I would like to express my appreciation to colleagues at the Centre for Behavioural Work with Families (formerly the Child Treatment Research Unit), notably Professor Derek Jehu, Dr Keith Turner, Dr Roger Morgan, Dr Carole Sutton. I owe a particular debt to Dr Dorota Iwaniec whose clinical skill has been an inspiration to her students and myself.

Contents

Preface   v
Acknowledgements   vii

SECTION 1   BASIC ASSUMPTIONS   1

SECTION 2   INTRODUCTION: INITIAL SCREENING   8

            Step 1   Explain yourself   11
            Step 2a   Identify the problems   12
            Step 2b   Identify the child's assets   14
            Step 3   Discover the desired outcomes   15
            Step 4   Construct a problem profile   17
            Step 5   Teach clients to think in ABC terms   17
            Step 6   Establish problem priorities   22

SECTION 3   FROM DATA COLLECTION TO
            PROBLEM FORMULATION   25

            Step 7   Specifying situations   27
            Step 8   Assess the extent and severity
                        of the problem   29
            Step 8a   Provide client with appropriate material   31
            Step 8b   Find out the frequency of the behaviour   37
            Step 8c   Find out how intense the problem is   42
            Step 8d   How many problems are being
                        manifested by the child?   44
            Step 8e   There are two 'duration of problem'
                        questions   49
            Step 9   Assess the contingencies   50
            Step 10a   Identify reinforcers   56

Step 10b   What *sense* or meaning is there in the
           problem behaviour?   60
Step 11   Assess organismic variables   61
Step 12   Arrive at a diagnostic decision   65
Step 13   Formulate the problem   70

SECTION 4   THE INTERVENTION   82

Step 14a   Plan the treatment programme   83
Step 14b   Formulate objectives   88
Step 14c   Select your procedures and methods   91
Step 14d   Treatment plan   94
Step 15   Work out the practicalities of the
           treatment programme   95
Step 16   Evaluate the programme   98
Step 17   Initiate the programme   109
Step 18   Phase out and terminate treatment   110
Step 18a   Fade out the programme gradually   113

SECTION 5   FAMILY-ORIENTATED BEHAVIOURAL WORK   116

Illustrative Case studies: 125
1. Treatment of conduct disorder   125
2. Treatment of emotional disorder   141
3. Treatment of child abuse   144

SECTION 6   METHODS OF TREATMENT   151

Methods for increasing behaviour (Procedures 1 to 7) 151
Methods for reducing behaviour (Procedures 8 to 22) 183

APPENDIX I   Guide to the Application of Procedures   235
APPENDIX II   An Interview Guide   239
APPENDIX III Handouts for Parents attending the Centre 243
APPENDIX IV   Relaxation Training   252
APPENDIX V   Monitoring and Analysing Behaviour
              and Knowledge   256

References   262
Further Reading   270
Index   272

SECTION 1

Basic Assumptions

---

1. *Good theory generates good practice.*

A consistent theoretical framework is desirable in order to change children's (and sometimes, their caregivers') problematic behaviour. Such consistency demands a clear conceptualization of what constitutes a psychological problem and how it comes about.

2. *Childhood behaviour problems, by and large, are exaggerations, deficits, or handicapping combinations of behaviours common to all children.*

After all, we are talking about phenomena such as aggression, disobedience, fear, depression, school refusal, shyness, stealing. The evidence suggests that there is no absolute distinction between the attributes of those who come to be labelled 'problem children' and other unselected children. Most problematic conditions differ quantitatively from the normal in terms of severity and of accompanying impairment—the sort of difference there is between (say) a somewhat anxious child and a child with a school phobia.

No child is *all* problem! Minor variations of behavioural problems can be identified in most essentially 'well-adjusted' children. A majority of children have tantrums (to take an example) at one time or another. Some, however, display incessant and extreme explosions of temper. In other words normality and abnormality are viewed as the extremes of a continuum; normality merges almost imperceptibly into abnormality so that any child may be more or less problematic—but only with regard to particular characteristics. It's a matter of degree.

But if it is a matter of degree, how do you draw the line?

3. *The criteria are social ones and therefore relative.*

The word 'norm' means a standard—in the Latin from which it derives. To be abnormal implies (the prefix 'ab' means 'away from') a deviation from a standard. People, as individuals or as members of groups (families, neighbourhoods, religious communities, societies), make the rules and set the standards of behaviour. For this reason, therapists must beware of their personal and social biases, not to mention prejudices in making judgements.

Not only is problematic (abnormal) behaviour in children on a continuum with non-problematic (normal) behaviour, but it does not differ, by and large, from normal behaviour in its development, its persistence, and the way in which it can be modified.

It is hypothesized that a major proportion of a child's behaviour is learned, maintained, and regulated by its effect upon the natural environment and the feedback it receives with regard to these consequences. Behaviour does not occur in a vacuum. It is a result of a complex transaction between the individual, with his or her inborn strengths and weaknesses, acting and reacting with an environment which sometimes encourages and sometimes discourages certain actions.

4. Many behaviour problems are the consequences of failures or distortions of learning.

The laws of learning which apply to the acquisition and changing of normal socially approved behaviour are assumed to be relevant to the understanding of socially disapproved (problem) actions. Unfortunately—and it is the case with all forms of learning—the very processes which help the child adapt to life can, under certain circumstances, contribute to maladaptation. An immature child who learns by imitating an adult is not necessarily to comprehend when it is undesirable (deviant) behaviour that is being modelled. The youngster who learns (adaptively) on the basis of classical and instrumental conditioning processes to avoid dangerous situations can also learn in the same way (maladaptively) to avoid school or social gatherings. A mother or father may unwittingly reinforce immature behaviour by attending to it.

But there is much more to learning—and learning to behave dysfunctionally—than is conveyed by these examples as we shall see in Point 5.

5. Behavioural work as described in this manual is based upon the assumption that cognitive processes are critical in human learning.

A cognitive behavioural approach emphasizes, indeed depends upon, an explicit understanding by the client of procedures and goals, responsibilities and risks. It is assumed, at the 'microlevel' of teaching new responses and strategies, that learning and conditioning in humans is produced most often—perhaps invariably in adults—through the operation of higher mental processes. Awareness on the part of the child is particularly encouraged.

6. A social learning approach is particularly relevant.

Learning occurs within a social nexus; rewards, punishments and other events are mediated by human agents and within attachment and social systems, and are not simply the impersonal consequences of behaviour. Human beings do not simply respond to stimuli; they interpret them. As Bandura (1977a) puts it: 'Stimuli influence the likelihood of particular behaviours through their predictive function, not because they are automatically linked to responses by occurring together. In the social learning view, contingent experiences create expectations rather than stimulus-response connections'.

7. *There is a reciprocal influence and relationship between behaviour and environment.*

Bandura (1977a) states that the dictum 'change behaviour and you change contingencies' should be added to the better known 'change contingencies and you change behaviour'. By their *actions* (and humans are active agents not simply passively reacting organisms) people play a *positive* role in producing the reinforcing contingencies that impinge upon them.

8. *Behaviour modification (behaviour therapy) is an educational and a therapeutic process.*

There are three main settings in which behavioural work with children takes place. Therapy based on the dyadic (one-to-one) model tends to take place in the clinic. The treatment of 'neurotic' and stress disorders (with varying degrees of involvement of parents) is likely to occur in the clinic, although there is nothing absolute about such a demarcation. These problems tend to be of relatively short-term duration (Herbert, 1974). Behavioural training based on the triadic model (using significant caregivers or teachers as mediators of change) generally takes place in the home or in the school. Although the distinction between treatment and training is, at times, indistinct, the treatment model is most appropriate to the 'emotional' disorders of childhood (fears and phobias etc.) the training model to the longer-term problems (antisocial behaviour and mental handicap).

9. *The behavioural approach has crucial implications for the way in which therapists work, as well as where they work.*

It affects the manner in which they listen to the caregiver's complaints about the child's behaviour, and the methods by which they later explore the specific details of the problems.

If it is accepted that problematic behaviours of childhood are acquired largely as a function of faulty learning processes, then there is a case for arguing that certain problems can most effectively be modified where they occur, by changing the 'social lessons' the child receives. The clinician mobilizes, and capitalizes on the significance of parents and other significant caregivers for children's development and mental health.

Several lines of reasoning converge to reinforce the logic of the triadic approach of involving parents (and others in the natural environment) in the work with psychological problems of childhood. First, prevention is better than cure! As parents and teachers exert a significant formative influence during the impressionable years of early childhood, they are usually in a strong position to enhance satisfactory adjustment and moderate the genesis of behaviour problems. Secondly, they are in a good position to generalize beneficial changes (brought about in therapy) to other children in the family, and to various life-situations.

10. The triadic model facilitates long-term change.

Home-based therapy/classroom based behavioural work is geared to the only people — parents and teachers or substitute caregivers — who can intervene often enough and long enough to produce the long-term changes in what are often (especially in the case of the more serious problems of childhood) matters of faulty socialization. After all the parents are 'on the spot' most of the time to initiate and consolidate social learning experiences.

11. All this presupposes a cooperative working alliance between the parent and the helping professional, both of whom are interested in the welfare of the child.

By no means are all caregivers motivated to change, or to care for their children; and casework may be necessary to bring them to the point of working on their interactions and relationship with their offspring.

12. Maladaptive behaviour can most effectively be changed by the therapeutic application of principles of learning.

Inappropriate behaviour that has been learned can be unlearned or modified directly (often in relatively brief periods of treatment) on the basis of applied learning principles. Behaviour that has not been learned (and where the deficit constitutes a problem) may be acquired by training.

13. To simplify: there are certain basic learning tasks that are commonly encountered in child therapy:

(a) the acquisition (i.e. learning) of a desired behaviour in which the individual is deficient (e.g. compliance, self-control, bladder and bowel control, fluent speech, social or academic skills);
(b) the reduction or elimination (i.e. unlearning) of an unwanted response in the child's behavioural repertoire (e.g. aggression, temper tantrums, stealing, facial tics, phobic anxiety, compulsive eating) or the exchange of one response for another (e.g. self-assertion in place of tearful withdrawal).

14. *Each of these tasks may be served by one or a combination of four major types of learning:*

(a) classical conditioning;
(b) operant conditioning;
(c) observational learning; and
(d) cognitive learning.

15. *Behaviour modification (or behaviour therapy) provides us with the practice 'know-how' for using these learning (and other psychological) principles for therapeutic (or, as some problems represent deficits) educative and training purposes.*

16. *All parents are informal learning theorists and all are in the business of behaviour modification (i.e. changing behaviour).*

They use various techniques to teach, influence and change the child in their care. Among those used are material and psychological rewards, praise and encouragement, giving or withholding approval, and other psychological punishments such as reproof or disapproval. They give direct instructions, set an example and provide explanations of rules (i.e. inductive methods). Of course they do not always use them systematically and certainly not on the basis of a theoretical knowledge-base or a planned assessment. Although parents are unfamiliar with the 'small print' of learning theory, *behavioural methods* do tend to have face validity for many of them. They are, in essence, so much like the methods they use day-to-day, but of course, without the technical jargon.

There are wide variations, in terms of type and extent of parental involvement in therapeutic work in the natural environment, ranging from carrying out simple instructions in contingency management to a full involvement as co-therapists in all aspects of observation, recording, programme planning and implementation.

17. *Behavioural work starts from a clear objective of producing change.*

The assessment in which the child and his or her parents (and perhaps teachers) are closely involved, attempts to identify precisely what behaviours are to be changed. What can be said about these behaviours—the subject of this manual—is that they bring disadvantage and disablement to a multitude of troubled and troublesome children, and indeed, their families.

18. *Behaviour modification, however, is not only about changing the undesirable behaviour of 'problem children'.*

We have already stressed the fact that learning occurs in a social context; children are interacting with, and learning from people who have meaning and value for them. They are attached to some, feel antipathetic to others; they may perceive a gesture of affection from the former as 'rewarding', but from the latter as 'aversive'. Even infants are not simply passive reactors to events; they initiate actions and make things happen. Not surprisingly, behaviour modification does not concentrate only on the 'unacceptable' behaviour of the child. It is also about altering the behaviour of the persons — parents, teachers and others — who form a significant part of the child's social world.

Here is a crucial source of human variety — the susceptibility of people to many different types of environment. It provides their source of strength and (of course) weakness. The human ability to learn afresh new ways of living or to unlearn self-defeating means of coping with existence makes behaviour modification an optimistic and exciting venture.

19. *Therapy must be an ethical endeavour; behavioural work can (and must) have a human face.*

Behaviour modification, like all other therapies, is open to abuse. However, it should constitute a compassionate and moral response to the need for help of children and families in acute distress. The moral and ethical issues will be dealt with in detail.

20. *Behaviour modification is a craft; that is to say it is, or should be, a subtle amalgam of art and applied science; as such it requires careful study and apprenticeship — which in turn imply supervised practice experience.*

The latter is not always available. The trouble with a manual as a guide is the author's inability to pre-empt all the essential questions the reader would like answers to, let alone those important supplementaries — points of clarification or elaboration, and those unexpected, unplanned for, exigencies of practice. The manual cannot legislate for those times when one should be flexible in the approach; it cannot indicate when the nature of the problem being dealt with or your level of experience, makes it appropriate to take 'short cuts' (i.e. to compress or, indeed, leave out certain steps). Nor does it tell you when extra information not mentioned in these pages is required.

Certainly, the writing of this manual as a training and practice guide does not imply a slavish conformity to the sequence of work set out in the flow charts, nor an over-inclusive search for every bit of data mentioned. But, most of all, it fails if it leads to some facile 'cookbook' application of techniques, or a mechanical insistence on numbers and measurement. The virtues of operationism *can* turn into quantiphrenia, which acts to the detriment of warm empathic interactions with parents and children. The emphasis on rigorous thinking and scientific assessment in this book is not meant to be at the expense of clinical art and sensitivity. 'Scientism', a

Pharasaical adherence to the letter rather than the spirit of scientific method is to be avoided at all costs.

No manual can replace supervised practice experience. The complexity of behavioural interventions requires intensive study, structured sequential learning experiences and many opportunities for informed practical application.

SECTION 2

Introduction: Initial Screening

In trying to learn about the behaviour of other persons, the two principal ways are through questioning and observation. We 'ask them' and 'watch them'.

(a) *Direct Observation*: Go and see for yourself at home, school, etc. what and where problematic behaviours are occurring.

(b) *Record Keeping*: Ask the client to keep a diary and/or chart indicating when/with whom/under what circumstances it occurs.

(c) *Interviewing*: Interviewing (because of the opportunity it gives to question and observe a client) is one of the prime instruments of psychological assessment.

You may regard verbal report as a good predictor of real-life behaviour, but do not rely entirely on it (and that means the interview) for your data. Clients may not notice things, they may misperceive events, they may forget significant details and emphasize irrelevant points. Embarrassment or guilt may lead to errors of commission and omission in information-giving. If the crucial behaviour consists of overlearned responses, the client may be quite unaware ('unconscious') of his or her actions. So go and look for yourself and/or train the clients to observe so that you can see things through their informed eyes.

Questions, conversations, and direct observation are part and parcel of the various steps described in the following pages, in order to help you conduct a behavioural assessment. Steps 1 to 6 (the initial screening) and later steps 7 to 13 (data collection) rely on interviews, informal observations in the clinic or natural environment, and also formal recordings made by yourself, and/or your clients as part of their 'homework' assignments.

An initial interview guide is provided in Appendix II. In Fig. 1 you will find a ground plan or 'conceptual framework' for the data you are likely to be teasing out and the inter-relationships of the various items of information obtained.

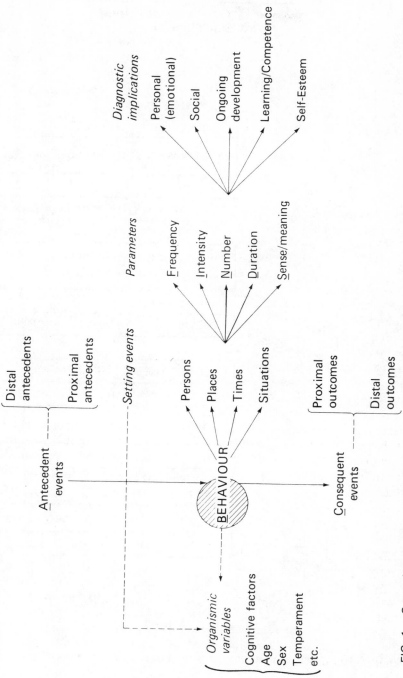

FIG. 1. General assessment guidelines: this provides you with an overview or groundplan to assessment, the first stage being an initial screening of your clients.

INITIAL SCREENING

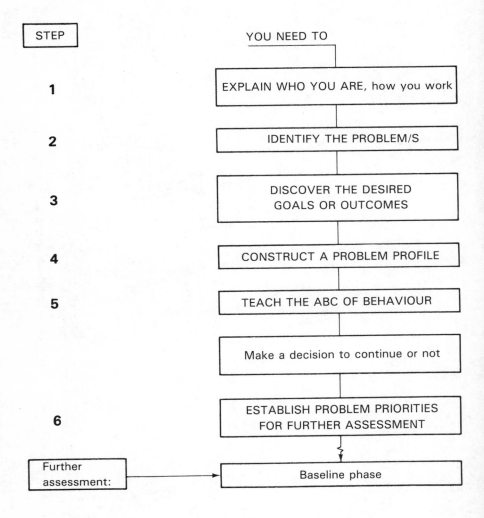

FLOW CHART 1   Assessment steps for the initial screening interviews.

> **Step 1** EXPLAIN YOURSELF: Who you are and how you work
>
> *Without being patronizing, use simple language, i.e. don't use jargon.*

During the initial contact with (preferably) both parents (or other caregivers), give a brief account (with down-to-earth examples) of how problem behaviour, like normal behaviour, can be acquired through failures or anomalies of learning and how such problems might be alleviated by practical strategies based on theories of learning and development.

You might find it helpful to provide the parents with a concise explanatory handout. Build up your own store of examples and metaphors in order to illuminate your explanations.

The Interview

The guided (semi-structured) interview is the main vehicle for the *preliminary* assessment of the areas outlined in the diagnostic guide in Fig. 1. Such interviews provide chiefly two kinds of information:

(a) They afford an opportunity for direct observation of a rather limited sample of behaviour manifested during the interview situation itself (e.g. the individual's speech, his or her style of thinking, competence, poise and manner of relating to the child).

(b) The interviewer seeks to secure directly as much information of a factual or personal nature from the client as is relevant to the purpose of the interview (e.g. information about the problem, opinions, relationships, parental skills, experience). A particularly important function in a clinical or social work setting is to elicit life-history data. What the individual has done in the past is thought to be a good indicator of what he or she may do in the future.

Remember: People, despite their generalized personality styles, still react to situations in highly idiosyncratic ways. Each situation requires an individual analysis. It has been calculated that if the total variance in behaviour is 100%, then an average of about 13% of this variance is due to the person (personality traits), 10% due to the situation and 21% to the interaction

> *between persons and situations. Although a detailed and specific assessment plan is de rigeur in behavioural work, it should not preclude opportunities for the 'person' as a personality and individual to express feelings and attitudes.*

Emphasize that if (after assessment) a behavioural treatment is felt to be appropriate, then it is likely to involve altering the consequences of the child's problem behaviour. But the child will not be the only focus of attention: family interactions are important and parents should be prepared not only to change their present *responses* to the child's supposedly maladaptive behaviours, but also to initiate new behaviours provided that they are not required to do anything distasteful or contrary to their values as parents.

There is evidence that sharing information with clients reduces the likelihood of their dropping out from treatment. An 'open agenda' and one which prepares the client for change (never a painless process) should pay a dividend in client motivation and cooperation.

Step 2a   IDENTIFY THE PROBLEM/S Keep asking 'What . . .'

Obtain information about all aspects of a child's behaviour which are considered to be problematic by his or her parents, by any other persons (e.g. teachers), agencies (e.g. medical or educational) or the child himself.

Method: It is useful to begin with an open-ended question: 'Tell me in your own words about what is worrying you about X's behaviour? Do take your time.'

Later: 'Are there any other matters you'd like to go into?' Encourage your clients to speak freely. Pause at suitable intervals to summarize what the clients have told you. Say: 'I would like to stop for a moment to see whether I have understood properly the points you have made.' Don't give the impression that the clients cannot express themselves clearly, but rather that what they say is worthy of being treated with due concern and seriousness.

Avoid: For the moment, the more fascinating 'riddle' question, 'Why?', and interpretations and speculations . . . at this stage, anyway.

> Be careful not to focus prematurely on specific problems at the expense of an initially open-ended and reasonably full exploration of the range of difficulties being expressed.

In order to get a good intellectual grasp of what a child is doing and why, it is necessary to have detailed and specific information (whenever possible, by direct observation) about the child's behaviour in his various life situations. The parent is encouraged to translate inferential statements into descriptive examples of the problem, in other words to define what she means in specific terms when she uses a particular label. If the informant says: 'Lorna is very aggressive', ask: 'In what way is she aggressive? Tell me what she says and does that makes you describe her as aggressive.' Also: 'Give me some examples (preferably recent ones) of what happens when she behaves like this.'

It is crucial to specify the problem in terms of observable responses which are accessible to other people (e.g. parents) as well as the child; 'public events' such as her striking, pinching or swearing at another person make for a more precise and consistent definition of the problem behaviour than a global statement that she is aggressive or filled with hostility. They can be verified by other observers. Find out while specifying what the problems are and what the desired outcomes might be, the steps taken to eliminate the former and bring about the latter. What methods have (say) the parents tried, and with what consequences? Such information is important in influencing your own treatment decisions and choices. Have other agencies been consulted? If so, will they give you permission to contact them?

Difficulties and indeed failures in the treatment of children's behaviour problems can frequently be traced back to a lack of precision during the crucial assessment (or diagnostic) phase of a therapeutic contact. The analysis of a problem situation and the planning of a treatment programme probably require more knowledge and skill than any other aspect of the behavioural approach. Sadly, what happens all too often in diagnostic conferences is an unwitting 'distancing' of the problem. This comes about, first of all, because of a tendency to describe the problem in terms which are too fuzzy or vague to allow for the rigorous formulation of clinical hypotheses which can be put to the test. The serious pitfall of using diagnostic labels such as minimal brain damage or hyperactivity is the illusory impression they give the user of having explained the behaviour.

Avoid: Being trapped into premature 'explanations' or 'prescriptions' by anxious clients. Also avoid letting parents or teachers focus exclusively on what the child *is* and *has* ('he is immoral; he has no conscience'); steer them towards describing what he or she *does* and *says*.

> ## Step 2b   IDENTIFY THE CHILD'S ASSETS Note and record prosocial behaviour
>
> *Seek out the child's 'good points'. Parents may be surprised at how many 'virtues', strengths and resources the child possesses when you encourage them to think about them.*

Method: Ask the parents to imagine a credit and debit balance sheet with two columns (see below). Make a list. You most probably will have to say: 'There's a long list of items on Peter's debit side; what can you think of to his credit?'

Balance sheet

Credit	Debit
He is generous	He's always fighting
He is good at his schoolwork	He's disobedient

Parents usually come to a clinic or agency with a mental set for discussing the negative aspects of their child's behaviour. There are advantages in asking them to talk about and observe (by monitoring at home) those areas in which his behaviour is socially appropriate. They may be surprised at how much prosocial behaviour they have overlooked. This may increase their own self-esteem as parents and also help them to establish a more balanced view of the child's behaviour. If parents focus their attention more on the positive behaviour, even if of rather poor quality, this behaviour is quite likely to increase and therefore leave less time for antisocial behaviour.

When carrying out treatment an emphasis on the positive is crucial in balancing out the efforts to reduce deviant behaviour. If the child acts in a silly or 'clownish' way to obtain attention and self-esteem, it would be short-sighted (not to say unethical) to 'extinguish' this inappropriate behaviour without providing him with skills and a behavioural repertoire which will earn him attention and esteem in more appropriate ways. In any event, failure to do this would not be very effective. The child might find other ways to seek these 'payoffs'.

Remember: While specifying the child's strengths and weaknesses ask what methods clients have tried in dealing with the problem so far and with what consequences?

Step 3 DISCOVER THE DESIRED OUTCOMES
While collecting early statements of 'problems' also tease out statements about
'desired outcomes'

*Parents express their concern about their child's
shortcomings in different ways; they may make
statements about:*
(a) problems: 'She is so thoughtless' and/or
*(b) desired outcomes: 'I wish she could be more
helpful and cooperative'.*

---

*Initial comments about desired outcomes provide the raw material for the
formulation (later) of more specific goals and objectives.*

Goals are the behavioural changes to be sought; they define how the behaviour
is to be changed. So ask parents in what way they wish things to be different,
how they would like the child to behave in order to allay their concern. How
do *they* need to change in order to bring about a better relationship with
their offspring.

There are, broadly speaking, three classes of problematic behaviour:

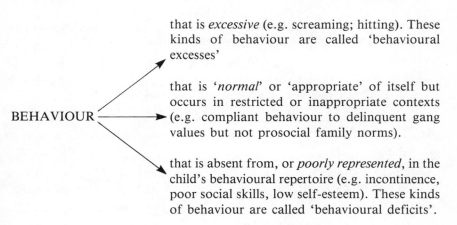

that is *excessive* (e.g. screaming; hitting). These
kinds of behaviour are called 'behavioural
excesses'

that is '*normal*' or 'appropriate' of itself but
occurs in restricted or inappropriate contexts
(e.g. compliant behaviour to delinquent gang
values but not prosocial family norms).

that is absent from, or *poorly represented*, in the
child's behavioural repertoire (e.g. incontinence,
poor social skills, low self-esteem). These kinds
of behaviour are called 'behavioural deficits'.

Behavioural and emotional problems, signs of psychological abnormality are,
by and large, exaggerations, deficits or handicapping combinations of
behaviour patterns common to all children.

Goals are thus generally formulated in terms of increasing, decreasing,
maintaining, establishing or expanding particular target behaviours. After all,

you are going to ask the clients to make a sizeable emotional and time investment in the programme so the goals must seem salient. It will help if you can point out that the 'costs' of the present problems outweigh the costs of the commitment to the therapy. Draw your clients' attention to longer-term benefits.

The evaluation of normality and abnormality within a developmental framework requires a familiarity with *general principles* of development, with particular reference to personality. It necessitates a comprehensive knowledge of children — how (in general terms) they look, think and talk, their skills and limitations at various ages, their typical repertoires of behaviour and the life-tasks and crises that they confront. Such a comparative or normative approach needs to be complemented by an idiographic analysis which takes into account biographical and other intrinsic influences which give individual children their *unique* quality.

Setting goals

Setting goals is at the centre of the attempt to solve problems; your help in this matter could be invaluable to your clients be they parent, child or teenager. A *workable* goal is an accomplishment that helps the individual manage problematic situations. The goal is achieved when he or she has acquired new skills, practised them, and actually used them to solve or manage the situation causing all the difficulties. This accomplishment is often referred to in counselling as the new (or preferred) scenario.

Here are some scenarios based on questions children, adolescents and parents (respectively) can usefully ask themselves:

Q: What would the problem situation be like if I could cope better?
A: I'd be able to talk to others without feeling awkward and tongue-tied; I would not spend so much time on my own.

Q: What changes would take place in my lifestyle?
A: I'd go out steady with a nice girl. I'd be more ambitious; take an interest.

Q: What would be happening that is not happening now?
A: I'd go to concerts, the cinema and plays instead of always moping about at home looking after a child who is so difficult I can't get a baby-sitter.

Scenarios and set goals can help clients who are in difficulty in four ways:
1.   They focus the person's attention and action. They provide a vision which offers hope and an outlet for concentrated effort.
2.   They mobilize energy and help pull the worrier out of the inertia of helplessness and depression.
3.   They enhance the persistence needed for working at the problem.
4.   They motivate people to search for strategies to accomplish their goals.

> ## Step 4   CONSTRUCT A PROBLEM PROFILE
>
> *Draw up a problem profile to take account not only
> of the problems of the child, but in addition those
> ascribed to others in the family. In this way you will
> have a record of perceptions of all members of the
> family.*

You are beginning (by now) to find out, and the profile will help you specify clearly

(a) who is complaining about particular problems;

(b) who desires a given outcome;

(c) the level of agreement/disagreement between (for example) parents and child, or parents, as to how they would like things to be different;

(d) the implications of change in the direction of the desired outcome. Who benefits? Does anyone lose? Your overriding concern is that a programme should benefit your client in the short term *and* the long term. When your clients are a young child *and* her parents you may have to adopt a role of advocacy on the part of the child. Be on your guard against designing programmes that make life easier for staff (e.g. institutional staff) to the detriment of the client.

Having narrowed your focus for a more detailed problem definition, move on to Step 5.

Remember: *You may have to back-track as you collect more information.
You may find that you have chosen an inappropriate behaviour (or
indeed person) on which to concentrate.*

> ## Step 5   TEACH CLIENTS TO THINK IN ABC TERMS
>
> *Begin with the B term.*

Antecedent events
↓
BEHAVIOUR _____ The behaviours being complained of
will be called 'target' behaviours
as you put them in their context
↓
Consequent events

Problem profile: Lorna's family

Problem as defined	Who complains	Who manifests the problem/to whom	Examples of problem	Settings	Desired outcome
Defiance	Mother	Lorna/Mother	Lorna ignores Mother's requests or says 'No'.	Bedtime, home; supermarket; visiting.	More obedient.
Demanding	Mother	Lorna/Mother	Mother has to 'obey' Lorna's commands or there is a temper tantrum.	Home; supermarket.	More patient.
Self-centredness	Mother/Father	Lorna (whole family)	Lorna is aggressive.	Home and elsewhere.	More thoughtful and unselfish.
Aggression	Mother	Lorna/whole family	Lorna pulls mother's hair, pinches back of her knees, hits her (to a lesser extent father and sister).	Home; in the car.	Stop lashing out for nothing.
Attention-seeking	Mother	Lorna/Mother	Follows mother everywhere, hangs onto mother, demands mother's attention when attending to others.	Home.	Give mother some peace.
Rudeness	Father	Lorna/Father	Make contemptuous remarks to father, e.g. 'you're stupid'.	Home.	Learn politeness.
Opting-out	Mother	Father/Mother	Father rushes off to work as if glad to get out of the house.	Home.	F to help more.
Depression	Father	Mother	Mrs. G. doesn't enjoy life; no energy for anything.	Everywhere.	Be her old self.
Inconsistency: reinforcement of deviant behaviour	Therapist	Mother and Father with regard to Lorna	Parents give in to Lorna if she is coercive; attend to her when her behaviour is deviant.	Most interactions.	—
Infantilizing	Lorna	Father/Mother	'They treat me like a baby.'	Playgroup/home. When I don't want to play with other children.	Treat me like my sister
Rejection; spoiling tactics	Her sister	Lorna vis-à-vis Father and Mother	'They have no time for me. Lorna spoils everything.'	Home.	Treat us the same.

Remember: The key word in this phase of assessment is still 'what'. The behaviour therapist asks: 'What is the person doing? Under what conditions are these behaviours emitted?'

You are beginning to introduce parents (or teachers) to the basic learning equation: the ABC analysis.

The analysis is *functional* in that it provides a description of the elements of a situation and their interrelationships. Thus diverse attributes (for example, actions such as hitting, kicking, pinching, swearing) would be considered to be members of the same response class ('aggression') because it could be shown that they enter into the same functional relationships: antecedent, concurrent and consequent stimulus conditions. Speaking more figuratively:

(a) The child is not simply a 'small volcano' erupting with 'bad' behaviour at the most inconvenient times. In other words, the 'problem' (in this case, aggression) does not reside within him like some figurative equivalent of molten lava, seemingly out of touch with surface events, but emanating from subterranean sources alone.

(b) His behaviour occurs in a social context.

(c) It is a *function* of the sort of person he is, and the situation he finds himself in.

In a functional analysis the importance of genetic predispositions and biological differences is recognized but the focus is on learned behaviour. It is based on the concept of a functional relationship with the environment in which changes in individual behaviour produce changes in the environment and vice versa.

All this can be said in the following shorthand:

$$\underline{A}\text{ntecedent events} \longrightarrow \underline{B}\text{ehaviour} \longrightarrow \underline{C}\text{onsequences}$$
$$\uparrow$$
$$\text{Organismic (state) variables}$$

Method: You will have to see (over a period of interviews, role plays and observations):

(a) What events precede, lead up to, set the stage for — Antecedent events ↓

(b) the behaviour that is being complained of? (*What* is it? *What* happens?) — Behaviour ↓

(c) And what are the social (or other) consequences/outcomes that flow from a display of problematic behaviour? What happens after the event? — Consequent events

In the jargon: the ABC sequence is referred to as the 'three-term contingency'. The child's behaviour is linked to *contingencies* in the environment, as well as *states* of mind, mood and health (etc.) within the child—the so-called organismic variables.

Remember: His behaviour may act as an antecedent to, and 'shaper' of (say) his sister's behaviour.

Here is a fairly typical sequence of behaviour—referred to by Patterson and Reid (1970) as 'the coercion process':

(a) John annoys Sally by grabbing her toy.
(b) Sally reacts by hitting John.
(c) John then stops annoying Sally, thus negatively reinforcing (see Section 6, Procedure 2) Sally's hitting response.

Sally has coerced John into terminating his annoying behaviour. A vicious circle is quite likely to be set in motion, an escalation of attack and counter-attack. To continue the sequence:

(d) John may, of course, react to Sally's hitting, not by desisting from his grabbing at Sally's toy, but by hitting back in an attempt to terminate Sally's aggression.
(e) Sally now responds to John's aggression with more intense counter-aggression.

This exchange could continue until it is interrupted by an adult or until one of the antagonists is negatively reinforced by the cessation of warfare on the part of the other child. We can see how it carries within it the seeds for a perpetuation of aggressive behaviour in the child's repertoire.

Method: Indicate in a reassuring manner, if clients find it difficult to describe problems or to conceptualize them in ABC terms, that the subtleties and complexities of behaviour problems are difficult to put into words, and for this and other (diagnostic) reasons you will have to ask many questions and a number of supplementaries. Try to avoid a manner which implies that the clients are being cross-examined; they already feel, more likely than not, embarrassed, guilty and apprehensive.

Interlude

Organismic Variables have been mentioned in connection with the ABC analysis. These 'internal' aspects of the child's environment are dealt with in Step 11. However it is worth mentioning four aspects — intrinsic features of the young person — which affect his 'processing' of information about the world, and the way in which the world perceives and 'labels' the child.

Age and sex appropriateness
What is normal at one age in a child may not be normal at another age. Temper tantrums are extremely common at age two and, in that sense, fairly 'normal'. Frequent temper explosions at age 13 would seem rather problematic. Girls are much less likely to respond to frustration with a temper tantrum than boys at that age.

Congenital factors
Information about genetic or congenital factors aids the fuller understanding of problem behaviour. Interpretations of socialization in terms of social reinforcement have shared (in the past) a common view of the infant as an essentially passive organism whose character is moulded solely by the impact of environment upon genetic predispositions. There is evidence (see Herbert, 1974, 1980) that the direction of effects of socialization is not always downward — from parent to child — and parents are not the sole possessors of power and influence within the family. Children exert an influence on significant adults in their lives and, in a sense, socialize them into a parental role. What is obvious from recent studies is that important individual differences are manifested in early infancy, among them being autonomic response patterns, temperament, social responsiveness (cuddliness), regularity of sleeping, feeding and other biological patterns, and perceptual responses. These can influence the way in which parents respond to, and manage (or mismanage) their offspring (see Bell and Harper, 1977).

Brain functioning and integrity
Damage to the brain is one of several main types of congenital abnormality in babies. Congenital, a word that means 'born with', is used in medicine to describe inborn diseases or defects. Congenital defects may, but need not, be inherited.

As advances in medicine have brought infectious diseases under control, an increasingly large proportion of ill health in childhood has been caused by congenital defects.

Even a sturdy organ like the brain can have its functions adversely affected by injuries (such as a blow, a fall or some penetrating wound), oxygen deprivation (for example, asphyxia at birth), infections, tumours, degenerative diseases and mechanical trauma (brought about by difficulties during birth). Brain injuries or defective functioning of the central nervous system can have an influence on the emotional stability of the child, on his motor and sensory abilities. They may also impair the processes he relies on to interpret the messages from his environment and those which coordinate his reactions to such information. This can be very disabling as can be seen in autistic and spastic children — for differing reasons. Apart from the adverse consequences for the child's emotional intensity and control which can follow directly from injuries to the brain, the physical difficulties (e.g. clumsiness and overactivity) so often associated with brain damage may provide another (if indirect) route to emotional maladjustment.

> **Step 6   ESTABLISH PROBLEM PRIORITIES**
> **Discuss with the family the priorities for further assessment**
>
> *It is important to select (after negotiation with the family) the problems on which to concentrate — at least initially.*
> *(a) Establish a hierarchy of problems/outcomes in order of their importance to the parents.*
> *(b) Establish your own hierarchy of problems in terms of their implications as you perceive them.*

Ask: (a) 'If I had a magic wand and could wave it so that things could change for the better in the situation you've been describing to me, what would you change first? . . . and after that? . . .' etc; or

(b) 'Which aspect is the greatest worry to you at the moment?'; or

(c) 'Which of the desired outcomes you've mentioned would you regard as your top priorities?'

Criteria

Here is a list of criteria for choosing among alternative outcomes;

(1) Annoyance value of the current situation to the client.
(2) Danger value of the current situation.
(3) Interference of the current situation in the client's life.

(4) Likelihood that the outcome will be attained with intervention.
(5) Centrality of the problem in a complex of problems.
(6) Accessibility of the problem. (Can you get close enough to it?)
(7) Potential for change. (Can you do something about it; do you have the resources and skills?)
(8) Probable cost of intervention (time, money, energy and resources).
(9) Relative frequency, duration or magnitude of the problem.
(10) Ethical acceptability of the outcome to the therapist, client and significant others.

Ethical imperatives

Because behaviour modification is very directive and often quite powerful, it should only be employed as a specific treatment or management procedure after full and careful consideration of the desirability of the proposed changes. The objectives are decided primarily on personal, social and ethical grounds. The clinician has the special responsibility of acting, in a sense, as an 'advocate' for the child. This is particularly the case with the younger child who cannot speak for himself and defend himself against the sometimes unreasonable demands made of him.

Critics accuse behaviour modification of a variety of failings, but none so passionately as its alleged unethical manipulativeness. There is justifiable concern that the behavioural approach might encompass the ideology that people are mere pawns of the environment or that it imposes control where no control previously existed. This notion that people are mindlessly manipulated without their choice or say so, is, in fact, misleading, not to say insulting; it is almost impossible to change someone's behaviour *significantly* without his awareness. Of course, all therapists are in the business of trying to produce change, as are all helping professionals, no matter what their orientation. However, they are out to change behaviour, not deep structures of personality. It can be argued that the practice of behaviour modification respects the integrity of parents and children by focusing on observed behaviour and limiting itself to helping diminish unconstructive functioning and increase adaptive functioning. The clients should be active participants in the selection of objectives/goals within a behavioural model of intervention—a choice which is likely to be obscured if the therapy is based on the therapist's interpretation of hidden motives and desires of which the clients themselves are unaware.

The idea that controlling behaviour is in itself somehow immoral ignores the reality, as Bandura (1969) reminds us, that all behaviour is inevitably controlled and the operation of psychological laws cannot be suspended by romantic conceptions of human behaviour any more than an indignant rejection of the laws of gravity can stop people falling. From the therapist's point of view the issue to be resolved, with any kind of treatment, is not whether behaviour is to be controlled but where the controlling forces lie and to what extent he or she should intervene or encourage others to intervene in their operation. The moral issues of whether to intervene and if so what the aim of intervention should be, can only be answered with reference to the individual therapist's value base and that of his or her profession.

The source of influence in behaviour modification is well recognized and quite explicit. The approach should encourage the therapist to take care not to influence the parents unduly in the selection of treatment goals and to make his or her thinking about the problem explicit. Non-recognition of influences allows their use in an unsystematic, covert way—the so-called hidden agenda. Behaviour modification is not an intervention entering a vacuum of free will. Its working philosophy can be deliberately underlined in order to enhance personal freedom of choice for the client; this is done by trying (in part) to analyse the processes of unwanted influence. Personal freedom of choice is further extended by the particular concern of behavioural therapists to provide the client with the ability for greater self-direction, by means of self-control and problem-solving training. (See Erwin (1979) and Stolz *et al.* (1975) for full discussions of these complex and crucial issues.)

Note: *Your decision to continue or not will depend on your assessment of the likelihood that new behaviours will be functional (i.e. have reward, survival and life-enhancing value) for the child. They should have a reasonable chance of being maintained when the intervention ends. If you decide to go ahead avoid trying to obtain a detailed assessment of too many problems. The effect of this could be to 'swamp' the parents with too much data-collection, making it unreliable and possibly engendering resistance to the programme.*

SECTION 3

From Data Collection to Problem Formulation

___

The baseline

The period of careful and controlled data collection stemming from the early interview is called the baseline (see Flow Chart 2). You will plan your baseline as part of, and flowing from, your assessment interview/s and personal observations. You are now moving from the more static collection of data (interview) to the more active, dynamic form of information gathering.

Remember: Behaviour modification is about changing behaviour; the frequency with which the child (for example) displays the behaviour may have to decrease, or increase depending upon its nature. On the other hand, it may not be a matter of doing something less or more often, but of manifesting an action with different intensity.

In order to change behaviour from some level to another level, you need to be clear about the definition of the problem and to know how much there is of that problem. In this way you will know:

(a) whether the problem is as extensive as parents say it is:

(b) whether your therapeutic programme (when it gets going) is producing real change.

The baseline is discussed in some detail in Step 8. If the target behaviour is occurring with some degree of consistency a week may be sufficient for the collection of data: if it is highly irregular you may require two or more weeks so as to get a picture of the day-to-day variations in the occurrence of the problem.

You may have to dispense with (or keep brief) the baseline period, if you are dealing with a problem that is dangerous to the client herself or to others. If, for *good* reasons, you have to dispense with a baseline, an estimated

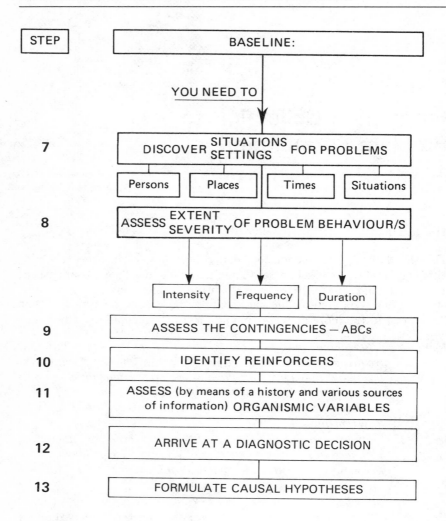

FLOW CHART 2   Further assessment.

retrospective 'baseline' (based on the verbal report of a responsible informant) is better than none. Accept it as the most tentative of estimates unless the target behaviour had a 100% or zero rate of occurrence (e.g. a child bedwetting every night: no incidence of speech at all in an elective mute).

Step 7   SPECIFYING SITUATIONS (SITUATION SPECIFICITY) Discover the situations in which the problematic interactions/feelings/behaviours occur

Behaviour is not usually manifested on a random basis: the probability of a specific action occurring varies according to the surrounding environmental cues. If you are to understand, predict and prescribe, you need to find out how behaviour covaries with different environmental stimuli, i.e. how antecedent situations affect a particular action.

Setting Events:

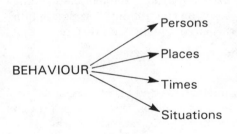

BEHAVIOUR
Persons
Places
Times
Situations

Find Out:
(1) whether there are particular persons with whom . . . places at which . . . times when . . . and situations in which . . . the problem behaviours are displayed:
(2) whether there are particular persons with whom . . . places at which . . . times when . . . and situations in which the problem behaviours are *not* manifested:
(3) the setting events for each problem separately. The problems may be related in the sense of occurring in the same settings.

You need to find out about the child and her responses to a variety of situations and environmental settings. A child referred for troublesome behaviour may display this kind of behaviour in her home, her school classroom, her playground, and perhaps on the streets of her neighbourhood. Furthermore, there may be refinements of such specific situations in which the problem behaviour occurs. For example, the child with severe temper tantrums solely at home, may show them only at bedtime and at mealtimes. She may be quite cooperative and pleasant at other times of the day when she is at home.

The best way to predict how a child is going to behave tomorrow in a particular situation is to observe how she behaves in that situation today. Parents, too, may behave in ways that vary more than the impression of consistency and generality that they convey in your interviews with them. This is where direct observation is so potentially revealing. For example, their handling of the 'target' child may be very different than that of their other offspring and they may be quite unaware of it.

Methods

Ask questions in the interview which lead to 'hypotheses' you can check by direct observation and *in situ* testing. A useful question to ask is whether there are particular persons (grandmother, sibling, parent, uncle, friend) who get the 'best' out of the child, in the sense that she does not display her problem behaviour with them. If so, the interactions of those persons with the child are worth studying. This question needs a good deal of tact in the asking. 'You say she is *always* disobedient. Try to think of situations in which she *is* obedient . . . What do you do differently in these circumstances compared with those in which she regularly disobeys you?' (You might conduct a small experiment, when you have the parents' confidence, by getting them to instruct the child to do X or Y so you can test out their description of the confrontation. You might ask them to try doing it in a different way.)

Narrative recording: a typical day

A technique used to tease out family interactions and behaviours is the so-called 'typical day' in the life of the child and family. It is worked through in minute behavioural detail, pinpointing those areas which cause confrontations and concern. It also provides the times and places at which, and the persons with whom, they occur. A 'blow by blow' account is sought of the events surrounding problem behaviours. You might introduce some role-play at the point of major confrontations so you can 'see' what happens. The therapist might refine the parent's complaint that 'he is always shouting and banging about', which is both inaccurate and vague, to: 'This boy has temper-tantrums, involving screaming, crying, hitting other children, and throwing property, lasting an average of 10 minutes on each occasion and occurring on average four times per day. They occur when he is thwarted such as when he is made to . . . etc., etc.'

The typical day (or days) makes for a reasonable sampling of the child's antisocial and prosocial activities as perceived by parents or other significant adults (e.g. the child's schoolteacher). Don't neglect the child herself as a potential informant. Her points of view, her perception of events are important sources of data in your assessment. Not all children are articulate. This is where behaviour itself, even more than usual, must be 'interpreted' for what it 'tells' you about the problem and its function.

Remember: Behaviour is reactive to observation. You may not see typical or representative interactions on your first visit(s). So ask parents: 'Is this what it is usually like?' 'How would it differ if I wasn't sitting here . . . would it be better . . . worse?' You might suggest that parents ask the child (say a disobedient one) to fetch something for them, in order to provide an 'experimental' observation.

Step 8   ASSESS THE EXTENT AND SEVERITY OF THE PROBLEM   Explore the parameters of the problem behaviour

This is still part of the specification of the 'What' questions: the specification of the dimensions (and, indeed, the seriousness) of the problem.

The acronym FIND refers to the specification of the target behaviours (problems) in terms of their frequency, intensity, number and duration, and the sense they make from the client's point of view. After an initial report from the clients, e.g. from parents (or teachers), you require careful and controlled observation of the behaviours you think are important, as they are presently occurring. Flow Chart 3 will help you get started.

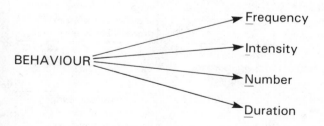

BEHAVIOUR

Frequency

Intensity

Number

Duration

Note: The dimensions (frequency, intensity, etc.) along which you quantify the behaviour depends upon the nature of the problem. Don't get bogged down by taking on too much at once. Record two or three target problems at first.

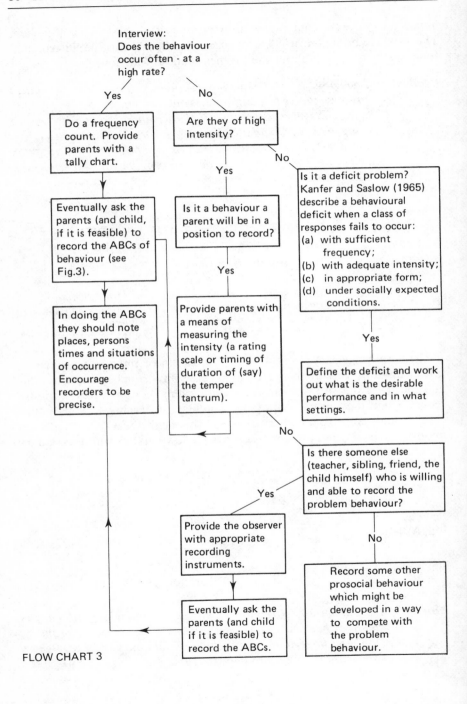

FLOW CHART 3

Step 8a	PROVIDE CLIENT WITH APPROPRIATE MATERIAL (CHARTS, NOTEBOOKS) TO RECORD PROBLEM BEHAVIOURS, FEELINGS, INTERACTIONS He thus 'FINDs' out more about the parameters of the problem
	This marks the beginning of the so-called baseline period.

The baseline period is not necessarily therapeutically inert as self-observation (or observations of a child) — especially when based upon more precise definitions of the behaviour — may produce 'insights' which predispose to beneficial effects. Some therapists claim that behaviours which can be quantified and counted are easiest to change: indeed that problem behaviours which cannot be observed and counted are not likely to be changed by the therapeutic agent.

Methods: (a)   To do all this, you *train* the parents (and not infrequently, the child) to observe behaviour so that, in a sense, you can observe things through their eyes during the time you cannot be 'on the spot'. The very fact of the client being able to interpret behaviour sequences with greater accuracy and sophistication, seems conducive to change.

         (b)   Give the parents a tally-sheet (a chart) so as to keep a record themselves (Fig. 2).

         (c)   Write down the behaviour to be recorded (with symbols and definitions) as a reminder to the parent. You might simply ask them to keep a count in the first week (Fig. 2) and then a more detailed ABC diary the next week (Fig. 3).

         (d)   Go and record or observe for yourself — if possible.

There has been considerable research (see Appendix V) into the measurement of behaviour by direct observation. Home (and, where necessary, school) observations are made prior to treatment and they contribute to the initial behavioural analysis. A painstakingly detailed interview about the child's typical day can produce reliable and valid data supplemented by parent and teacher observation records and diaries.

No one method of recording is suitable for all problems or situations. There are many ways of monitoring behaviour — from the molar to the molecular — some of which (and the sheer amount of time given to which) are more suitable for clinical research than busy day-to-day service delivery.

Mandy's Chart   Date: Week:

	Mon.	Tues.	Wed.	Thurs.	Fri.	Sat.	Sun.
7-8	T, D	C	T, D / T	D / T	D, T	C	C
8-9	C		T	T	T, D		
9-10						T	
10-11							
11-12							
12-1						D, T	D
1-2							
2-3							
3-4							
4-5	D / T	D, T	D	D, T	D		
5-6	T, T	T, T	D, T	T	T	D, T	D
6-7		D	T (long one 25 mins)	T	C		C
7-8							C

Code: T = temper tantrum = mandy screams, lies on the floor, kicking, banging her head, banging her fists.
D = disobedience/defiance = M ignores request (ie after one repetition). M says 'no' / shakes head - refuses to obey.
C = cooperation behaviour = M helps mother (or others) as defined in contract.

Fig. 2 Daily counting chart to show how often a child does something within a given time period.

Prepare parents for this eventuality of home visits and explain why you wish to observe and how. Try always to be as natural as possible and thereby unobtrusive as well. Keep your own remarks and interactions to a polite minimum, when observing interactions between family members. Discuss your, and their record with them. Ask: 'Is this what it is usually like?

Parents who find their child's behaviour intolerable tend to overestimate the actual frequency of its occurrence. There are, on the other hand, parents who do not want to admit that their child has problems. They deny the frequency (or intensity) with which a behaviour is occurring. Not surprisingly, the results of 'objective' observation and recording often differ markedly from the estimates of those involved. They also tend to underestimate the child's acceptable behaviour. Ask them to 'catch' the child out in good behaviour, and record it.

It might be impossible or unethical to observe certain problem behaviours or they may be distorted or inhibited by the process of observation. Questionnaires or interviews may have to serve.

CHART: *Mandy's*   DATE: 7/5 → 13/5   WEEK: 2

OBSERVER: *Mrs Sinclair*

BEHAVIOUR:
1 *temper tantrum* = *Mandy screams, lies on the floor,*   CODE: 1 'T'
2 *kicks, makes high pitched sounds;*   2
3 *bangs head / fists on floor.*   3
4 *Disobedience* = *Mandy ignores request (ie after one repetition)*   4 'D'
5 *Mandy says no / shakes head - refuses to*   5
6 *obey request / command (as defined in contract)*   6
7 *Cooperation* = *Mandy helps mother (or others) in ways*   7 'C'
8 *defined in contract.*   8

ANTECEDENT EVENTS (BEFORE)	BEHAVIOUR	CONSEQUENT EVENTS (AFTER)
May (10⁵⁰) I refused to buy Mandy a chocolate at the pay counter at the supermarket.	D, T	She kept pestering me. I kept telling her 'no'; she could have an apple at home. She went on and on. I tried to coax her out of it. M. began to scream and stamp her feet. I felt awful, everyone looking. In the end I compromised. I brought her some chewing gum to keep her quiet.
Eveng. (7⁰⁰) M helped me of her own accord to wash the dishes.	C	I praised her; scolded her a bit for being clumsy.

FIG. 3 A detailed ABC diary.

Data collection

Equipment

Paper and pencils are much in evidence in busy day-to-day assessment. Other equipment includes stopwatches and counters to provide time samples and event recordings of behaviour. Portable video equipment can be useful, providing parents and children with feedback about their relationships and interactions. To see yourself as others see you is sometimes the beginning of a decision to change.

Tracking behaviour

The following methods (there are references for further reading) provide you with different means of obtaining vital data for your casework (or research). Try to obtain reliable data without making 'heavy weather' of it for your client/s.

(1) Time budgets

A record is made of the time the person devotes to his various daily pursuits. Such a record kept over many days is likely to betray significant interests and reinforcers as well as personal idiosyncracies (distractibility, procrastination, preoccupation and the like).

(2) Time sampling/interval recording

This procedure involves direct observation of the person's behaviour: the attention of observer and analyst is fixed upon selected aspects of the stream of behaviour as they occur within uniform and short time intervals. The duration, spacing and number of intervals are intended to obtain representative time samples of whatever is being investigated. Such 'field observations' may involve records of children at home, in nursery schools, boys in camp, patients in hospital, students at their studies, and so on. In other words, they represent a sampling of natural, everyday situations.

Many behaviours are not clearly discrete in nature. Some responses have no clear-cut beginning or ending. Time sampling provides the clearest analysis of such behaviours. For example, in the case of a student who makes many loud, disruptive noises, such as yelling out across the room, hitting his neighbour and pinching him, and shuffling his chair around, it might be difficult either to make a tally of the number of times such responses occur or to measure their duration. After all, when does one instance of chair shifting end and another begin? However, it is feasible to record the presence or absence of such responses within a short time-span at intervals during (say) a classroom lesson.

Interval recording and time sampling are among the most popular methods of data collection. With the one-zero method of time-sampling (Tyler, 1979), the occurrence or non-occurrence of particular actions is scored for each successive time interval (often a period between 10 and 30 seconds in length). An act is scored once irrespective of the number of onsets within the interval or the amount of the interval that an activity occupied. From this a score of Hansen frequency (Hansen, 1966) which is equivalent to the total number of intervals in which a particular act has occurred, is worked out. What is being recorded then is not the 'true' frequency of each type of behaviour but the frequency of intervals that include any amount of time spent in that behaviour.

This method tends to underestimate the 'true' frequency of acts and overestimate time spent in an activity, although in certain circumstances this may give a better guide to the relative representation of a behaviour (Slater, 1978).

The advantage of using the 'one-zero' sampling convention is its simplicity and ease of use with a checklist (Hutt and Hutt, 1970) and its high reliability of measurement compared with other observational techniques. Provided that the time interval is short compared to the duration of each behaviour, the score will approximate the 'true' frequency.

(3) Instantaneous and scan sampling
Here the observer records an individual's current activity at preselected moments in time. When this instantaneous sampling method is used on groups, it is termed 'scan' sampling. Each individual is watched for a specified time and the observer focuses on each individual in turn. Once this 'scan' has been completed (say, the members of a family), then the sequence is repeated. The percentage of time that individuals devote to various activities can be estimated from the per cent of samples in which a given activity is recorded (Bekoff, 1979).

During direct observation, a time marker is required to register the beginning and end of preselected time periods or intervals. Many studies report the use of a stopwatch for this purpose, but this distracts the observer's attention away from the behaviour under investigation. A *Behavioural Timer* could be used to indicate the beginning and end of the time periods. This consists of a pocket-sized electronic device with an ear-piece attachment. The electronic timing mechanism is preset for the interval required. After each successive time interval has elapsed the machine 'bleeps' to indicate the end of the previous time period and the onset of the next. This sound is audible to the observer alone, through a small ear piece.

(4) Event sampling
This is like the classical method of natural history research in biology. It begins with a plan to study events of a given kind, e.g. outbursts of temper tantrums in children or cooperative acts by adolescents doing some common task in the work situation. The investigator stations himself where the people involved can be seen and heard, waits for the events to happen and then describes them in great detail.

(5) Trait rating
The observer goes, say, to a school playground and after several days of observation uses a rating scale to sum up what she has seen of the child's traits, e.g. friendliness, competitiveness, conformity, jealousy and so on, having defined them first in operational terms, i.e. in terms of observable behaviours.

(6) Sociometry
This so-called 'nominating technique' is a procedure in which each member of a group (classroom, family, playgroup) is asked to name the members of the group with whom he would like to work, play or engage in other designated activities. Naming may not always be the method used. An observer may simply plot the interactions of a group of, say, children to see who is isolated, popular, gregarious, etc.

Recent developments in data collection

The direct observation of behaviour is labour intensive both in data collection and analysis. However with the recent development in battery-powered portable microcomputers there is a potential to automate the direct recording of behavioural events both for laboratory and field work. They can provide an effortless way of obtaining a 'complete record' of behaviour, and can be equipped with a built-in printer, microcassette drive LCD screen, and a full size keyboard compact enough to rest on the observer's lap.

More elaborate and time-consuming methods of recording and analysing observations are provided in Appendix V. To give but one example, Browne and Madaley (1985) have developed a software package for use with the portable EPSON HX20, which affords the ability to rapidly record predefined behaviours with minimum keyboard input. For each behaviour key pressed the sequence and elapsed time from start are automatically recorded up to seven times per second. This can be done for single subject observations, for observations of several subjects, and for interactions between subjects functioning in their natural environment. The recorded data may be immediately printed out and stored on microcassette for later transfer to a larger computer.

Software packages are available for the collection and analysis of observational data with laboratory-based microcomputers (Flowers, 1982). In addition, there are programmes for the analysis of verbal interaction (Hargrove and Martin, 1982), and the calculation of interobserver reliability statistics (Burns and Cavallaro, 1982).

Remember: What you are particularly interested in is behaviour variability, i.e. the correlation or covariance between the rate of a target behaviour as displayed during one observation session, and the rate of the behaviour during previous or subsequent sessions (high correlation = low variability). Variability in observational data may be due to (i) variations in environmental influences (including your intervention), (ii) natural characteristics of the behaviour, or (iii) reactivity to the observation methods being employed. You have to take this variability into account when attributing change to your therapy.

Step 8b   FIND OUT THE FREQUENCY OF THE BEHAVIOUR

(a) Ask how often the problem occurs (interview).
(b) Record how often the problem occurs (baseline).

Method: Discover:
(a) The frequency of the problem.
(b) The overall rate at which the behaviour occurs — i.e. how often. The usual means of expressing this is frequency/time, e.g. confrontations per day, tantrums per day.
(c) Whether there is a tendency for the problem to occur episodically.
(d) Whether there is any evidence of a clustering of behavioural events.

The observation and recording of problem behaviour and its attendant circumstance by the therapist, the child or others, may be facilitated by suitable coding systems. Methods for coding behaviour in families (Patterson, 1982) or at school (Ray *et al.*, 1970) have been developed.

In Table I we see one example of a system for coding observations of social interactions of problematic children. This sort of system may save observer

Table I Some noxious behaviours (Patterson, 1982)

Noxious behaviours	Definitions
Disapproval	Verbal or gestural disapproval of another person's behaviour or characteristics.
Negativism	Making a statement with a neutral verbal message, but which is delivered in a negative tone of voice.
Non-compliance	Not doing what is requested.
Tease	Teasing another person in such a way that the other person is likely to show displeasure and disapproval or when the person being teased is trying to do some behaviour but is unable to because of the teasing.
High rate	Behaviour that if carried on for a long period of time would be aversive, e.g. running back and forth in the living room, jumping up and down on the floor.
Physical negative	Attacking or attempting to attack another person. The attack must be of sufficient intensity to potentially inflict pain, e.g. biting, kicking, slapping, hitting, spanking, and taking an object roughly from another person.
Yell	Whenever the person shouts, yells, or talks loudly. If carried on for a sufficient time it would be extremely unpleasant.
Whine	When a person states something in a slurring, nasal, high-pitched, falsetto voice.
Destructiveness	Destroying, damaging, or trying to damage any object.
Humiliation	Someone makes fun of, shames, or embarrasses another person intentionally.
Cry	All forms of crying.
Command negative	Command in which immediate compliance is demanded and aversive consequences are implicitly or actually threatened if compliance is not immediate. In addition, it is a kind of sarcasm or humiliation at the receiver.
Dependency	Requesting assistance in doing a task that a person is capable of doing himself; for instance, a 16-year-old boy asks his mother to comb his hair.
Ignore	When person A has directed behaviour at person B, and person B appears to have recognized that the behaviour was directed at him, but does not respond in an active fashion.

and recording time. But keep it simple for parents. Perhaps the greatest merit of direct observation techniques is that they provide basic data about problems as conceptualized by the parents or teachers themselves. The child may also be involved in monitoring his own behaviour. It is always wise to check on the reliability of the client's observations by doing home or school visits and

	Monday						Tuesday						Wednesday						Thursday						Friday						Total
	1	2	3	4	5	6	1	2	3	4	5	6	1	2	3	4	5	6	1	2	3	4	5	6	1	2	3	4	5	6	
On-task	✓	✓		✓	✓						✓	✓	✓	✓	✓	✓			✓	✓	✓	✓	✓		✓				✓		15
Out of seat		✓								✓	✓				✓	✓			✓										✓		7
Inappropriate talking					✓		✓	✓																				✓	✓		5
Hitting									✓												✓					✓					3

FIG. 4 A classroom chart.

observing how they observe and record. Or, at the very least, check their recordings by discussing criteria with them.

Quantifying frequency

It is important to determine the frequency of a problem in quantifiable terms. This should include not only the overall rate (i.e. how often it occurs on average—hourly, daily or weekly), but also any tendency of the problem to occur episodically (i.e. at particular times). Any evidence of clustering of behavioural events should lead to further investigation. A frequency recording procedure is the simplest type of data analysis. It is nothing more than a *tally* method. Figure 2, Step 8a, provides an example of a tally chart. What the therapist does is to count the number of occurrences of the behaviour, as he or she has defined it. Recording the time at which the response occurred enhances the frequency data system.

Methods

(a) Interval method
Break the observation period down into small equal intervals and record the chosen behaviour as occurring or not occurring during each interval up to one minute in duration, depending upon the rate of the response and the average duration of a single response.

(b) Time sampling
Record the presence or absence of the target responses during a short time period or interval. In order to obtain a representative sample of observations one might record the presence or absence of the behaviour within short, uniform time intervals, such as the first ten seconds in every five minutes of a half-hour classroom period. Just such a classroom chart is given in Fig. 4.

On one of your home visit observations you might record the interactions of a child and (say) her mother in ten second samples (on every minute) according to your own pre-coded categories (see Fig. 5).

	10	20	30	40	50
Sarah	T O S H	T O S H	T O S H	T O S H	T O S H
Mother	O V N P	O V N P	O V N P	O V N P	O V N P
Sarah	T O S H				
Mother	O V N P				

FIG. 5 Interaction chart. Time sampling: Sarah and mother at home. *Code:* Sarah: T = throwing objects; O = no problem behaviour; S = shouting, screaming; H = hitting mother. Mother: O = no response; V = verbal interaction; N = near Sarah; P = punishment.

(c) Use of graphs (see Fig. 6)
Graphs basically tell you 'when' and 'how much' X, Y or Z occurred at a glance. Plotting behaviour rates across observation sessions may indicate trends (look for positive or negative slopes) in the frequency or intensity of the behaviour over time. A negative slope — in this case a reduction of target behaviour — is illustrated in Fig. 6.

It helps you to see what the data you have collected looks like, if you can bring it all together and summarize it in graphical form. Figure 7, for example, 'tells a story' about Andrew's progress with regard to his aggressive behaviour. (The scores represent ratings of his behaviour at a certain time each day, i.e. the average number of aggressive episodes recorded at a particular hour over a period of a week.) We see a marked improvement during treatment which is maintained at a slightly more modest level on follow-up, after four months.

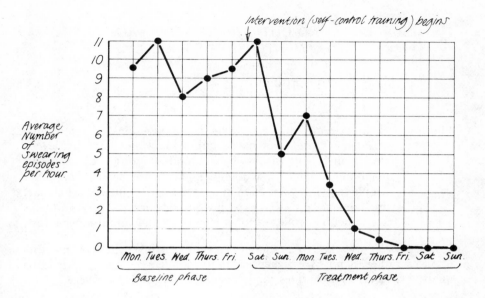

FIG. 6 Try to graph your data. See Gelfand and Hartmann (1975) for interpretation and construction of graphs. There are various methods (Glass *et al.*, 1973) for analysing slopes.

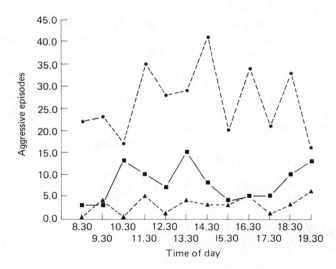

FIG. 7 Andrew's aggressiveness (weekly average) during: ●----● baseline; ▲----▲ termination week of treatment; ■——■ four-month follow-up.

> **Step 8c   FIND OUT (WHERE APPROPRIATE) HOW INTENSE THE PROBLEM IS**
> This is another index of the severity of the problem.

Find out: How extreme the behaviour is. Expressions of emotional and behavioural acts have certain allowable intensity levels. Very 'high' intensities—behavioural responses of excessive magnitude—which have unpleasant consequences for other people (e.g. incessant screaming, overactivity, fidgety behaviour) are likely to be viewed as behavioural disorder. These problems are sometimes referred to as 'aversive behavioural repertoires'.

It may be appropriate to measure the level of the problem in terms of its intensity rather than its frequency. Intensity can be assessed by asking two questions: (1) How long does the behaviour last? (2) How severe is it?

(1) *Duration:* Some problems are most usefully described in terms of how long the behaviour lasts. A stopwatch is run continuously while the behaviour is occurring during an observation period of a specified length.
(2) *Severity:* This can be measured by constructing *ad hoc* severity rating scales of a graphical, numerical, or some other kind. Find out also when the problem is stronger in intensity, when it is less severe. Why are there these *contrasts* in expression . . . with whom . . . and in what circumstances?

Remember: A child (and his environment) may suffer not only because he is (say) over aggressive (sadistic) but because he is under aggressive (not sufficiently self-assertive). Some appropriate responses may be entirely absent from his behavioural repertoire; let alone too weakly manifested (a knowledge of developmental norms is crucial). These problems are sometimes referred to as 'deficient behavioural repertoires'.

Ask: Whether there are actions and skills which the parents would like the child to display, which he shows little or nothing of.

Methods: (a) *Rating Scale:* If the child is, say, anxious about making journeys and is old enough to rate himself, construct a simple *ad hoc* scale and put it on cards, so the child can assess his anxiety responses to different journeys he makes, in subjective units of anxiety (0 to 100). (See Fig. 8.)

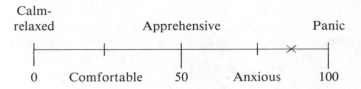

Date: Tues. 7th; Comment: Hemmed in in front of school bus.

FIG. 8.

(b) *Direct Observation:* Rate for yourself (or ask parents to rate) episodes of so-called deviant behaviour. The dimensions will be suggested by the nature of the problem.

Interlude

Rating methods

These come closest to the common, everyday practice by which one person arrives at conclusions about the traits of another person with whom he is acquainted. The judgement he makes is likely to be one of two extremes; the person is regarded ('mentally rated') as bright and dull, friendly or unfriendly, and so on.

Only when the observer begins to compare two or more individuals, or when he is *forced* by circumstances to make finer distinctions, is he likely to do so. Then he recognizes the appropriateness of speaking of *more or less* of some attribute. He is now on the way to making a judgement that has numerical properties.

There are several types of rating scales (5 point scales to be most efficient).

(a) Numerical rating scales
The rater assigns to each ratee a numerical value for each attribute. The numerical values may be defined in verbal terms. For example: a rating on serious-mindedness of 7 might mean 'takes everything as if it were a matter of life or death'; of 4 'neither serious nor unconcerned'; of 2 'ordinarily unconcerned and carefree'; of 1 'seems not to have a care in the world', etc. Such ratings would best be anchored in agreed and clearly observable behaviours.

(b) Graphic rating scale
This is a variant of the numerical scale. The judgement is made by marking a point on a line to define the client's position between two extremes

How depressed is the client?

:   ×   :   :   :   :   :

Extremely Very Some Mildly Not at all

(c) Personal concept tests
There are a number of techniques available (e.g. the Q-sort technique, the Semantic Differential and the Repertory Grid), which allow for the direct expression of the personal conceptual system — the manner in which the individual 'sees' or conceptualizes himself, people and the world he lives in. They may reveal concepts, and relationships between concepts (constructs), that the person is barely aware of, or which function normally at the emotional rather than the verbally explicit level. For example, an individual may be construing her husband in much the same way as her father and a test like the Repertory Grid helps to point out such connections.

Step 8d	HOW MANY PROBLEMS ARE BEING MANIFESTED BY THE CHILD?
	List or check off (Table II) the number of problematic behaviours/emotions.

Remember: There may be a tendency for parents to raise of their own accord only the more 'visible' and irksome problems. Without a full picture of the child's anti- and prosocial behaviours, the therapist's assessment will be partial and his or her treatment programme may run into trouble.

Remember: The number of deviant behaviours coexisting in the child is an index of maladjustment. The more problematic behaviours reported as such by parents, the greater the likelihood that the child will be found to have an emotional or behavioural disorder on clinical examination. Isolated 'symptoms' are very common and usually of little clinical significance.

Table II A checklist of how often problematic behaviours occur:

Behaviour	Never	Sometimes	Often:	Is it seen as a problem by the parent? Yes/no
Attention demanding				
Destructiveness				
Disobedience				
Disturbing dreams				
Enuresis				
Excessive modesty				
Excessive reserve				
Food finickiness				
Insufficient appetite				
Irritability				
Jealousy				
Lying				
Mood swings				
Nailbiting				
Negativism				
Overactivity				
Overdependence				
Oversensitiveness				
Physical timidity				
Reading difficulty				
Restless sleep				
School refusal				
Shyness				
Soiling				
Somberness				
Specific fears				
Speech				
Tempers				
Thumbsucking				
Wandering				
Whining				

Table III provides you with information about the problems of British school-going children, as manifested at different ages.

The point was made in the enumeration of the basic assumptions of this book, that no child is *all* problem. Indeed, there is relatively little overlap in the populations of children who show problems at home and those who display problems at school. This is why you should tend to 'sit up and take notice' when the child manifests behavioural disorders in both settings. And you would certainly do so when you note behavioural consistencies such that the child's typical behaviour pattern tends to be deviant across a wide variety of situational contexts.

Table III   Percentages of children recorded as showing 'extreme' types of behaviour at each age from five to fifteen (from Shepherd et al., 1971)

GIRLS (age in years:)	5	6	7	8	9	10	11	12	13	14	15
Very destructive	2	—	1	—	*	*	—	*	—	1	—
Fear of animals	5	5	3	3	3	1	2	2	1	1	7
Fear of strangers	1	*	2	2	*	2	1	1	1	2	—
Fear of the dark	11	5	8	7	8	8	6	5	4	5	4
Lying	2	2	1	1	3	1	3	1	1	3	2
Dislike of school	1	3	2	4	3	2	3	3	5	7	4
Stealing	1	—	—	—	*	—	—	*	—	1	—
Irritability	10	9	9	10	12	10	12	10	11	16	11
Food fads	20	19	20	22	21	23	17	17	15	17	09
Fear of other children	—	*	1	1	1	1	*	1	*	1	1
Always hungry	5	6	6	10	9	10	10	13	15	11	16
Small appetite	21	17	21	18	13	12	12	8	7	8	5
Worrying	5	7	4	4	6	4	7	5	1	4	5
Whining	7	5	5	4	6	2	5	4	3	5	5
Restlessness	20	16	20	16	13	13	13	11	11	10	4
Underactivity	—	2	1	1	2	3	3	4	7	7	5
Jealousy	8	4	5	5	6	3	4	3	3	6	4
Wandering	*	*	—	1	1	*	1	3	1	2	4
Withdrawn	2	1	2	2	3	2	2	3	2	3	7
{ Disobedient	10	10	8	8	11	7	10	10	12	14	14
{ Always obeys	8	7	7	9	9	8	14	11	12	10	12
Truanting—at all	*	1	1	*	1	*	*	·1	1	3	4
Tics	1	—	—	1	1	*	—	*	—	1	—
Mood change	5	2	4	3	5	3	5	5	7	7	14
Reading difficulty	5	7	14	14	10	13	10	11	5	7	4

BOYS (age in years:)	5	6	7	8	9	10	11	12	13	14	15
Very destructive	3	2	2	—	2	1	1	1	2	1	2
Fear of animals	3	3	2	1	1	2	2	1	1	1	4
Fear of strangers	2	1	1	1	—	*	*	1	—	*	2
Fear of the dark	9	6	8	8	10	7	6	5	2	2	4
Lying	5	3	5	2	3	3	3	5	4	2	2
Dislike of school	4	5	5	3	5	5	5	6	7	10	4
Stealing	—	1	1	1	1	*	1	1	2	*	—
Irritability	10	7	13	11	12	14	11	14	11	9	16
Food fads	19	20	22	22	22	18	23	19	17	17	16
Fear of other children	1	*	—	—	*	1	1	1	1	*	—
Always hungry	11	10	10	14	16	13	16	19	15	23	39
Small appetite	11	13	17	14	11	10	13	9	7	5	—
Worrying	4	5	5	7	6	5	3	3	5	4	5
Complaining	7	6	8	5	4	3	4	4	3	2	2
Restlessness	23	19	25	21	22	19	20	18	15	17	20
Underactivity	1	2	1	1	1	2	2	2	3	6	2
Jealousy	6	2	4	4	4	5	3	4	2	3	2
Wandering	3	1	2	3	3	3	3	4	4	8	2
Withdrawn	2	1	4	3	3	3	2	3	3	2	2
{ Disobedient	17	11	14	12	12	13	13	14	11	12	7
{ Always obeys	8	7	7	8	7	6	7	7	9	9	9
Truanting—at all	1	—	1	—	*	2	—	2	1	4	16
Tics	*	1	1	2	1	2	1	2	2	1	2
Mood changes	4	3	3	2	5	3	4	4	2	2	2
Reading difficulty	7	18	21	27	25	17	21	22	13	13	9

Note: * = less than 0.5 %.

Also remember: In checking for problematic behaviours look for 'interfering' behaviours, that is to say, actions which preclude or compete with the learning and performance of socially adaptive behaviours. These actions are sometimes manifested so often and intensely that they reduce dramatically the probability of alternative responses being made.

Reliability

We referred briefly to this issue earlier on. There is little point in training caregivers to observe (itself a skill with a therapeutic pay-off) if the observations are not reliable. Methods for checking on observer reliability can be studied in Gelfand and Hartmann (1975); the more elaborate methods for calculating reliability will not be feasible for the busy therapist (although it may be a useful occasional team exercise—as a refresher or training task). However, it is a good idea (if you are an experienced observer) to record simultaneously with a parent, a sequence of behavioural events. Reliability for event recording can be calculated as follows:

$$\frac{\text{Number of agreed events}}{\text{Number of agreed events} + \text{number of disagreed events}} \times 100 = \% \text{ agreement}$$

A rather more precise assessment of agreement between observers can be obtained by use of an interaction matrix. You assess agreements and disagreements for each sampling interval rather than overall observer agreement on event totals over an observation session (as above). Both observers mark 1 for the first interval observation: 2 for the second: and so on—in the appropriate interactional cells. Agreement is defined as both observers marking the same cell during the same sampling interval. Percentage agreement is worked out as above (80% or above is generally considered a satisfactory level).

The issues of reliability, internal consistency and interobserver agreement are important aspects of behavioural observation but are too complex to deal with in depth in a pragmatic guide like the present one. The question of validity—the degree to which measured differences represent true differences—cannot be taken for granted, simply because you have carried out direct observations of behaviour. As a busy therapist you may not be able to implement all the 'niceties' of quantification and checking used by the researcher, but this is no excuse for not being aware of the problems and pitfalls of attaining reliable and valid data. Chapters 5 and 6 in Haynes (1978) are recommended to the reader in pursuit of such an awareness.

Haynes and Horn (1982) review that major threat to the internal and external validity of behavioural observation: reactivity, the phenomenon in which an assessment procedure results in modification of the behaviour of the persons being assessed.

Remember: *to take account of the reactive effects associated with behavioural observation. They might involve:*

(1) Increases in rates of behaviour;
(2) Decreases in rates of behaviour;
(3) Differential effects on rates of behaviour for different behaviours within the same person;
(4) Differential effects on rates of behaviour for different individuals;
(5) Increased variability in rates of behaviour.

Note: *It is possible to minimize or control the reactive effects of observation by:*

(a) the use of participant observers (e.g. parents) who are normally part of the individual's (e.g. child's) environment;
(b) the use of covert observation;
(c) instructions to subjects to act 'naturally';
(d) minimizing the intrusiveness of the observers and the process of observation;
(e) using telemetry, video cameras or tape recorders;
(f) using several observers or procedures so that differential effects cancel out one another;
(g) allowing time for the 'reactive slope' to dissipate with familiarity.

Step 8e **THERE ARE TWO 'DURATION OF PROBLEM' QUESTIONS:**

(a) Target behaviour duration: how long the behaviour lasts (say, a temper tantrum).
(b) Time-since-onset: the date of the onset of the problem/s.

Duration 'When Jenny has a fit of screaming, how long does it go on for?'

(a) Ask parents to time samples of the tantrums.

(b) This will provide baseline data as well as diagnostic information.

BEHAVIOUR

Duration 'When did the problem begin?'

Note: *Many of the problems of childhood are the emotional equivalent of 'growing pains': they are transitory. Problem behaviour is sometimes a 'normal' reaction to a difficult phase of life. They will 'grow out of it' given sensitive and sensible home and/or school management. The clinician refers to this phenomenon as 'spontaneous remission'.*

   Given that the persistence of behaviour problems is the exception rather than the rule, the duration of the problems should be estimated; it may serve as an index of the seriousness you ascribe to it.

Ask: The parent 'Has the problem gone on for so long that, on balance, there are more incidents of high tension, in which you are at odds with your child, than moments of relaxed enjoyment of him?' If the answer indicates that the balance has tilted badly in the direction of long-enduring aversion, your diagnostic 'mental alarm system' should start sounding.

Step 9   ASSESS THE CONTINGENCIES; IDENTIFY THE ANTECEDENT, AND CONSEQUENT EVENTS (CONTINGENCIES)

Having gathered all the information you can about the problem and its settings, in order to put forward hypotheses about the conditions influencing the behaviour you need to identify the functional relationships between As and Bs and Cs.

(a) What happens just before the behaviour occurs; what sets it off?

(b) What happens immediately following the behaviour; what happens as a result of the behaviour?

	Name of Pupil:	*John Simpson*					
	Date: *24/6*			Stage: *Baseline*			
	Recording/observation time: *2×3 minute sessions per subject*						
	Mon	Tues	Wed	Thurs	Fri		Total (by subject/per week)
1	1' 2"	1' 15"	2' 15"	1' 2"	40"	Maths	*11' 34"*
2	50"	1' 2"	1' 18"	2' 5"	55"		
1	10"	40"	55'	1' 10"	1' 10"	History	*6' 56"*
Week 1 2	1' 30"	30"	1' 13"	40"	38'		
1	—	1' 10"	10"	—	1' 0"	English	*3' 40"*
2	1' 10"	10"	—	—	—		
Total	4' 42"	4' 47"	5' 51"	4' 57"	4' 13"	Weekly percentage 27 %	

1	50"					Maths	
2	40"						
1	42"					History	
Week 2 2	55"						
1	1' 15"					English	
2	5"						
Total (all subjects)	4' 27"					Weekly percentage %	

Problem definition: *Poor attention = off task behaviour*
= doing things / tasks not given
daydreaming
talking to others
looking out of window / at others
playing with objects (pencils, etc)

Fig. 9 An illustration of one way of collecting information (in this case, duration of 'off-task' behaviours) to answer the question, 'How much of the problematic behaviour does the child show?' Record the proportion of time spent on a particular set of actions out of the total possible time (i.e. the time available).

Antecedent events (prior stimulation) are the antecedent stimulus events which reliably precede the (target) behaviour. They may be functionally related to the behaviour by:
(1) setting the stage for it (discriminative stimuli); or
(2) evoking it (eliciting stimuli).

What factors (situations, persons, etc.) can 'push' or 'pull' — make more or less severe — the level of the problematic behaviour? In other words, what sets off the behaviour; what moderates it?

Consequent events (outcomes) refer to the new conditions which the target behaviour was instrumental in bringing about. The effects of this behaviour on the person's internal and external environment are crucial determinants of whether or not the behaviour will recur. What conditions seem to be maintaining the problematic behaviour; what are the positively reinforcing and/or negatively reinforcing consequences of the troublesome actions?

> **Remember:** *Parents are often conscious only of the child's problem behaviour; to them he seems to erupt unpredictably with 'bad' behaviour. They cannot always tell you of the events which precipitate (or indeed) ameliorate a sequence of troublesome behaviour. It is up to you to tease out the information by precise interviewing, or by observation (theirs and/or yours). They may be too bound up in the problem to see their own role in triggering or prolonging the events. Teach parents to observe so that with your help they can identify the conditions that elicit, cue, or promote deviant behaviour.*

You may attempt to measure or obtain an estimate of:

(1) the overall rate of antecedent events (e.g. commands per hour; affectionate overtures per day);
(2) the overall rate of consequent events (e.g. praises or punishments per hour; response costs per day);
(3) the ratios of antecedents to behaviour, behaviour to consequents (e.g. what is the probability (rate) of obedience or disobedience following a command and what is the ratio of verbal reinforcement following these two behaviours).

A major difficulty for inexperienced behaviour analysts (not unlike the parents) is the 'I can't see the wood for the trees' problem. Paradoxically, the very richness of the data becomes an embarrassment. They don't know where to start. Work slowly and systematically. Take one target behaviour at a time. Write it down in ABC terms. Tease out all the implications you can.

Don't stop at one consequence; *follow* the chain of outcomes. For example:

Student: My client steals games and sweets from the supermarket.
Q: Then what happens?
A: He brings them home.
Q: And then . . .?

A: He is punished.
Q: How and by whom?
A: His mother tells him off.

It might be tempting, apart from getting more detail, to leave the sequence there . . . but what about the stolen items?

Q: What happens to the sweets and games?
A: In the evening the family eat the sweets and settle down with the child to play the games.

This *true* sequence, with its final sting in the tail, puts a different complexion on the episode as a learning experience about theft for the child. Antecedents too, may be traced some way back through chains of overt and covert events.

Illustration

Here is an example of an ABC analysis (obviously a small illustrative fragment) for a child named John, aged six, and his 'demanding' behaviour.

A. Antecedent events

Demanding occurs in and out of the house, but more frequently and intensively in public places like shops or friends' houses. At home it can happen any time, but more often when mother has got company or is very busy, cooking, washing, telephoning. Tea-times and mornings are particularly difficult. Demanding occurs seldom with his father and is less frequent when father is present. It never occurs with people he does not know well and never at school. Demanding is triggered off if mother doesn't respond immediately to his request or if she says 'no'.

B. Behaviour

John will demand that mother give or buy him something, ask her to let him do something or go somewhere, things of which she does not approve, or demands she cannot fulfil immediately. He will go on and on repeating his 'request', getting very angry so that the request becomes a querulous command. He follows the mother, pulls her, eventually screams and shouts at her or becomes destructive throwing things about, etc. The frequency is seven times a day on average, each episode lasting up to 20 minutes at times, and is very intensive — depending on what he wants and where it happens.

C. Consequences

Mother interacts a good deal with John during these episodes, she pleads with him, disputes with him, tries to distract him, getting angrier and more frustrated, threatens him (threats are seldom carried out), screams and shouts at him, and occasionally hits him. He obviously gains a lot of attention. Eventually she gets tired and just for peace and quiet she gives in. In a public place, e.g. shops, she gives in quickly to avoid embarrassment, criticisms from other people and scenes. She gets very upset and at times ends up in tears.

Recording adult behaviour

You may get a hunch that (say) the mother's moods are part of the stimulus configuration of antecedents leading up to problematic behaviour on the part of the child, or fraught interactions between parent and child. Try to quantify your hunch by getting the mother to keep a diary (see Fig. 10).

There is evidence that self-monitoring can be an accurate method of assessment. You must be cautious, however, as it is reactive to various factors (see Haynes, 1978). Intermittent monitoring and reinforcement of the process (by the therapist) can facilitate accuracy.

Stimulus control

Antecedent events or stimuli with potential stimulus-control properties are many and various; the concept of multiple or compound stimulus-control is thus useful in assessing the behaviour of children in the home or classroom. You might be looking at the parents' verbal messages (tone and content), physical gestures, eye-contact and so on (see Forehand and McMahon, 1981). Other antecedents could be the particular persons or number of persons present, their age and sex; their relationship to the child. There are those stimuli which derive their behaviour-control potency through association with different contingency (reinforcement) probabilities. Others are, to an extent, non-contingent in their behaviour-control properties, e.g. states brought about by illness, drugs, alcohol, rejection, and so on.

Many problematic behaviours are the final events in a sequence of behavioural 'happenings' which may have been provoked in another place

DIARY RECORD: *Mrs Val Smith*   STAGE: *Baseline (1st week)*
(self-report)

MORNING	AFTERNOON
1 24/3 Am feeling irritable and low. Real 'blue monday'. Have to shove a lot to get Pauline ready for school. P fractious, defiant – refused to get dressed. We had a real set-to.	Feel a bit brighter. Still worried about the bill. But something will turn up. Did my relaxation exercises. No problem with P since coming from school. Thank Heavens!
2 Period pains!! Feel v. tense. Pauline annoyed me, not sure if she got out of the wrong side of the bed... or I did? P dawdled over breakfast. Argy Bargy.	Nothing eventful – P. OK.
3 Feeling depressed. Had an argument with Frank over shouting at the children (Had to shout at P – fighting with Barbara I don't seem to be able to manage. Bit tearful.)	More relaxed. Did relaxation exercises with tape recorder on. Pauline in good mood; amused herself.
4 P's defiance is really getting me down. It tires me out. She just won't listen. After a restless night my nerves are raw.	Feeling OK; Pauline a bit whiny but not bad. I'm so much better when she's behaving, or is it the other way round?!
5 No change. P horrible. I could have 'murdered' her this a.m. I nagged at her. Frank left for work in a mood.	Blessed peace P out with her gran. Feel a bit guilty saying that.
6 Sat. Usual hell. P played up at the supermarket, wanted things. Ended up feeling embarrassed.	Feeling tired. P wouldn't eat her lunch. In the end left it to Frank. Threatened to leave them all.
7	

CHOSEN TOPICS:
1. My moodiness (getting irritable and depressed)
2. Pauline's behaviour (defiance and fighting)
3. Frank's attitude to me and the girls.
4. Any random thoughts and feelings
5.
6.
7.
8.

FIG. 10 A self-report diary.

and at another time. A careful tracing of such behavioural chains is necessary because an early intervention in a chain may successfully pre-empt the problem behaviour.

Up to now we have been referring to proximal antecedents (see Fig. 1) which are close in time to the actual behaviour. The distal antecedents refer to the more distant (historical) events in the client's life. The child's past and present development is described in terms of the known medical history as well as parental reports of the child's early behaviour patterns, his growth and developmental milestones.

An analysis of these factors is not necessarily a condition of successful interventions — distal antecedents, after all, are more or less removed in time from the events of the client's life-situation. An analysis of these factors is, however, a valuable exercise. Haynes (1978) lists four advantages:

(1) it may suggest conditions under which the behaviour problem may reappear after successful modification;
(2) it may provide clues concerning controlling variables;
(3) understanding of how behaviour problems begin is very instructive to clients; and
(4) the historical information may be relevant to behaviour theory and to the development of preventative programmes.

Step 10a   IDENTIFY REINFORCERS

Children are 'turned on' and 'turned off' by different things; so find out what the child (and the parents) find rewarding.

(a) You need to identify reinforcers (rewards). Children find different things pleasurable or aversive. After all, they have different kinds of genetic constitution and reinforcement histories. The important thing is to use reinforcers that are effective for the client you are working with.

(b) You need to know something of the child's reinforcement history. The analysis of outcome controlling factors (consequent events) includes an assessment of why, when and how parents (and others) reward the child. This means finding out whether rewarding the child is contingent on her behaving in a certain way; whether rewards are applied indiscriminately or whether there is any consistency in the pattern of rewarding. Indeed, is she ever praised or encouraged for behaving well, or does she only receive attention when behaving 'badly'? Using praise as a source of reinforcement may be counterproductive with some children when they have received so little in the past that they have not learned to value it.

(c) Timing of the rewards is also crucial. There should be as little delay as possible between the child's behaviour and its consequences. Human beings do have the ability to delay reinforcement or punishment because they have verbal means to mediate this delay. In fact, teaching a child to delay gratification is one of the major jobs of parents and society. We tend to think of adults who cannot do this as childish or immature. People do learn to work for distant goals such as a professional diploma. However, a careful examination of the situation surrounding such long range activities would undoubtedly reveal many reinforcements along the way that tend to maintain the behaviour.

(d) Do not underestimate the amount and frequency of reinforcement required when the child is learning new skills or tasks. (When the skill is acquired and has to be maintained the reinforcers are modified.)

(e) The reinforcing consequences should be very closely related to the desired 'terminal' behaviour (i.e. the particular and immediate treatment goal which is required) not the long-term objectives.

(f) Parents should be *clear* about what behaviours they are reinforcing and consistent (i.e. predictable in the consequences they apply to those behaviours).

(g) And they should make it plain to the child what it is they are reinforcing her for (cognitive structure).

The above assessments are made not only for the use of positive reinforcers but also for sanctions and punishments.

It is at this stage of the analysis (to take one example) that knowledge of the developmental literature is helpful. As the child matures, the way in which she cognitively structures (labels) a situation will determine whether or not anxiety about deviant acts is elicited or not. This has a bearing on whether she inhibits the 'immoral' act or not. What happens is that disapproved behaviours and the cues associated with the immediate antecedents of such behaviours ('impulses') come to elicit anxiety. Parents may have, in a sense, a choice of whether they bring out to lesser or greater degree one or other of the attributes of guilt and resistance to temptation, in their children. This will depend primarily on two things: the timing of the sanctions they administer for misconduct, and the nature of the explanations they provide when they do so. There is evidence that punishment which immediately precedes a forbidden act (i.e. as the intention to transgress is forming and becoming explicit) maximizes resistance to temptation. Punishment has undesirable side-effects when it is not modulated. Above a certain optimal level of intensity it produces a state of emotionality in the child which appears to interfere with learning. If discrimination of the punished choice is difficult, intense punishment is actually more likely to lead to transgression. A child must be able to distinguish what aspect of her behaviour is being punished if she is to be able to exercise control over the consequences of her actions.

Note: *Reinforcers and punishers (the C term in our ABC equation) are defined in terms of how they influence the child—the learner— and not how the therapist or parents think they might or should affect her. Reinforcers are individual to the particular child.*

You can identify reinforcers in the following ways:
(1) Observe the child's behaviour. What does she like doing most? What does she choose to do a lot of when she has the choice (high probability behaviours)?
(2) Ask the child . . . what she likes . . . likes doing . . . with whom.
(3) Ask those who know the child.

Table IV   Some suggested reinforcers[a]

	Home	Classroom
Things	Crayons, plasticene, note pads, play-money, football cards, charms, pencils, marbles, ball-point pens, comics, records, favourite meals, small toys, book/record tokens, models, puzzles, stamps, magazines, sweets, crisps, fruit, stars.	Good report to take home, loan of books, magazines, records. Tokens. Use of stimulating rarity-value items/equipment. Special place in the classroom.
Activities and games	Pictures to fill in — in stages,[b] cutting out pictures, drawing/ painting, stickers, watching TV, listening to records, playing monopoly, ludo, puzzles, etc. visits, helping mother/father.	Finger painting, quiz, writing on the board, being read a story, helping teacher, clay modelling, looking at magazines, listening to records, using the tape-recorder, other favoured individual group activities.
Privileges	Staying up late, choice of meal, extra pocket money, extra long story from parent, outing with father (football match, etc.), going to the cinema.	Longer recess, no homework, not having to take a test, outings, leaving school early.
Social	Praise, encouragement, hugging etc.	Attention, recognition praise.

[a]These items may be offered as part of a reinforcement menu (with a tariff) for older children, or put on display in a 'pretend shop' with its price list, for younger children.
[b]See p. 163 for an imaginative example of a reinforcement picture drawn by a child's mother.

(4) Table IV provides you with a few questionnaire/checklist items.

(5) Check on particular states of deprivation. Some children are deprived of so few of the 'goodies' in life that it is very difficult to find effective reinforcers.

(6) Premack's Principle: Therapists have made use of the principle that the opportunity, or privilege, to engage in preferred activities can reinforce activities or behaviours that are less popular. In other words, high probability behaviours can act as contingent reinforcers for low probability behaviours. The value to a child of reinforcing activities can be estimated by observing the frequency of behaviours in a free-choice situation. This principle is sometimes referred to as 'Grandma's rule'. It states that 'first you work, then you play' or 'you do what I want you to do before you are allowed to do what you want to do'. Clearly this notion, like so many other learning principles, has been known and practised by succeeding generations of child-rearers as simple common sense. However, it has been enshrined as a formal principle — the Premack principle — defining one type of reinforcer, following Premack's research into the problem of response probability and his search for an index that would predict between response preferences for a wide variety of topographically dissimilar behaviours.

Remember: Attention is very rewarding! Especially for children; and parents can (unwittingly) support disruptive behaviour by attending to it (scolding, nagging, distracting). Don't forget to look for what is reinforcing in the maladaptive, self-defeating behaviours of parents or parent-substitutes.

An individual's behaviour is affected by much more than the particular nature of reinforcements (pay-offs) or goals. The effect of reinforcement depends on whether or not the person perceives a causal relationship between his own behaviour and the reward. This perception may vary in degree from individual to individual and even within the same individual over time and situations. A truly significant influence on behaviour is provided by the person's *anticipation* ('expectancy') that his goals will be achieved. Such expectations are determined by his previous experience.

Remember: A child's alleged 'problems' may serve as an 'admission ticket' for parents who may have other problems they need to discuss. The hidden agenda may be family problems, the child with the so-called 'symptoms' acting unwittingly as a diversion from the recognition of such problems (marital or other). It is not unknown for the 'successful' treatment of the child to change the family

*system in a way that exacerbates other areas of tension; conflicts
between the parents may be laid bare. For these and other reasons,
do not neglect Step 10b.*

Step 10b   **WHAT *SENSE* OR MEANING
IS THERE IN THE PROBLEM
BEHAVIOUR?**

*(a) From the child's point of view. (What are
his perceptions of his behaviour and
situation? Does the problematic behaviour
have a pay-off? What function does it
serve for him?)*
*(b) From the family's point of view. (Is there
a pay-off for them in his problematic
status?)*
(c) From your professional point of view.

What a person tells himself about his experience affects his behaviour (see
Meichenbaum (1977) on cognitive aspects of behaviour modification).
Problems arise when he misperceives events and then bases his actions on
his distorted conception of a situation.

Because of the maturing child's capacity to anticipate events, conditions
of reinforcement also have potent incentive and motivational effects.
Although immediate reinforcement is (as we have said) particularly powerful,
especially with children, most human behaviour is not controlled by
immediate external reinforcement. As a result of prior experiences and
through the capacity to represent actual outcomes *symbolically*, future
consequences can be converted into current incentives/motivators that
influence behaviour in much the same way as *actual* outcomes. Cognitive
skills in the maturing child allow him to be foresightful.

The motivational function of reinforcement has implications for your
assessment. Problems arise when the incentive system is faulty, for example
when (1) social stimuli which are positively or negatively reinforcing for a
majority of persons (praise, attention, encouragement, blame, criticism,
disapproval) do not work for the client: (2) the potent reinforcers for the
client are deviant or harmful (drugs, alcohol, glue-sniffing, fire-setting):
(3) the environment (wittingly and unwittingly) is reinforcing maladaptive
behaviour: (4) there is a relative absence of reinforcement in the individual's
life-situation.

Motivational function of reinforcement

Reinforcement and its vicissitudes may play a part in the depressions manifested (fairly rarely) in children, and more frequently in adolescents. In the experience of the author, many parents (especially mothers) are reacting with depression and demoralization to the child and family problems they find themselves coping with so ineffectually. Depressive reactions may result from any one, or more, of the following situations:

(1) The individual's perceptions of his ability to control his life is distorted; he feels helpless or hopeless because of a perceived absence of any contingency between the person's own efforts and the reinforcing nature of the consequences that flow from them.
(2) The individual's efforts to bring about reinforcement are inadequate.
(3) His environment is providing him with scanty reinforcers.

Step 11   ASSESS ORGANISMIC VARIABLES (or obtain information from other sources)

You are not dealing with an 'empty vessel'; there are all sorts of things going on within the organism. The child's behaviour does not occur in a vacuum. He is responding to an external and internal environment as he grows up. An assessment of organismic factors tells us something of the intrinsic child.

Children respond to two environments — an inner and outer one — as they grow up. For example, adolescents are subject to dramatic changes in metabolism and body size and shape at puberty. These changes influence their body image and self-concept and, in turn, affect behaviour (Herbert, 1987). But the word *organism* must not be allowed to over-emphasize the *reactive (passive)* element, or understate the *agency (active)* aspects of human behaviour.

Certainly social learning theorists place great emphasis on the active, interpretive nature of learning and thus the cognitive component.

(1)   Cognitive factors

People learn many of their social and other behaviours (and psychological disorders tend to be socially defined) by following their instructions, by thinking through the implications of their observations of the significant people in their environment, learning from what they do and say. They are also demonstrably capable of regulating their behaviour 'from within'.

Part of the confusion about the role of cognition in contemporary behavioural work is the presumption of some psychologists that cognition refers not to a substantive aspect of behaviour explicable in terms of basic behavioural processes, but that it refers to another set of processes at another level of analysis (Morris, 1986). Morris states that cognition does constitute a substantive content-related domain of behavioural activity and outcome described in ordinary language terms (e.g. thinking, remembering, problem-solving). As he puts it: 'cognitive' is an adjective, 'cognitively' an adverb and 'cognitating' a verb—all denoting a particular kind of behavioural activity and context (e.g. remembering where we left the keys).

The influence of environmental events is strongly determined by cognition which, in turn, is based upon prior experience. It governs what events are attended to, how they are perceived and interpreted, whether or not they are remembered and how they might influence future thought and action. Bandura (1977b) does not restrict cognitive processes to the encoding of immediate environmental events. He claims that they also involve deliberate and self-referent thinking that regulates behaviour.

The cognitive construct of 'expectations' has been of importance in two mini-theories pertinent to psychological disorders: self efficacy theory (Bandura, 1977b); and learned helplessness theory (Seligman, 1975; Abramson et al., 1980). These theories have important implications for the style and content of any treatment programme; so do the developmental aspects of children's cognitions.

What children think may influence their performance of deviant behaviours. Thus knowledge of the ways the child perceives and structures events—say, a 'provocative' incident—may provide a clue to changing his behaviour, if it is self-defeating.

There are many factors including maturational processes which pre-determine the sequence and structure of developmental stages. Intellectual processes change qualitatively as the child grows up. It is important for the child therapist to know about these processes if she is to understand what sense and meaning the child is able to make of the physical, social and moral world he inhabits—at different ages and stages of development.

(2) Temperament

Information about behaviour style aids the fuller understanding of problem behaviour. For example, it is clear that early differences in temperament set the stage for varying patterns of interaction with the environment, leading to the shaping of personality along lines which are not predictable from knowledge of the environment alone.

An intensive study of 136 New York children (Thomas *et al.*, 1968) measured temperament in terms of nine descriptive categories: activity level, rhythmicity, approach and withdrawal, adaptability, intensity of reaction, threshold of responsiveness, quality of mood, distractibility, attention span and persistence. They classified babies according to clusters of temperamental characteristics; these groupings were referred to as 'difficult', 'easy' and 'slow to warm up' babies. The difficult child showed irregularity in biological functioning, a predominance of negative response (withdrawal) to new stimuli, slowness in adapting to changes in the environment, frequent expression of negative moods and a predominance of intense reactions. The easy child, on the other hand, was positive in mood, highly regular, low or mild in the intensity of his reactions, readily adaptable and usually positive in his approach to new situations. In short, his temperamental organization was such that it usually made his early care seem easy and pleasant.

There is evidence that even as early as the second year of life, and before the manifestation of symptoms, children who were later to develop behaviour problems showed particular temperamental attributes. Children with markedly irregular patterns of functioning, who were slow to adapt to new situations, whose emotional responses were usually at a high level of intensity, and whose predominant mood was negative were the ones who were most likely to come to psychiatric attention for later problem behaviour (70% of this so-called 'difficult' category).

Activity level is a temperamental attribute which tends to be stable over time. A mother will react to a child with a high activity level in a different manner than to a child with a low activity level. High rates of activity and high intensities of emotional expression in the repertoire of children tend to be aversive to adults, and, indeed, are among the most frequent complaints made by adults in referring children to out-patient clinics.

Hyperactivity is the name for one of the most trying problems a mother or teacher has to cope with: the overactive child, who seldom sits still. Such a 'hyperactive' child faces severe impediments to achieving success at school, because his problems militate against efficient learning. First of all, he suffers intense and disorganized overactivity. This, in turn, is associated with distractivility, a very short span of attention, and impulsiveness. Also, more often than not, children with these problems do not get on very well with their peers, being aggressive and rather destructive. Their control over their emotions may be limited, and trivial setbacks may trigger sudden and violent outbursts of rage, while stressful situations may precipitate panic attacks.

(3) Health and physical impairment

There is a variety of physical conditions, such as hunger, anaemia, mild infections and drug-effects, which can lead to lassitude — something often mistaken for laziness. If a child is to be successful at school, good health is vital; it provides the basis for the stamina demanded by long hours of concentration in the classroom. Regular attendance at school depends upon it, and effective learning, in turn, depends upon reasonably consistent presence at lessons. Some subjects (e.g. arithmetic, mathematics) are hierarchical in structure; that is, one step is logically preceded by, and dependent upon, another. So the child who misses a series of lessons (particularly the child who has chronic, recurrent illnesses) may experience great difficulty in catching up. Subjects like mathematics, which tend anyway to attract negative emotional attitudes, may (in the absence of an understanding teacher) become the focus of intense anxiety for the vulnerable child. Even the regular attender may not be able to learn efficiently if he is tired or apathetic.

The clinician needs to be alert to physical and intellectual limitations such as short-sightedness, epilepsy, slow learning and low IQ and the referral services available for dealing with these disabilities.

Physical problems are not only responsible for undermining scholastic endeavours; they may themselves be the consequence of emotional disturbance. If a child shows physical lethargy and a lack of interest, he may be depressed. In its milder forms, depression may show itself as a lack of physical energy and well-being. In its more severe manifestations, the child tends to be irritable and bad-tempered, and, when it is at its worst, he sleeps poorly, lacks an appetite and is always dejected, apathetic and lifeless. The child who is (for whatever reason) depressed refuses to meet the challenges of life; he ceases to strive and to use his full effectiveness in whatever sphere of activity he finds himself. An essentially emotional problem like this is often mistaken for a physical one.

(4) Autonomic response patterns

The control system responsible in large part for emotional reactions is the autonomic nervous system (ANS). It is also responsible for the more mundane day-to-day maintenance of the *internal* environment via the glands, blood vessels, smooth muscles and heart muscle. The activities of these effectors (as they are known) are controlled by the autonomic nervous system. Most of the motor impulses that control these internal organs (viscera) and keep us functioning efficiently operate below the level of consciousness.

This control system—a network of motor nerve cells—plays a large part, not ony in maintaining the individual's internal environment and homeostasis, but also in determining his response to emergencies, toning him up for maximum capacity to cope.

In many problems we see physiology (the ANS), behaviour, affect (feelings) and cognitions, all at work. For example, phobic anxiety in a child may involve avoidance or escape strategies, physiological signs of arousal, cognitive factors like faulty attribution, and feelings of helplessness, or combinations and permutations of all of them. Here then is a mixture of overt and covert events playing aetiological, maintaining or mediational roles in the manifestation of the problem. Any of them might become the focus of an intervention. A doctor might try to reduce a child's level of arousal (tension/anxiety) by prescribing tranquillizers; a psychologist might suggest relaxation training and an ABC analysis.

Step 12   ARRIVE AT A DIAGNOSTIC DECISION

Ask yourself:
(a) *Is one of your objectives to intervene and bring about some change?*
(b) *If so, specify precisely what the areas of change are to be; why they need to be brought about; and how these alterations are likely to change not only the child but the whole (family/classroom) system.*

There are essentially two issues to be resolved at this stage:

(a) *Diagnostic:* Is it a problem of sufficient seriousness to merit an intervention?
(b) *Ethical:*   Is it ethically right to intervene so as to produce changes in the direction of goals X, Y or Z?

Arriving at diagnostic criteria

Problems are so-called because they have a variety of unfavourable consequences: when they are not deficit problems (a failure to learn adaptive responses), they are conceptualized as strategies of adjustment which the child has learned to his own disadvantage (and often to the disadvantage of others) in the attempt to cope with the demands of life. They are therefore referred to as maladaptive strategies: they are inappropriate in terms of several criteria which are assessed by the clinician.

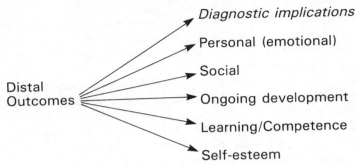

The diagnostic criteria are listed on the right of Fig. 1 (p. 9), with regard to (a) personal, (b) social, (c) developmental, (d) learning and (e) self-factors. They arise from a consideration of the longer-term consequences (distal outcomes) of the problem behaviours. You should have arrived already at some reckoning of the probability that you are dealing with a problem meriting serious concern—in your working out of the FIND parameters (Step 8).

Ultimately, the professional judgement of a child's mental/behavioural well-being is made in individual terms, taking into account the child's unique personality, his particular circumstances and the opportunities, privations and stresses associated with them. (On another level, similar questions can be asked of the family unit in which he resides.)

Ask yourself: What are the implications of the child's (and his family's) life style? More specifically, what are the consequences—favourable or unfavourable—that flow from the child's ways of behaving and his interactions with others?

You must establish what the implications of his behaviour are for the following factors:

(a) His personal well-being (his emotional state)

Ask yourself: Is he in a state of distress: anxious, discontented, unhappy, morbidly preoccupied, hostile, insecure, overly dependent, guilty?

(b) His social development

Ask yourself: Does he get on with other children, with adults? Can he go out and enjoy himself or is he socially restricted in some way? Can he make and keep friends?

Immature, self-centred children are not always able to manage the give-and-take of friendship. Exchange theory gives us pointers to why this should be so; it provides one method of evaluating friendships. Those theorists who employ 'exchange theory' in analysing aspects of social behaviour and friendship, view social interactions as a social exchange somewhat analogous to economic exchange; people are influenced (consciously and unconsciously) by the ratio of 'rewards' and the 'costs' incurred in the interaction.

In the assessment of the implications for social relationships, it is useful to draw up a balance sheet. On the debit side, the term 'cost' is applied to deterrents that may be incurred in contacts with another person—such as hostility, anxiety, embarrassment, and the like. For attraction to a potential friend to occur the reward–cost outcome must be above the 'comparison level', a standard against which satisfaction is judged.

Technique: *Do a cost-benefit analysis* to evaluate the desirability of changing the target behaviour as it affects the child, the caregiver (parent/teacher) and oneself (or the agency).

Costs to the child might include being singled out (and embarrassed) as needing help; benefits anticipated might include happier relations with siblings, less failure at school.

Costs to the caregiver (say teacher) may involve distraction from teaching duties to other children in the classroom; benefits (in the longer term) might include more time for creative teaching in the absence of disruptive interjections by the target child.

Note: Ways should be worked out to minimize costs.

(c) His ongoing development and maturation

Ask yourself: Do the child's problems interfere with the forward momentum and course of normal development? Are they causing him to 'regress', or slowing him down? Do they represent a 'cul-de-sac', taking him in the direction of a self-defeating life-style?

(1) Is the child's adaptive behaviour appropriate to his age, intelligence and social situation?
(2) Is the environment making reasonable *demands* of the child?
(3) Is the environment satisfying the crucial *needs* of the child, i.e. the needs that are vital at his particular stage of development?

The family (or some other agent of socialization) may be dysfunctional. Thus, if the child's behaviour is abnormal (unusual), troublesome and self-defeating—and the answers to questions 2 and 3 are 'No'—then you are still faced with a problem. However, it is more of a 'problem situation'

Table V Behaviour problems shown by one-third or more of normal boys and girls aged 21 months to 14 years (behaviour problems shown by one-third or more of the boys and girls at each age level) (MacFarlane et al., 1954)

		Age 1¾	3	3½	4	5	6	7	8	9	10	11	12	13	14
Enuresis (diurnal and nocturnal)	B	+													
	G	+													
Soiling	B														
	G														
Disturbing dreams	B										+				
	G						+				+	+			
Restless sleep	B	+													
	G														
Insufficient appetite	B														
	G						+								
Food finickiness	B		+												
	G	+	+	+											
Excessive modesty	B														
	G														
Nailbiting	B													+	+
	G									+		+	+		
Thumbsucking	B														
	G		+												
Overactivity	B		+	+	+			+	+	+					
	G		+	+	+	+									
Speech	B						+	+	+						
	G				+	+									

Overdependence	B										
	G										
Attention demanding	B										
	G										
Oversensitiveness	B	+ +	+ +	+ +	+	+ +	+ +	+ +	+ +	+ +	+ +	+
	G	+ +	+ +	+ +	+	+ +	+ +	+ +	+ +	+ +	+ +	+
Physical timidity	B			+	+							
	G	+										
Specific fears	B	+ +	+ +	+ +	+ +	+ +	+ +	+	+ +	+ +		
	G	+ +	+ +	+ +	+ +	+ +	+ +	+	+ +	+ +		
Mood swings	B			−	−	− −	−	−	+	+	+ +	+
	G			−	−	− −	+	+	+ +	+	+	
Shyness[a]	B	−	−	−	−	−	−	−				
	G	−	−	−	−	−	−	−				
Sombreness	B				+		+					
	G				+		+					
Negativism	B	+		+			+					
	G	+		+			+					
Irritability	B											
	G											
Tempers	B	+ +	+ +	+ +	+ +	+ +	+ +	+ +	+	+	+	
	G	+ +	+ +	+ +	+ +	+ +	+ +	+ +	+	+	+	
Jealousy	B		+	+		+	+	+ +	+	+	+	+
	G		+	+		+	+	+ +	+	+	+	+
Excessive reserve[a]	B	−	−	+ +	+ +	+	+	+	+	+ +	+ +	+
	G	−	−	+ +	+ +	+	+	+	+	+ +	+ +	+

[a]Data not obtained

than a 'problem child'. In a sense this is always the case, and it is a matter of judgement as to where the emphasis in treatment will be.

A feature of much problem behaviour in childhood is its transitoriness. So mercurial are some of the changes of behaviour in response to the rapid growth and the successive challenges of childhood that it is difficult to pinpoint the beginning of really serious problems. A long-term study (MacFarlane et al., 1954) of the development of 126 American 'run-of-the-mill' children provides us with information (see Table V) about the incidents and shifts in their problem behaviours as manifested at different ages between 21 months and 14 years.

It would be helpful if we could identify the periods when a child is most vulnerable to emotional problems, and concentrate our efforts and resources so as to help him (and his parents) through such crises (Herbert, 1974). Some theorists talk of 'developmental discontinuities'. One of the chief types of developmental discontinuity is brought about by significant and relatively rapid shifts in the individual's biosocial status (e.g. adolescence).

(d) His learning skills, competence and self-esteem

Perhaps one of the most serious consequences of emotional and behavioural disorder is its deleterious effect on the child's learning in the classroom and hence, his achievement. Even highly intelligent, maladjusted pupils tend to have real difficulties in school performance. The greater the number of problems reported, the poorer, on the whole, is school performance.

Some children, for a wide variety of reasons, lack skills which are essential in order to cope with growing up in a satisfactory manner. Physically handicapped children, for example, are massively overrepresented in the population of youngsters with behaviour problems. If such children behave dysfunctionally in response to a variety of stresses, frustrations and humiliations, it is hardly surprising. They can be helped to become more competent and thus have less need of what proves to be counterproductive problem behaviour.

Seligman (1975) suggests that what produces self-esteem and a sense of competence in the quality and consistency of his early and ongoing experience at home and at school.

Step 13	FORMULATE THE PROBLEM
	Put together your information and collate your data so as to make sense of your clients' problem. Present them in such a way that they generate possible solutions.

The formal or main phase of assessment can be said to be over when you have a reasonably clear picture of your clients' difficulties, their assets, social setting and background. You should have a sense of how the problems developed and how they 'look' against a framework of normal development.

The problem is formulated usually in systemic terms, that is to say as it affects people rather than one person (client) and as it impinges on a *family system* rather than an individual alone.

The formulation provides a summary of the salient information you have collected; it is 'formulated' in the sense that you put forward an 'explanatory story' (hopefully a valid one) to impose meaning on your data. It consists of a series of hypotheses which are statements about how the problem arose, when and where it occurs, and why it is maintained.

This is a precursor to formulating a strategy to solve the dilemma. A clear formulation should generate effective treatment methods.

Bromley (1977) describes the required steps for the explication of the individual case:

(1) State clearly the problems and issues.
(2) Collect background information as a context for understanding (1).
(3) Put forward *prima facie* explanations (conjectures/hypotheses) and solutions (programme formulation) with regard to the client's personality and predicament — on the basis of information available at the time, and on the basis of the *principle of parsimony*. Examine the simple and obvious answers first. They may, of course, have to be rejected if they don't stand up to critical examination. This guides the:
(4) Search for further/additional evidence. New hypotheses/explanations will have to be formulated and examined.
(5) Search *again* for, and admit for consideration, sufficient evidence to eliminate as many of the suggested explanations (hypotheses) as possible; the hope is that one of them will be so close to reality as to account for all the evidence and be contradicted by none of it. The evidence may be direct or indirect; but it is vital that it should be admissible, relevant and obtained from competent and credible sources.
(6) Enquire critically into the *sources* of evidence, as well as the evidence itself. Bromley (1977) makes the point that in the case of personal testimony, this is analogous to cross-examinations in a court of law; otherwise it amounts to checking the consistency and accuracy of all items of evidence.
(7) Examine carefully the internal logic, coherence and external validity of the entire network of associations and hypotheses formulated to explain the client's predicament and proposals to solve the problems.

(8) Select the 'most likely' interpretation, provided it is compatible with the evidence (some lines of argument will be obviously inadequate whereas others will be possible or even convincing).

(9) Work out the implications of your explanations for intervention/treatment or some other action (or, indeed, inaction).

Always ask yourself about the implications (e.g. the risks involved) of making Type I as opposed to Type II errors in your assessment. Is it more damaging to your client if you risk Type I errors (i.e. asserting relationships falsely) than if you risk Type II errors, which deny relationships that do actually exist? The academic psychologist tends to minimize errors of incautious assertion at the expense of relatively common Type II errors. The clinician often acts on the basis of weakly supported propositions because of the dangers of ignoring potentially significant associations. But of course there may also be some risks in presuming relationships which do not have any basis in reality.

This step requires that you

(10) Work out the implications in *specific* terms.

Levels of explanation

The trouble with the search for reasons or explanations is that there are several levels of explanation which may be applicable to a particular problem. This is illustrated by a young child, Pam, who has a learning problem which is affecting her ability to read. On top of this, she has certain behavioural problems, as constant failure is causing her morale to sink lower and lower. Diagnostic tests carried out by the educational psychologist show that she has a visual-perceptual handicap. Remedial treatment is available to help her overcome her reading problem. The remedial teacher could teach her to recognize words and their meanings through the medium of her other sensory modalities. Here, the visual handicap is one explanation of the reading difficulty. Some clinicians would rest content with this level of causal explanation, justifying their decision on the grounds that they have sufficient knowledge to intervene therapeutically and help the child. This has been called the 'instrumental' level of explanation. The explanation is sufficiently precise to be instrumental in planning some therapeutic measures to mitigate the cause-effect sequence of events. Or it may simply be instrumental in providing the individual with a satisfactory account of some event. It is sufficient in that it *explains*, and raises no further questions in his mind.

While this explanation provides an account of an important antecedent condition in the problem—in this case the visual-perception handicap—other workers might claim that the diagnostician should search for the *original* cause. In this case they would feel it necessary to determine whether the visual problem was organic — a case of *brain damage*. Be cautious about labelling or you may find it difficult to begin, let alone finish, therapy. Behavioural theorists find labelling almost entirely unnecessary, as becomes obvious from a study of the functional analysis of problems carried out by practitioners. Being tautologies (re-namings) in most instances, they tell us very little about the child and only too often are therapeutically pessimistic.

Parents and teachers are sometimes told that a particular child's difficulties at home and at school are 'a result of brain damage', suffered perhaps as early as at birth. This is no more helpful than for a general practitioner to tell a mother her child is 'physically ill' when she takes her along for a diagnosis of a bodily malaise. Certainly no programme of rehabilitation — remedial teaching or behaviour modification — could be planned on the basis of such a vague diagnosis as 'brain damage'. What is needed, in describing a child, is not a meaningless label but precise information about her specific physical and intellectual problems, and also about any emotional difficulties which have a bearing on her ability to learn. The resistance in behaviour therapy to labels reduces the possibility that such labels will become self-fulfilling prophecies setting up a chain of responses that reinforce expected patterns of dysfunctional behaviour.

A classic example of this last situation can be seen in the case of Robert, an 'autistic' ten-year-old boy referred to the Centre. His parents were told that to expect anything other than bizarre and aggressive behaviour from an 'autistic' child was being unrealistic: as a result, for years, they made no attempt to check or prevent his more antisocial behaviour.

This child was successfully treated using a behavioural programme which assessed his difficult behaviour in the same way as any other behaviour would be assessed. By changing certain antecedent and consequent events the therapist was able to reduce his 'irrational aggression' (which in behavioural terms could be quite rationally explained by looking at the reinforcement it was receiving) and similar antisocial behaviours. Eventually, he was able to start mixing socially with peers, and begin to develop the potential he did have, without the label 'autistic' getting in the way.

Note: *In your attempt to arrive at an explanation of the problem before you, don't neglect the client's point of view: Ask parents/teachers if they have a theory (or hunch) as to why the problem is occurring. You might say: 'I'm sure you've given the matter a lot of thought; have you any ideas or hunches about why she is so rude and aggressive?'*

Conceptual background to the causal formulation of the problem

It is useful to distinguish the distal or historical and the contemporary or proximal causes of problem behaviour (see Fig. 1, p. 9). Early formative (distal) influences have an historical but not a functional connection with present behaviour. The distinction between distal and proximal factors in the explanation of the client's behaviour is crucial. Proximal causes are direct in their effect, precipitating or instigating problem behaviour in a manner that is susceptible to testing in the way that a putative relationship between certain independent and dependent variables are subject to manipulation and testing in the laboratory. Distal causes have an indirect predisposing influence. They cannot be modified or manipulated directly. Historical causes may have affected the client's bodily functioning as in the cases of some genetic factors, injuries or infections, or they may have consisted of certain experiences through which he has learned particular attitudes or unacceptable ways of behaving, in certain situations.

Contemporary influences determine whether the child will perform the behaviour he has acquired, factors such as opportunity, the presence of discriminative stimuli signalling potential reinforcers, and so on. The contemporary causes of problem behaviour may exist in the client's environment or in his own thoughts, feelings or bodily processes, and they may exert their influences in several ways. The effectiveness of change endeavours entails gaining control over as many of the factors influencing the situation as is possible (see Fig. 11 below). Whenever possible this means placing such control in the hands of the client himself, otherwise the results of the intervention will terminate with the departure of the therapist.

Contingent reinforcement

Adult attention is a primary source of reinforcement for children. Social interactions can be beneficially or adversely affected by the reinforcement history experienced by the growing child. Bandura (1969, 1977a) has listed a number of ways in which lack of learning or faulty social learning could occur:

1. Insufficient reinforcement may lead to the extinction of appropriate behaviours. The child might receive little attention or reward from unthinking, harsh or neglectful parents. Such children may not be able to behave in a way that attracts social reinforcement from others and which may cause the child to become withdrawn and apathetic.
2. The child may receive inappropriate reinforcement for what is generally considered undesirable behaviour. Reinforcement of socially prohibited behaviours such as rudeness, aggression, or refusal to comply with adults'

instructions can teach children to behave in a manner that is socially inappropriate. In addition, parents alternatively rewarding, punishing and ignoring the same types of child's responses can prove confusing to the child. Such inconsistent handling fails to teach the child to discriminate how to behave in different circumstances in order to obtain reinforcement.

3. Fictional reinforcement contingencies can exert powerful control over some children's behaviour. Beliefs that other children are dangerous can lead to avoidance of the playground, parties, and so on; many other irrational beliefs may be acquired through the remarks and teaching of other people or may be self-generated. These fictional reinforcement contingencies can be even more powerful than *real* external reinforcing conditions.

4. Faulty self-reinforcement can occur when children hold unrealistically high standards for themselves and remain chronically dissatisfied with their achievements. Such low self-efficacy expectations may lead the child to stop trying to succeed since success seems impossible (Bandura, 1977b). Alternatively, some people have over-generous self-standards and are satisfied with nearly any form of their own behaviour whether selfish, gauche, heartless or insensitive. Self-standards are learned from others through modelling and through direct reinforcement.

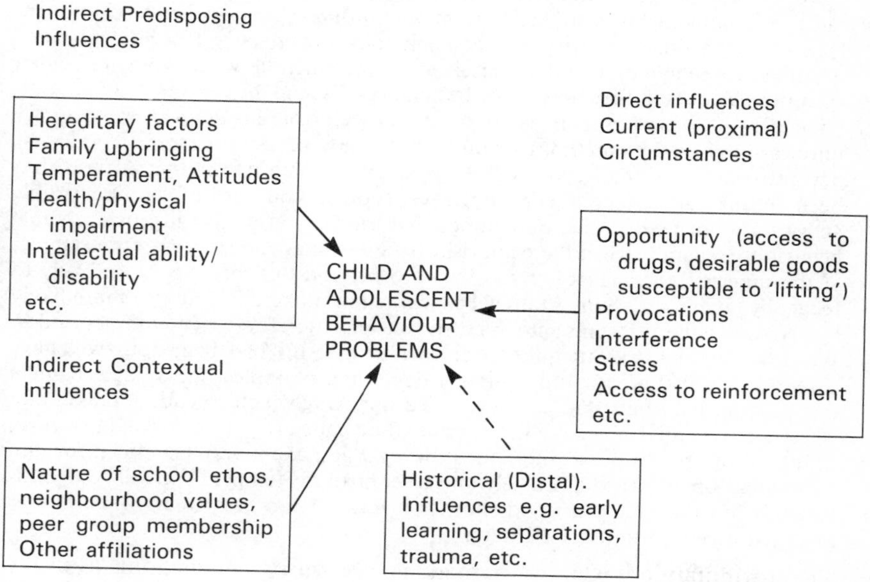

Fig. 11 Levels of influence on child and adolescent problem behaviour.

This list of factors is far from complete. In trying to explain problem behaviour you might draw on a wide range of possible influences: indirect predisposing, and indirect contextual influences, historical (distal) and direct (proximal) factors (Fig. 11).

A particular skill you require is (essentially) an editing one. It involves the identification of the *important* influences and *controlling* variables — among, potentially, so many — in order to plan an effective intervention. The principle of parsimony is helpful here; you invoke those causal factors that are sufficient to facilitate such an intervention. Avoid the wastefulness and risks of overinclusiveness (that is to say excessive complexity) and also simple-mindedness.

Explaining to parents

The attempt to 'make sense' of complicated problems for (say) parents and teachers, depends upon the particular circumstances of the case. However a general account of causation (a handout) used by the author is provided in Appendix III.

A more specific formulation which meets the particular case might sound something like this:

'Andrew has not yet learned to control his temper. He "lets go" in a frightening tantrum — banging his head, kicking, screaming and yelling — when he cannot get his own way: as when you try to insist on him doing something, refuse his commands or attend to people other than himself at a time when he wants your undivided attention. The result (usually) is that he achieves his goal, he coerces you both into giving way — a very rewarding state of affairs seen from his point of view; a very unrewarding (and sometimes humiliating) state of affairs seen from your perspective. Occasionally you stick to your guns which means that Andrew has been getting rather inconsistent messages: the consequences of his undesirable actions are not predictable. Sometimes (but rarely) you punish his unacceptable behaviour, generally when there are visitors. Sometimes you ignore it, for example, at the supermarket. Generally you "reward" it and thus make it more likely to recur, by giving in to him. Andrew has learned to make this outcome more likely by escalating the tantrums into very violent and therefore frightening episodes. We now have to make it quite clear to him that his bad behaviour will have consequences that are not only unrewarding, but also unpleasant enough to make him relinquish his tantrum. You have tried smacking which you admit makes him worse and you miserable. We will use a method called response-cost — in essence, fining his tantrums. But at the same time we will make it very beneficial for him to be more obedient, to ask nicely and to control his temper. We will record his successes on this star chart and show him how he can earn treats when he has collected a certain number of stars.'

The formulation given to parents is obviously couched in ordinary language. Your own more technical account might include some of the following elements:

Most problem situations can be analysed in terms of antecedent events, consequent events, organismic, cognitive and self*-variables.

(1) Certain antecedent conditions may be eliciting or reinforcing problem responses, especially those of an emotional kind, while other such conditions may involve some lack of appropriate discriminative stimulus control over the client's instrumental responses.

(2) 'Inappropriate stimulus control of behaviour' (where a normally neutral stimulus acquires the capability of eliciting a dysfunctional response like anxiety) may arise — in part — from a history of classical conditioning. 'Defective stimulus control' (see Fig. 12) over behaviour (notable for the inability of a stimulus, normally associated with a pattern of behaviour, to cue this pattern in a person) may stem from inconsistent discipline, *laissez faire* parenting, extreme permissiveness, or the lack of outcomes to actions — such as to make discriminating behaviour irrelevant or unimportant. There may be outcome conditions which either reinforce problem behaviour, or punish or extinguish desirable responses. 'Aversive behavioural repertoires' (such as violent actions, extreme dependency behaviours) may originate from learning conditions such as these and others.

(3) Any of these inappropriate forms of antecedent or outcome control may be operating in the client's symbolic processes, rather than in his external environment or physiological changes. In the case of 'aversive self-reinforcing systems' the youngster sets high standards in evaluating himself, thus leading to self-depreciation and criticism rather than self-approval. Such punitive cognitions can originate from an early history in which the individual was taught to rely on stern standards of self-appraisal. (Example: depressed, suicidal individuals; youngsters low in self-confidence.)

(4) 'Defective or inappropriate incentive systems' (as we saw above) are characterized by the failure of rewards, normally capable of acting as an incentive, to influence a youngster. (Defective incentive systems are to be seen in the aloof and isolated child, the child who is indifferent to achievement and learning; inappropriate incentive systems are to be seen in the cross-dresser and some delinquents.) These developments may originate from early disturbances in the reinforcement history when primary and secondary reinforcers are evolving.

The explanations of maladaptive behaviour given so far are usually grouped under the formidable heading of 'inappropriate' or 'defective' stimulus control of behaviour. All this means is that faulty learning has taken place; irrelevant behavioural responses have become accidentally associated with consequences that are rewarding, or, as happens most frequently, learning has occurred in aversive (e.g. fear-provoking or conflictual) conditions and

*To be fair, many practitioners would dispense with inferential constructs like self.

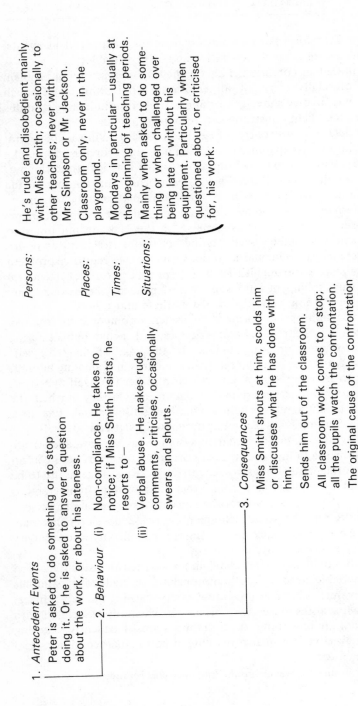

1. *Antecedent Events*

Peter is asked to do something or to stop doing it. Or he is asked to answer a question about the work, or about his lateness.

2. *Behaviour* (i) Non-compliance. He takes no notice; if Miss Smith insists, he resorts to —

(ii) Verbal abuse. He makes rude comments, criticises, occasionally swears and shouts.

3. *Consequences*

Miss Smith shouts at him, scolds him or discusses what he has done with him.

Sends him out of the classroom.

All classroom work comes to a stop; all the pupils watch the confrontation.

The original cause of the confrontation is forgotten.

Persons: He's rude and disobedient mainly with Miss Smith; occasionally to other teachers; never with Mrs Simpson or Mr Jackson.

Places: Classroom only, never in the playground.

Times: Mondays in particular — usually at the beginning of teaching periods.

Situations: Mainly when asked to do something or when challenged over being late or without his equipment. Particularly when questioned about, or criticised for, his work.

FIG. 12 Lay-out for a preliminary analysis of a problematic classroom situation involving defective stimulus control.

rituals and avoidance responses have been acquired because they prevent unpleasant outcomes.

Temporary states of the organism can affect learning (see Vila and Beech, 1978). We know that symptoms of distress (e.g. an inability to go out of the house or to meet others socially without feeling anxious) may be preceded by a period of general tension and emotional upset. This kind of disturbance is quite commonly experienced by women who suffer in the few days prior to menstruation from pre-menstrual tension. If this condition is a good parallel to the situation in which abnormal fears can arise, then it should be possible to show a propensity for 'defensive' or 'adverse' learning in pre-menstrual days which is not present at other times in the cycle. This is, in fact, what has been found. The evidence indicates that the state of the organism at the time when some noxious event is present will not only determine the speed at which learning takes place but also any tendency for the learning to be preserved over time. It is as if such states prepare the ground for certain kinds of learning to take place—as if such states put the organism on a defensive footing, ready to react adversely to relatively minor provocation.

The adolescent may be vulnerable, because of the rapid physical changes taking place in his organism and the dramatic changes occurring in his psychosocial status, to the acquisition of emotional problems.

Many of the problems that people have are not due to the individual learning *inappropriate* responses, but are the consequences of the failure to learn the *appropriate* behaviour. It has been noted by research workers that there is an important difference in the nature of many maladaptive behaviours in children and adults. Many behaviour problems in children (especially in the early years) are associated with inadequate skills or behaviour controls. These deficiencies are often connected with the activities of eating, sleeping, elimination, speaking and expressing aggression. In most instances the problem arises because the child had failed to develop an adequate way of responding, for example in bedwetting (enuresis), the inability to read (dyslexia) or certain disturbances of eating (anorexia). The over-aggressive child has failed to learn the socially desirable restraints over his hostile acts.

In adults, most problems seem to be concerned with maladaptive behaviours which arise because inappropriate responses have become attached to stimuli. Problems, such as chronic muscular tensions, intolerable anxiety reactions (and other forms of exaggerated activity of the autonomic nervous system), and symptoms of a wide variety of physical upsets such as chronic fatigue, insomnia, stomach and bowel disturbances may be at least partly understandable as conditioned emotional reactions. So may be many of the obsessions, compulsions and phobias of childhood (e.g. school refusal).

Has to wake up on time → Get bathed, dressed, breakfasted → Leave the house on time → Make a journey → Enter the school gates → Go to assembly → Stay in the school → Go home at appropriate time

School phobia?

(1) Does he wake on time? If not, why not?

(2) Does he get enough sleep? If not, why not (going to bed late; lying in bed unable to sleep because of morbid pre-occupations, tense, depressed?)

(3) Anyone to structure his day at home, e.g. supervise his getting ready ('push')?

(4) Is he sick/anxious/panicky?

(5) Any reason he needs to be at home (care for a sick member of the family; parents keep him at home to look after siblings, etc.)?

(6) Is he afraid to leave home because concerned about his mother's health, afraid of an accident befalling her (preoccupation with death, separation, anxiety)?

(7) Is he depressed, overwhelmed by apathy, helplessness, inertia?

Truancy?

(8) Is he teased/bullied on the way to, or at school?

(9) Claustrophobia/clothing (adequate for school?)/homework

(10) Is there anything to keep him at school (interests, friends, teacher)?

(11) Deviant models (peer group) for truanting

(12) Other 'pull' factors absent? (Is he under-achieving grossly at school, bored?)

(13) Does anyone really know him or take an interest in him at school?

FLOW CHART 4.

'Unpacking' the problem

In the case of complex problems like school refusal it is sometimes an aid to assessment and formulation to break down the processes underlying the problematic situation into their constituent elements. Thus with a school refusal problem you might ask yourself: What does a youngster have to do in order to go to school (successfully), stay at school, and then return at the appropriate time? This analysis suggests pertinent questions to ask your clients. There are a variety of 'push' and 'pull' factors which operate to impel, attract most pupils/students to school, and hold them there.

Flow Chart 4 illustrates the many stages in getting a child to school, at which things can go wrong.

SECTION 4

The Intervention

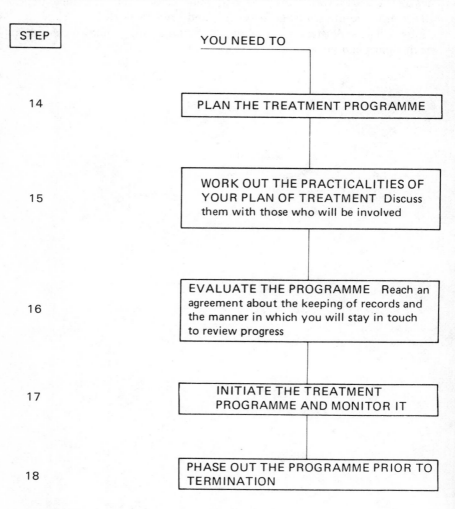

STEP	YOU NEED TO
14	PLAN THE TREATMENT PROGRAMME
15	WORK OUT THE PRACTICALITIES OF YOUR PLAN OF TREATMENT Discuss them with those who will be involved
16	EVALUATE THE PROGRAMME Reach an agreement about the keeping of records and the manner in which you will stay in touch to review progress
17	INITIATE THE TREATMENT PROGRAMME AND MONITOR IT
18	PHASE OUT THE PROGRAMME PRIOR TO TERMINATION

FLOW CHART 5   Treatment: how to proceed.

> ## Step 14a   PLAN THE TREATMENT PROGRAMME
>
> *Behaviour modification is an educational exercise. Indeed, you may not always be able to fathom out the causes of the problem, and yet still be able to do remedial work by using the behavioural approach. The point is that behaviour modification provides new learning experiences. These experiences include a wide range of specific behavioural procedures that are in some degree related to the basic learning models of observational learning, classical and operant conditioning, and self-regulation. Examples of such specific procedures include modelling, imitation, desensitization, flooding and reinforcement techniques.*

Rationale

Behaviour therapy has become so variegated in its conceptualizations of behaviour, research methods, and techniques, that no unifying scheme or set of assumptions can incorporate all extant techniques. Although behaviour therapy emphasizes the principles of classical and operant conditioning it is not restricted to them; it draws upon principles from other branches of experimental psychology such as social and developmental psychology. The importance of 'private events' or the cognitive mediation of behaviour is recognized; and a major role is attributed to vicarious and symbolic learning processes, for example modelling.

But what does it matter if the critics are correct in saying that behaviour therapy has no adequate unifying theory? Why not simply consider behavioural treatment as a technology? After all, the techniques can be utilized and researched *without* commitment to any distinctive foundational theory. As it happens there are powerful arguments and evidence which make it inappropriate to view behaviour therapy simply as a technology. Its claim to scientific status arises from the fact that:

1. Behaviour therapy practice and research is guided in part by specific experimental findings; the conceptualizing of assessment and the methodology of behaviour therapy are rigorous and sophisticated, building (as they do) on statistical–experimental foundations.
2. The empirical evidence that has been gathered in support of specific therapeutic claims is impressive; when behaviour therapists confirm the

efficacy of particular techniques they may be confirming causal hypotheses and thereby offering explanations of behavioural change.

3. There are many behaviour therapists who add to their derivations from the learning theory literature, by developing their own explanatory theories and testing them.

Operant conditioning

We are on fairly firm ground when we look at the kind of techniques which involve the systematic manipulation of the behaviour's consequences so as to modify subsequent behaviours of the same type. This may involve the removal of rewards (positive reinforcers) that customarily follow a maladaptive response or the provision of a reward following the display of a desirable response.

Classical conditioning

We have seen that emotional behaviour can be controlled by different stimulus sources (e.g. the emotional arousal evoked directly by conditioned aversive stimuli). To eliminate maladaptive emotional responses in children, repeated non-reinforced exposure to threatening events (either directly or vicariously) has been used as the main thrust of treatment. However, clear evidence for the effectiveness of any variant of desensitization with children is still lacking (see Hatzenbuehler and Schroeder, 1978). Some case studies suggest the successful reduction of avoidance behaviour; others have failed. Evidence suggests that it may be preferable with the child who shows intense avoidance behaviour so that his voluntary participation is inhibited, to emphasize (initially) responses (e.g. relaxation) which are antagonistic to anxiety. With moderately avoidant children, according to Hatzenbuehler and Schroeder (1978), active participation is preferable because of the assured advantage of behavioural rehearsal.

Modelling

This involves the systematic demonstration in actuality (or symbolically, on film) of a model displaying the required behaviour: a skill, an appropriate pro-social action, a coping strategy.

Most complex and novel behaviour (be it adaptive or maladaptive) is acquired by watching the behaviour of exemplary models. These may be people the child observes in his everyday life or they may be symbolic models that he reads about or sees on television. This process is called 'observational learning': it is considered by social learning theorists to be the cornerstone of learning for socialization, and a significant basis for therapeutic interventions.

A basic distinction is made between the acquisition and the performance of the imitative response. Acquisition is thought to result mainly from the contiguity of sensory events. When the observer performs no overt imitative response at the time of observing the model, he can acquire the behaviour only in cognitive representational form. During the *acquisition* phase the child observes a model and the stimuli are coded into images or words which are stored in memory: they now function as mediators for subsequent retrieval and reproduction of the observed behaviours. The *performance* of observed acts is thought to be influenced by the observed consequences of responses, that is to say, operant conditioning (see Bandura, 1977a).

Behaviour rehearsal is based, in part, on observational learning. It involves providing a model to demonstrate a skill or prosocial action or some coping behaviour. The child is encouraged to practise the skill, perhaps by role play at first, then in 'real life'. She is provided with accurate (and supportive) feedback with regard to her performance. The modelling and behaviour rehearsal are paced very carefully.

Cognitive learning processes

The charge often levelled at the behavioural approach is that it ignores or devalues the conceptual thinking that is so peculiarly and significantly human. This is a misunderstanding of the current situation in behaviour modification.

Cognitive explanations

The learning theorist Estes (1971) writes that for the lower animals, for very young children, and to some extent for human beings of all ages who are mentally retarded or subject to severe neurological or behaviour disorders, behaviour from moment to moment is largely describable and predictable in terms of responses to particular stimuli and the rewarding or punishing outcomes of previous stimulus–response sequences. In more mature beings, much instrumental behaviour and more especially a great part of verbal behaviour is organized into higher-order routines and is, in many instances, better understood in terms of the operation of rules, principles, strategies and the like. Bandura (1977a) points to a therapeutic paradox, when he comments that '. . . explanations are becoming more cognitive. On the other hand, it is performance based treatments that are proving most powerful in effecting psychological changes. Regardless of the method involved, the treatments implemented through actual performance achieve results consistently superior to those in which fears are eliminated to cognitive representations of threats' (p. 78).

Critics insist that learning is not simply something that happens to an individual, as in fundamentalist versions of the operant conditioning model, but something which he or she themselves make happen by the manner in which they handle incoming information and put it to use. While not denying the potential importance of the stimulus and the reinforcement in the S-R paradigm, they consider that operant theorists pay insufficient attention to the element that comes in between, namely the learner's own behaviour (B). This behaviour is not simply something 'elicited' by a stimulus and strengthened or otherwise by the nature of the reinforcement that follows; it is in fact a highly complex activity which involves three major processes, namely (1) the acquisition of information; (2) the manipulation or transformation of this information into a form suitable for dealing with the task in hand; (3) testing and checking the adequacy of this transformation.

Interestingly, behavioural procedures may be among the most powerful methods of actually activating cognitive processes. Not surprisingly they are recruited for the remediation of a wide range of intra- and interpersonal problems. There is an irony in the burgeoning literature on the cognitive aspects of behaviour therapy. Nowadays the approach encompasses a plethora of techniques that depend upon those mediating processes and private events which were once so passionately repudiated as 'ghosts in the machine'. Thus self-verbalizations, illogical thoughts, misperceptions and misinterpretations, attributions and self-appraisals (in other words what the client thinks, imagines, and says to himself) prior to, accompanying, and following his overt behaviour, become a primary focus for a therapeutic intervention.

Essentially, it is being claimed that people can be taught to eliminate some of their maladaptive behaviours by challenging their irrational beliefs and faulty logic or by getting them to instruct themselves in certain ways or to associate wanted behaviour with positive self-statements, and unwanted ones with negative self-statements.

Self-variables (e.g. self-control/self-mastery)

There are several other applications of self-directed procedures relating to antecedent and consequent (adverse) events. It is possible to manipulate those eliciting or reinforcing stimuli in the client's symbolic processes which influence his or her maladaptive behaviour. It is also possible to teach the client to rearrange contingencies that influence behaviour in such a way that he or she experiences benefits (see Karoly, 1977).

There have been many studies of the influence of the therapeutic relationship and such factors as the clients' expectations (expectancies) of receiving help. This matter of the client's beliefs about therapy leads us neatly into one of the crucial developments within behaviour therapy—the growth of self-direction in both the theory and practice of the method. The therapist's influence upon the client may have its source in the provision of information or interpretations; changing behaviours, attitudes, values and perceptions; teaching problem-solving and social skills; altering the client's attributions concerning past and present behaviours.

The client's positive expectations about the outcome of treatment and his attitude toward the therapist have been shown to be important (but not all-important) elements in determining the success or failure of programmes (see Herbert, 1987a,b). There is a lack of consistency in the studies, which makes it difficult to give appropriate weight to the various components in treatment techniques. Erwin (1979) puts forward the possibility that clients who believe they will be helped may have the incentive to test their belief by exposing themselves to (say) a phobic situation; also the client is 'under more demand' to show improvement than is the one who does not expect to be cured. For some, it may be most convincing to accept that the therapy works, but is effective (at least in part) because of the client's *beliefs.*

Bandura's theory (1977b) suggests that psychological treatment methods work by altering the client's self-efficacy expectations. These expectancies derive primarily from the four sources of information: performance accomplishments, vicarious experience, verbal persuasion and physiological states. The more reliable the sources, the greater are the changes in perceived self-efficacy. An increase in perceived self-efficacy will affect both initiation (the willingness to get involved in otherwise daunting situations) and persistence of coping behaviour (in the face of aversive experiences).

There are many behaviour therapists (e.g. Phillips, 1981) who are concerned to arrest the 'invasion' of cognitive behaviour therapists because of the dangers of the trend toward clouded concepts and methodology. She has this to say in her conclusion of a review of work carried out by behaviour therapists in which there was 'cognitive content':

> Since the cognitive behaviour therapists reviewed above are really helping their clients (their mixed techniques seem to be effective in most of the cases cited) one might ask what is the harm in confounding techniques anyway? The harm lies in the confusion created in the professional community. Behaviour therapy is still misunderstood and not accepted by the majority of the psychiatric establishment . . . Rather than cloud the issues, we need to sharpen the precision of our concepts and techniques. More careful behaviour analysis should be carried out on individuals, clients and in research populations (p. 15).

Phillip's position is summarized in the following hypotheses:
  *'Cognition' is a category term which refers to a class of behaviours subject to external stimulus controls as are other behaviours.

*Private events are not ignored by behaviourists: they have as much access to them as do 'cognitivists', through verbal report of clients and direct experience of their own. The former simply require more precise, operational definitions of their constructs.

*Mediating responses categorized as images, perceptions, hypotheses, r_g-s_g's etc., are learned through interactions with the organism's external environment, as are more overt responses.

*There is no disagreement that cognitive behaviours are, and always have been an important part of behaviour therapy. There is complete disagreement, however, with the implication that they must be treated differently or belong to a different world and are governed by laws different from other behaviours (p. 6).

Step 14b	FORMULATE OBJECTIVES if and when you have made a decision that the problem requires an intervention.

Having selected the goals of treament it is necessary to specify them very precisely in terms of the responses to be produced and the conditions under which these should occur. An objective must contain four elements:
(1) Who will do
(2) What.
(3) To what extent.
(4) Under what conditions?

The goals of treatment are also specified as publicly observable responses. At the treatment level, a serious difficulty arises because of the tendency for therapeutic goals in some traditional therapies to be conceived in vague 'global' terms rather than specified as measurable targets. This makes it difficult to measure success or failure, and thus to validate or invalidate one's way of working. Or when improvement does not follow treatment it is easy to label the parents ('they're uncooperative, manipulative, ineffectual . . . etc . . . etc.') and their children, by way of exculpation. Such diagnostic labelling places the origins of the intractable problem within the child (e.g. an inadequate personality, a character disorder, poor motivation) or his family, rather than the interaction between the child and his environment. Furthermore, failure to get better can be attributed to the shortcomings of clients rather than to the therapist's lack of skill.

Practical guidelines to ethical issues

Obtain the full informed consent of the client or those responsible for him/her. Defining who the client is raises some complicated issues in family-orientated work.

Ask yourself: (especially where a child is concerned) Who benefits from the programme if it is implemented? Who should decide what behaviours are desirable or undesirable?
Who (if anyone) has the right to define the situations as problematic, and thus request a change?
Is the child old enough or responsible enough to have a say in the decision to intervene? (At the Centre the child is privy to all the discussions about the actual programme, but not to intimate marital or personal parental matters.)

There are no simple answers to these questions: they depend on varying circumstances in individual situations.

Choosing between alternative strategies

Any decision to change is likely to involve benefits and 'costs': benefits for clients (hopefully), for significant others, for their social network. There could be costs to clients, to others and to their social setting. Egan (1986) suggests a balance sheet to help the person work through the implications of his or her chosen course of action; it could be of particular help to parents in their quest for change within the family (see Fig. 13).

Egan, a theorist and practitioner in the field of counselling, writes that goals should preferably be:

1. *Specific*, a necessity if they are to be converted into actions.
2. *Measurable*, that is to say capable of providing feedback that change is occurring and, eventually, verifying that the objective has been accomplished.
3. *Realistic*, in the sense that the child and parent have the resources to achieve them; that external circumstances are not bound to thwart their accomplishment; that the goals are under the control (potentially) of the youngster/parent; and the cost of obtaining them is not too high.
4. *Pertinent to their problem* and not simply a partial solution or even a diversionary move.
5. *His or her own goals* and not those they simply adopt because someone expects them of him or her, or they are the line of least resistance.
6. *In keeping with his or her values.*
7. *Achievable within a reasonable time.*

If I choose this course of action:		
The Self		
Gains for self:	Acceptable to me because:	Not acceptable to me because:
Losses for self:	Acceptable to me because:	Not acceptable to me because:
Significant Others		
Gains for significant others:	Acceptable to me because:	Not acceptable to me because:
Losses for significant others:	Acceptable to me because:	Not acceptable to me because:
Social Setting		
Gains for social setting:	Acceptable to me because:	Not acceptable to me because:
Losses for social setting:	Acceptable to me because:	Not acceptable to me because:

Fig. 13 A decision-making balance sheet (Egan, 1986).

Once treatment goals have been identified, they are ranked according to the negotiated consensus as to what the priorities are. Balanced against the proposition that treatment must begin with the most troublesome behaviours is the proposition that the parents' first intervention attempts should hopefully be successful. Maximizing the chances of success may be more important than beginning with the parent's first choice, because they may already have a sense of failure in dealing with the child. If they experience failure at the beginning of treatment such an experience is likely to reinforce the sense of despair and helplessness which caused the parents to seek professional help in the first place.

Remember: Your behavioural objective is a carefully specified goal which describes:

(1) The nature of the desired behaviour (e.g. the child, whose target behaviour is disobedience, should comply with a parental request without saying 'No!' accompanied by verbal abuse).

(2) The situation in which it should occur (e.g. when mother asks him not to get up from the table when eating, or not to grab his sister's food from her place).

(3) The criteria for deciding whether the behavioural goal has been achieved (e.g. acceding to mother's specific request — without comment — immediately, or after one repetition).

Step 14c **SELECT YOUR PROCEDURES AND METHODS**

Section 6 presents a detailed list of available methods.

Some criteria for selecting procedures

A treatment programme may include various combinations of antecedent and outcome procedures, environmental and self-control methods. There is no generalized formula or simple recipe approach to the choice of treatment procedures, such as X methods for Y problems. The planning of a therapeutic intervention is based upon highly individual and flexible considerations. Morgan (1984) puts it in this way: 'Just as in a game of chess a limited number of possible moves are combined into a strategy which is adapted to fit a given situation, according to a behavioural analysis. A programme once initiated may continue or be adapted according to its progress or lack of progress, or unexpected practical exigencies.'

Remember: not to overlook direct and informal solutions. A child who is not getting enough sleep may be irritable and rude. An earlier bedtime may resolve the problem. Direct requests (or orders) to change may sometimes be sufficient, e.g. telling a child to stop picking his hair; explaining that blasphemy causes offence to some. Changes in the physical environment (separating two talkative children in the classroom) and changes in routine and responsibility (setting poacher to be gamekeeper) may work like magic in some instances.

In less straightforward cases, the therapeutic method will be determined—
in part—by the target problem in need of modification. You would not use
a technique like desensitization on a truant who deliberately opts out of school
because of boredom and under-achievement, rather than some fear of school-
going. You might well use it on a school phobic. Thus methods are selected
on the basis of knowledge of their therapeutic and directional effects, and
acquaintance with studies of the modification of particular problems (see
Ollendick and Cerny, 1982).

The behaviour therapist seeks out the *strongest accessible controlling
variables* in a problem situation, and in the light of this analysis, decides
on the most appropriate procedures to bring to bear on these influences.

*Remember: Problems occur not only in the client's overt actions but also
in her covert thoughts or feelings.*

*Remember: Learning always involves knowing what to do (the appropriate
response) as well as when to do it (under what stimulus conditions
the response is appropriate).*

As far as the child is concerned, there are three preliminary questions to
be answered:

(1) Does she know *what* to do?
(2) Does she know *how* to do it?
(3) Does she know *when* to do it?

When a benign therapeutic experience leads to a relatively permanent
modification of behaviour, attitude or knowledge, we say that learning has
occurred. We have to distinguish between *learning* an action or behaviour
and actually *performing* it.

There are (as was stated earlier) basic learning tasks that are commonly
encountered in child therapy. To be more specific they might involve
the acquisition or learning of desired behaviours in which the individual
is deficient such as compliance, self-control, bladder and bowel control,
fluent speech, social or academic skills, or the reduction or cessation—the
unlearning—of such undesired responses in the child's behavioural repertoire
as aggression, temper tantrums, stealing, facial tics, phobic anxiety,
compulsive eating. The exchange of one response for another (e.g. self-
assertion in place of timid withdrawal) is another therapeutic option.

Broadly speaking the therapeutic task with deficit problems is to increase
the strength of a particular behaviour (response increment procedures) or
to aid in the acquisition of new behaviour patterns (response acquisition
procedures); whereas with excess behaviours, the therapeutic task is to
eliminate them or reduce their strength (response decrement procedures).

Note: *Behaviour excesses (like aggression) may be related to behaviour deficits in the sense that if appropriate skills are absent, the only way that reinforcement can be obtained is through deviant actions.*

It is probably not an exaggeration to claim that in a majority of behavioural programmes the parents have been taught how to decrease unwanted behaviour rather than how to increase desired behaviour with positive methods. It is a good idea, however, to emphasize the latter. Parents are encouraged to 'catch' the child doing something praiseworthy, rather than 'catch' him out in something bad. The same applies to their own actions—so many lack self-esteem or self-confidence and tend to make negative, disapproving self-statements. Positive methods are generally more effective. Produce a more rewarding child and you'll produce a more rewarding parent (and vice versa). You will also tend to get beneficial results going beyond your original targets of intervention—a kind of 'snow-ball' effect. So build into your programme the kinds of interactions/situations in which the parents and child are likely to enjoy each other's company and in which it is probable that the youngster can be praised for desired alternatives to his present self-defeating behavioural style.

Further tasks

A child may know how to produce appropriate behaviour and when to perform it, and yet seldom, if ever, come up with the goods! Parents (and teachers) are faced with four more questions:

(1) How can I get him to do X?
(2) Now that he is doing X, how do I get him to continue doing X?
(3) How can I get him to stop doing Y?
(4) Now that he doesn't do Y, how can I get him to go on desisting from doing Y?

The choice of therapeutic approach will depend not only on the nature of the target behaviour to be modified and the stimuli which maintain it, but also on the age and maturity of the child, the circumstances under which the child manifests the problem behaviour and the aspects of the environment which are subject to the therapist's influence. All of this brings us to the next step: deciding who can best facilitate the realization of the chosen goals.

> ## Step 14d TREATMENT PLAN Assess the resources for treatment
>
> *Are the persons involved in the programme likely to give it the priority, support and concern it requires in order to 'get off the ground'? Motivation for treatment is a significant factor in the successful outcome of a therapeutic intervention, so the assessment of resources explores the child's (and his parents') personal attitudes, competencies, and limitations with regard to treatment.*

The child

Your assessment might include his degree of motivation, capacity for self-regulation, and any skills which might be capitalized on for treatment purposes. In the case of the younger child, there is the question of how much he should be directly involved in the intervention. There is also the issue of how intensive treatment should be. This will depend on the parents.

The parents

Ask yourself about the severity of the problem and current parent resourcefulness. Practical help like a playgroup or child-minding services may give an exhausted mother (especially in a single-parent family) the 'break' she needs to take on an onerous programme. Other significant persons in the family, such as grandparents or siblings can be an aid (and sometimes a hindrance) to the implementation of a programme. These matters must be calculated.

In some clients there is minimal responsiveness to social cues and reinforcements, a problem given the significant contribution of social persuasion and reinforcement in behavioural work.

There are various family attitudes to assess. How do they see the behavioural methods which have been explained to them? What is their attitude to the child and the work (and possible stress) a therapeutic intervention may involve? How realistic are parental (or teacher) expectations of the child and of the therapy? Persons suffering from serious personal problems or an unhappy marriage may find it difficult to act as agents of change for others. There are variations in the sophistication and comprehension of clients to take into account.

Staff

As assessment of staff and other resources (available for *this* case) in the treatment agency is another requirement. Part of the calculation must take into account the fact that behavioural treatments are not like fixed items on a medical prescription to be implemented in an inflexible manner. There is a creative element to the planning of an overall treatment programme and a human (and therefore fallible) component in its application.

Ask yourself: Who can best implement the programme—the client, a mediator, or yourself. A mediator is necessary if the client is unable to control the consequences of his behaviour, or is not in a position to implement the basic recording which is essential to the programme (e.g. very young children, mentally handicapped persons). The naturally occurring incentives for mediators of change in some working environments (e.g. some wards, residential establishments, classrooms) are few and far between. This may be due to poor pay, lack of encouragment, low status, or indeed, plain overwork.

Step 15	WORK OUT THE PRACTICALITIES OF THE TREATMENT PROGRAMME

Work them out in detail and discuss them with your clients (let the child know what is happening).

Many a programme has foundered on some apparently trivial *practical* detail. But, first, a theoretical one; many children get 'worse' before they get 'better' when on an extinction programme; the theoretically predicted extinction burst. Warn parents of this or you will lose them.

Practical problems

Can the mother use time-out as a really viable strategy or is there no suitable room to use? If she lives in a thin-walled terrace house, a yelling child trying to coerce her into submission, could make time-out a tough proposition (one imagines phone calls to the NSPCC!). How do you get a heavy, resistant child to go into time-out? Anticipate the difficulties, but better still (being human and unable to foretell the future and every bothersome hurdle) stay in touch, especially in the early part of the programme. Try to 'nip in the bud' the unexpected problems, before they assume serious proportions.

A typed treatment script can be helpful. Here is an example from a colleague (Griffith, 1985):

"Reward Good Behaviour.

Lee is affectionate and enjoys pleasing his Mum and Dad, so we can easily reward him with cuddles, smiles, praise and by playing with him.

We reward him after good behaviour:
a) when he does what he's been asked to do;
b) when he's helpful;
c) when he's prepared to wait; or
d) when he plays quietly or co-operatively.

Apart from the social rewards above, you might also like to give him a small sweet or biscuit or sticker when you feel a behaviour is particularly good.

The stickers are symbolic rewards for his good behaviour. He can display these on his chart so that all the family can see his achievements and share in his successes. The chart should be in a prominent position.

Rewards should be given as soon as possible after a good behaviour, along with a short explanation as to why:

e.g. 'You are good, Lee, to come straight up to bed'
'That was kind to give Nina her dummy'
'Isn't it nice when you'll wait a minute for Mummy to see to you properly?'

This will teach Lee exactly which behaviours you wish him to repeat. With praise and encouragement, good behaviours will generalize over a variety of situations.

At the end of each day or each week, you could look at Lee's chart and discuss how his stickers were earned. You might like to offer a larger material reward for overall results. This could be Dad's task. Anything from a balloon to a toy car or an outing to the park or the swimming pool might be appropriately awarded.

The discussion will help Lee to think through how you want him to behave. Try to avoid negative comment at this time.

Ignore Bad Behaviour.

Just as we use attention to encourage some behaviours, so we use ignoring to discourage others. We remove the audience. So let us — up to an agreed point — ignore Lee when he is misbehaving. We can ignore by pretending not to hear or see, by turning away or walking away.

Avoid:
Scolding, smacking and shouting. They are all forms of attention. If we use them, we may be unwittingly reinforcing the behaviours we wish to diminish.

Time Out + Temper Tantrums.
If Lee is ignored following a bad behaviour, he may accelerate his attention-seeking into tantrums or aggression. Where possible, tantrums should be ignored. If they *persist* or he becomes *aggressive* or *destructive*, we begin to operate Time Out. This involves removing Lee from the socially rewarding environment he is in and placing him in the hall by himself for a short time—3 minutes. Time Out is another form of ignoring in that it becomes useless for him to protest when there is nobody present to respond.

If Lee is behaving badly he should be told to stop. If he persists he should be warned: 'Lee, if you don't stop I shall need to put you in the hall'. If he stops, praise him: 'Thank you for "quietening down"' and introduce him to an alternative behaviour 'Come and play in the sink'.

If he persists, without saying anything to him, put him in the hall. On, closing the door, say to him; 'Lee, I am leaving you here for a short time so that you'll learn to remember not to "stamp and shout"'. Then leave quickly. It is important to ignore grumblings, shouting, banging, kicking, etc., on the way to or during Time Out. After 3 minutes, if Lee is quiet, let him out of the hall and encourage him to do something positive. If he is making a fuss in Time Out, say to him at 3 minute intervals: 'When you stop you can come out'. Then wait and let him out.

Demanding.
When Lee makes a request which you decide to refuse, he sometimes begins demanding. His frustration builds when his demands aren't met. Because of Lee's difficulties in communicating, it may be that at times he thinks you have misunderstood his request. At times you may not be sure yourself, as frustration is present on both occasions. Don't let this deter you.

Establish what Lee wants in your usual way, by letting him explain until you can repeat his request back to him. But as soon as you are sure you have understood him correctly, give your answer. If it is 'no', then give your reason for refusal kindly but firmly and then *ignore* any further demands. If tantrums or aggression follow, deal with them accordingly.

Defiance.
When we wish Lee to do something or not to do something, you again need to be kind but firm. And if Lee does *not* comply with your requests,

then *action* must follow. Lee then learns that you mean what you say and you will back up your words with action. You need to be *consistent* and *persistent* so that Lee will learn quickly. Couple this with praise for compliance . . . etc., etc.''

Remember: The importance of feedback. The significance of giving learners feedback accords with the cybernetic model of human behaviour which suggests that the behaviour of an organism depends upon the feedback information available to him about the accuracy of his performance. This stops him perpetuating errors which might interfere with additional learning. Knowledge of results may be very reinforcing especially if correct responses outnumber errors (another reason for the therapist's presence).

Step 16   EVALUATE THE PROGRAMME   Put your hypotheses to the test by monitoring what happens after the treatment intervention begins.

Without an objective assessment and record-keeping system, it is not possible to evaluate accurately and reliably the progress made by the child in the therapeutic situation.

In working out your treatment, delineate clearly, as a matter of fundamental principle how you will demonstrate that treatment has been effective. Change is the operative word for assessing your work and deciding on an appropriate point to terminate the programme. You might plan to make use of several indices of change (Gordon, 1975). The chosen intervention may bring about considerable changes in the home which are pervasive as well as specific. Multiple criteria are therefore suggested to assess the outcome of intervention:

You could show by means of graphs (see Fig. 14) based upon frequency counts or ratings (like the ones illustrated in Table VI) that the client's distressing problems have changed significantly in the desired direction. You would probably also wish to demonstrate that the improvement is stable and that the desirable behaviours have generalized outside the treatment setting and continue (at follow up) to persist over time. Naturally you would hope that new problems have not been created (interventions put a strain on families) in the course of your work.

There are three main sources of evaluation:

(1) *Therapist's clinical judgement.* This relates to the points enumerated above and is the therapist's assessment of the child and his family as

Table VI.

TREATMENT EVALUATION SHEET

The following questionnaire has been designed to enable us to assess your evaluation of the effectiveness of Janine's treatment programme.

Below are listed several aspects of Janine's behaviour. Please circle one figure in each area described to indicate any changes that *you* have observed since the beginning of assessment and treatment.

Name . . . . Date . . . .

	Severe Worsening	Slight Worsening	No Change	Slight Improvement	Good Improvement
Tantrums	−2	−1	0	+1	+2
Aggression	−2	−1	0	+1	+2
Defiance	−2	−1	0	+1	+2
Demanding	−2	−1	0	+1	+2
Speech frustration	−2	−1	0	+1	+2
Speech	−2	−1	0	+1	+2
Sense of humour	−2	−1	0	+1	+2
Patience	−2	−1	0	+1	+2
Co-operation at home	−2	−1	0	+1	+2
Co-operation when out	−2	−1	0	+1	+2

The following are goals that you indicated during assessment. Bearing in mind your consideration of acceptable '3 year old' behaviour, please circle to show whether or not you feel these goals have been attained.

functioning better or more happily than before intervention or the same, or worse, as the case may be. The judgement requires specific criteria which are of real clinical and social significance, i.e. they should represent meaningful gains in adaptive functioning.

(2) *Inspection of graphed records.* A significant change from baseline to termination, greater than fluctuations in the baseline, is required. An 'eyeball' test will probably have to suffice for the busy clinician.

(3) *Parents' assessment.* Parental perceptions of change are by far the most simple measures of outcome to obtain, and they should not be neglected.
   (a) The parents' evaluation of improvement (or its absence) in their child's behaviour and relationships with them, can be assessed using either a questionnaire or a structured interview.
   (b) Semi-structured interviews might provide information about changes in the family's social activities (e.g. visits outside the home; changes in the child's play and other social interactions with his peer group; enjoyable outings by the family; being able to leave the child with a babysitter, or take him to a supermarket or indeed, visiting).

Improvement may be defined as a change in the child's target behaviours toward the goals set for those behaviours; it may also be specified in terms of parental activities, or parent–child interactions. The goals may not be all met, but a definite change must be reported by the clinician, parents and be apparent in the graphical records.

The degree of improvement in (say) the child's behaviour might be refined into categories (as in the example provided in Table VI).

It is clear that many children's problems are transient, and often change can occur as a function of time and non-specific placebo effects. For these reasons, a controlled evaluation of the therapeutic process is essential. Objective data make possible two important objectives: determining whether a child in treatment is changing, and the direction and extent of change. They also make possible an assessment of the relationship between different kinds of intervention within the overall therapeutic programme.

An important function of the review of a programme, based upon data relating to the target behaviours is the indication that a change in the treatment plan is required. A programme should be flexible. If target behaviours are showing *no* signs of change within two or three weeks (depending on the problem — there is, in fact, no set time guide) you would be wise to review all aspects of the programme.

There are widely divergent views as to the purposes of psychotherapy. Differing conceptualizations of objectives lead inevitably to different therapeutic *operations*. Different goals lead to divergent *outcomes*. Global questions such as 'Is X therapy effective?', 'Does casework of the Y variety

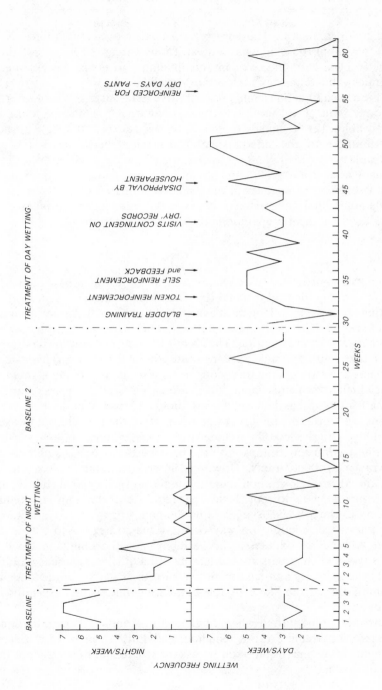

FIG. 14   A typical ABC design graph. Elizabeth aged 10 years. Frequency of nocturnal and diurnal enuresis.

work?' are meaningless. They beg several further questions: effective for whom: to what purpose, in what context, for how long . . . etc., etc. Failure to specify clear-cut objectives in therapy (and social casework) means one cannot validate or (more important) invalidate the way one is working. There is no need to define change in restrictive terms, as many behaviourists have done, but it is necessary to stipulate that (1) change must be demonstrable; (2) it must be relatively permanent; and (3) it must be attributable to the interpersonal transactions between patient and therapist.

What is needed is:

(1) an assessment of changes in the client over time, and
(2) a demonstrated link between these changes (dependent variables) and particular therapeutic operations (independent variables).

Baseline

The pre-treatment record, as we have seen, is known as a baseline and is useful in defining the problem and (by comparison with treatment records) indicating progress. How long must a baseline be to be sufficient for adequate data collection? This is difficult to answer and exposes the tension between a service *vs.* research orientation. The client's interests and your own purposes must be taken into account. Baseline (and other pre-treatment) assessment procedures serve to anchor behaviour in time so as to provide a *standard* against which to measure change. There are no hard and fast rules regarding the length of time baseline conditions should be followed. A theoretical guideline is to look for stability, to persevere until the behavioural measure varies only within a certain well-defined range. Sidman (1960) suggests preserving baseline conditions until the baseline behaviour is stable within a 5% range of fluctuations. However, in practice, stability remains an ideal rather than a realistic consideration in most psychological endeavours, and frequently we do not have the requisite technology to reduce variability to the 5% level suggested by Sidman. For hyperactive children, 'up-and-down' behaviour is a way of life. One strategy is to extend the baseline to understand better the variability of the child's behaviour. However, some behaviours are intolerable and a quick response is required from the therapist. He may have to be content with only a few days of baseline recordings, taking the slope of the best-fitting line as an indication of direction.

Treatment can be started when a baseline is ascending if the intention is to *decrease* the strength of the behaviour (say hitting), or when a baseline is descending if the intention is to increase the strength of the behaviour (say attention in class).

Ongoing measurements

Treatment records are meant to indicate progress towards a specified goal. The literature is replete with studies in which change has been demonstrated along only one dimension. It is generally agreed that it is preferable to evaluate the effects of intervention by multiple criteria. Child and family variables need to be assessed before, during, and after the parent-training programme, and the assessment designed to cover several dimensions of child and parent functioning. The change should have social *and* clinical significance. Measures should be based on instruments which are acceptable in terms of reliability and validity.

Side-effects of behavioural interventions

It would be naïve to assess the principal target behaviours alone as if changes in those areas can be encapsulated and isolated from any effects on behaviours of other kinds, in the child, and on the adjustments of other persons. A positive change in a target behaviour (say, a reduction in school refusal) if accompanied by negative features (say, an increase in disruptive classroom behaviour and consequent confrontations between teachers and parents) cannot be claimed as a 'success story'.

Given such possibilities you should build into your programme a systematic monitoring of behaviours and interactions which indicate acceptable and unacceptable side-effects of your intervention. Look out particularly for undesirable reverberations on the target child's siblings. They may feel that the client is monopolizing his parents' attention, or that he is rewarded for doing things that are taken for granted when *they* perform them (e.g. compliance to rules). Such complications require ingenuity on the part of the therapist and the parents to mitigate their effects.

Evaluation of interventions

How far you take this important principle of trying to validate your work (or invalidate it, in cases where you are getting it wrong) depends upon your role and function, and the opportunities you have to 'stand back' and examine the therapeutic process critically. You should *always* monitor your work at some level. If you are training students, or wish to publish your results on a particular client group or problem, or with regard to a new elaboration of therapy, then you should demonstrate your work by means of the appropriate experimental designs. In addition, parents and children might be interviewed before and after treatment, by an independent assessor not involved in the intervention; the purpose of such an enquiry would be to ascertain (in a detached manner) the significance of any changes that have occurred, as well as to assess their importance as viewed by the family.

None of the research designs will be of much use unless you ensure the highest degree of reliability for your data, as is possible (see Kent and Foster, 1977).

The most rigorous test of the usefulness of any treatment is long-term assessment. Follow-up visits (and/or phone calls) over gradually lengthening intervals should be conducted for at least 12 months in all cases, possibly as many as 24.

Systematic variation of treatment

A particular advantage of the single-subject ($N = 1$) experimental design (as it is known) is that it maximizes opportunity for innovation and flexibility in treatment, while laying the basis for the formulation and testing of hypotheses. There are problems connected with the approach but it does allow comparisons to be made between a child's behaviour under one condition and the same youngster's actions under different conditions. The manner in which the therapeutic interventions are systematically varied directly affects the conclusion that can be drawn from the manipulation.

AB and ABC designs

Symbol A represents a baseline during which the problem behaviour is monitored under uncontrolled conditions and the symbols B, C, D, etc., represent different treatment programmes (one may, of course, find one sufficient). The experimental design involves a comparison of (say) the frequency of the problem behaviour under a pre-treatment baseline condition and its frequency after the application of a treatment programme or a series of treatment strategies. Designs of this type determine whether a change in the level of the behaviour has occurred, and the approximate magnitude of that change. The child's behaviour is recorded, with the resultant scores (counts, or ratings) plotted graphically. When the therapist decides that the baseline measures represent the child's typical behaviour (and it has to be remembered that some children change during baseline recording) an intervention is initiated, designed to modify the deviant behaviour observed during the baseline period. Observations of the target behaviour are continued during treatment.

If you had a reducing baseline you would wait to see whether the improvement was consolidated over a period of time (and, indeed, discuss it with the family to try to work out the reasons for it) rather than starting a treatment programme.

Golden Rule: Don't interfere with something that is getting better; try to understand the process, capitalize on it, and if possible, consolidate it.

The principal limitation of both the AB and ABC designs is the inability to be certain that any reduction in problem behaviour is due to the therapeutic intervention rather than to other change-inducing influences. As service-oriented clinics are concerned primarily with treatment rather than with the constraints of research into its efficacy, this is not a vital limitation; nevertheless, it remains a useful routine check on the progress of your work.

Reversal designs

The reversal (or ABAB) design has a characteristic form; the baseline performance is measured first and identified as the A phase. Next the independent variable (behavioural intervention) is introduced. This is the B phase. Then the independent variable is removed. The return to baseline conditions when the independent variable is temporarily removed is frequently referred to as the reversal or the probe. Because these conditions are allegedly 'identical' with the baseline conditions, the phase is also labelled A. The independent variable is once more introduced. This reintroduction of the treatment condition is again labelled B. You will see how the reversal design comes to be referred to as an ABAB design. If, during the third stage when the intervention is discontinued, the target behaviour does indeed approximate to the original baseline level, then you have support for the notion that the problematic behaviour would have persisted without the treatment. The fourth stage should be followed by another reduction in the deviant behaviour. If such a result is obtained, it *suggests* that it is the intervention which is producing the change in behaviour. What this kind of design yields is essentially correlational evidence of an association between a treatment and a reduction in problem behaviour.

However, it is still not *certain* that fluctuations in target behaviour which accompany the application and withdrawal of the treatment are in fact a function of this treatment. The changes might still be due to the operation of other factors which happen to covary with the treatment and baseline conditions. In any event, because behaviour does not always reverse when the treatment contingency is altered or withdrawn, the reversal design may not always demonstrate a causal relationship between behaviour and therapeutic events, even when a contingency *was responsible* for the initial change. There are situations in which the logic of the reversal design breaks down because the target behaviour would not necessarily be expected to reverse in a reversal phase. The aim of treatment is usually to produce an

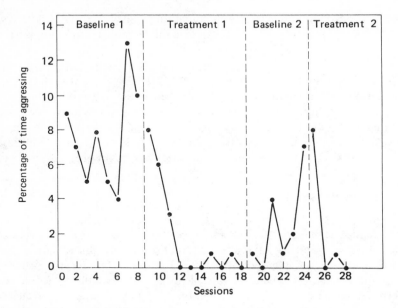

FIG. 15 Rate of aggressive responding during treatment periods when positive responses were awarded and injurious actions were punished by brief social exclusion. The figure shows the reductions in physical aggression achieved by a mother in her five-year-old son (Zeilberger *et al.*, 1968).

irreversible reduction in some target behaviour — one which persists after treatment ends. If this is done successfully, then it will not be possible to return to the original baseline level of behaviour by withdrawing treatment in the third stage. Certain behaviours, once developed or altered, are maintained by beneficial and rewarding consequences which result directly from their performance. Figure 15 gives you an idea of what a reversal design record looks like.

Perhaps a more important problem related to the use of reversal designs in treatment is the ethical dilemma of deliberately attempting to reverse any beneficial therapeutic changes by successive replications of the baseline conditions. Even if willing, parents and teachers as contingency managers, may be unable to behave in the same way they behaved before an intervention. They may become more authoritative, confident, rewarding, in a way and to a degree, that there is no 'going back' to being tentative, fumbling or punitive.

Successive replications may also train the child to return to his deviant behaviour more quickly, and may make it more resistant to extinction because the replications constitute an intermittent reinforcement schedule. They may

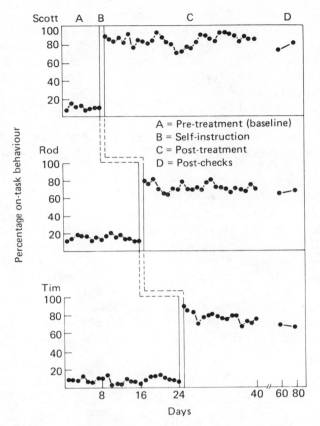

FIG. 16   Daily percentage on-task behaviours for Scott, Rod and Tim across experimental conditions (from Bornstein and Quevillon, 1976).

also breed distrust and suspicion in the child because of the apparent capriciousness of the adults operating the programme.

Multiple-baseline designs

Multiple-baseline designs involve comparing and contrasting change in those behaviours which have been treated, with other behaviours which have not been treated. For example, a child who manifests three relatively discrete behaviour problems such as aggressiveness, oppositional behaviour, and extreme attention-seeking might be treated specifically for the oppositional behaviour and extreme attention-seeking; changes in respect to these behaviours can then be compared with fluctuations in the problem which has been left untreated.

If, however, only one category of deviant behaviour (say aggression) was involved, the same treatment is applied in sequence to several baselines for different forms of aggressive behaviour. Alternatively, an intervention can be made across a number of behaviours but in only one of several settings, while the behaviour is monitored in all the settings. For an example of the design across children, see Fig. 16.

There are two more designs you might consider in monitoring specific behaviour problems:
(i) the changing-criterion design (Hall and Fox, 1977); and
(ii) the alternating treatments design (Barlow and Hayes, 1979; Watson *et al.*, 1985)

The analysis of change
Curve fitting is the simplest and best known approach to the analysis of your data, and is one way of analysing the structure of a baseline (Gottman *et al.*, 1969). It involves fitting the data to the *least squares* straight lines. In this procedure the slope and intercept of the best-fit straight lines obtained during baseline and intervention are calculated. A test of significance is performed on the difference between these two lines.

There is insufficient space to elaborate these statistical (or design) methods here. They require a study all of their own! (See Gottman and Leiblum (1974) for the 'know-how' to assess the statistical significance of post-baseline changes.)

For practical purposes
In the reversal and multiple-baseline designs, a comparison is made within individuals or groups. The extent of behaviour change is indicated by comparing performance during baseline with performance during the treatment phase. What is the degree of change needed to provide a convincing demonstration that behaviour has reliably improved? Within-subject designs usually use the *raw scores* to assess change. The therapist assesses differences in average scores between baseline and treatment intervention or present rate changes (Risley and Wolf, 1967).

Some studies simply give a graphical presentation of data with no statistical analysis performed. For this reason, correct graphic methods are vitally important. In many cases, behaviour change is dramatic. Careful visual inspection of a graph sometimes reveals that behaviour during baseline does not overlap with behaviour during the treatment phase. In other words, during the programme the rate of behaviour does not approach the baseline. In instances such as these there would be a consensus that change has occurred. There may be changes which are less clear-cut, thus necessitating more subjective evaluation.

A common mistake is to use units of measurement which do not reflect equal amounts of observation time. For example, it is misleading to quantify the home-based number of aggressive episodes on a daily basis, when the child is at school Monday to Friday and is only observed for five hours per day as compared with 13 hours on Saturday and Sunday. Some form of ratio unit (e.g. aggressive episodes per hour expressed as an average) is required.

Bloom (1975) has published a step-by-step guide for the practitioner to evaluate his/her marginal results based upon single-case designs. Of course statistics are not everything. An essential criterion for deciding whether a significant behaviour change has occurred or not, is its *practical* importance. If the behaviour has been altered enough to satisfy parents, school teachers, and the therapist, then *that* criterion has been met. Such a criterion of clinical and social significance should be decided, as far as possible, before the treatment programme; this is to avoid any subsequent bias in assessing the results.

Control group design

The most efficient procedure to control for systematic differences between groups (before a treatment programme is evaluated) is to randomly assign children to one of the two groups. One receives the experimental therapeutic programme (the experimental group) and the other does not (the control group). If subjects are not randomly assigned to groups, the likelihood is greater that the groups may differ in terms of the target behaviour prior to the therapy being implemented. And, if so, any differences (changes) in the target behaviour that you achieve may occur for reasons other than the effect of the therapeutic intervention.

Step 17   INITIATE THE PROGRAMME — with a good deal of help to the clients

---

There are many things that can go wrong in the early stages of a programme. There is a great deal of unpredictability in the effects of behavioural interventions. The therapist soon learns that techniques which yield the most impressive results are not always effective with all types of problem or with all children. Furthermore, to his (and everyone else's) frustration, a given technique may, on one day, produce complete control in the case of a particular child, but on the next have no apparent effect at all. It is one thing to plan the campaign quietly around a table; it is another to put it into effect in the hurly burly of family life. It is also useful to hand out highly structured sheets with instructions and/or record forms to be filled in for the following week's consultation.

Criteria of behaviour for rewarding or sanctioning no longer seem so clear. Parents may require prompting, reassuring. It is helpful to be around when the programme begins or within reach for consultation.

One of the frustrations of doing home-based behaviour modification is the 'I've tried it' syndrome! This is the price of using concepts and methods that are on a continuum with their day-to-day child-training practices. 'Time-out', 'Oooh, I've tried that'; 'Response-cost', 'I've tried that'; 'Over-correction', 'That didn't work', and so on. Of course, parents may not be aware of the small print of learning principles: matters of definition, of timing and the need for careful specification and contingency analysis. It is just these issues that require careful monitoring if the programme is to be successful.

Several of the procedures described in Section 6 are usually combined into a comprehensive treatment programme for implementation in an atmosphere of concern and care for the child. The actuality of behavioural work (as opposed to the neat and 'tramlines' way it is often written about) is a highly individualized, proactive but also reactive, undertaking. A programme once initiated may continue, or be adapted according to its progress or lack of progress, or unexpected practical obstacles.

Each programme is designed to produce an enduring decline in self-defeating actions together with the acquisition, performance and maintenance of acceptable alternatives. This behavioural approach can be contrasted with more traditional attempts either to suppress unacceptable behaviour by means of physical punishment, or to encourage its expression (in cases like aggression) in approved situations (the sports field) in the hope that it will decline elsewhere.

Step 18	PHASE OUT AND TERMINATE TREATMENT Do this with care: the durability of any improvements depend upon it

---

The decision to terminate treatment should be made jointly with your client. The time for the programme to end depends upon the goals established at the beginning of treatment.

Try to ensure natural, intermittent reinforcement in the child's different settings. A guideline is to teach only those behaviours which will continue to be rewarded after training, provided they are adaptive in the sense of contributing to the child's well-being and efficiency, and that of the community.

If a behaviour is defined as part of the treatment goals but is not functional (i.e. useful and rewarding) for a child, then a treatment programme may produce only a transitory effect. When the therapeutic procedures are withdrawn there may be nothing to maintain the behaviour and it will disappear.

Note: *Parents should not (and usually do not) expect the child to acquire and maintain certain lessons without setbacks and frequent reminders. Although some therapists pay lip-service to returning the child to an environment which will 'naturally' maintain the target behaviours, precise attention is not always paid to whether this actually happens. And when it does not, the therapy of the child has somehow failed. What has failed is the modification and maintenance of an environment that will promote the new behavioural repertoire of the once-deviant child.*

Parents tend to take a long-term view of rearing their offspring, continually encouraging their desirable actions, while chiding them for 'deviant' behaviour—month in and month out, and sometimes year in and year out. This goes on until the child has certain crucial social behaviours (or the control of antisocial behaviours) as habitual (internalized) parts of her repertoire. Other behaviours will always remain, to varying degrees, under the control of external contingencies. Time-scales vary, depending on the age and maturity of the child and the nature of the behaviour or task.

The termination of a programme is set—in theory—in advance of the treatment programme, by the negotiation of objectives. In practice it is a bit like jazz, a matter of 'playing it by ear'. It is so difficult to be precise, despite one's best efforts, in setting goals for future behaviour; *skills* are somewhat easier to specify. Deciding whether problematic behaviour (especially ones like aggression, manifested to some degree by all children) has changed enough is difficult. A clinician needs to know how different the terminal behaviour is from what is 'normal' for a child of the client's age and sex, and in his particular situation. How far should the changes go? The *total* elimination of anxiety or (in a three-year-old) of tantrums—as a treatment objective—would be extreme, unrealistic and unattainable. So you might decide to terminate when there has been an improvement. But what constitutes an improvement? How much of an improvement will suffice? Should certain problem behaviours be eradicated altogether in all situations and forever? Or should the therapist be satisfied with a more modest reduction in the frequency of deviant behaviour, say, a 25% or 50% decrement. There is no simple answer. It depends on the problem behaviour, its implications, the context within which it occurs and so on. As with the criteria of what constitutes a problem it is more a value/social question than a scientific one; as at the diagnostic phase of your contact with your clients you have the special responsibility of acting as an 'advocate' for the child.

Facing failure

Sadly for you, and more distressingly your client, you are going to fail on occasions to achieve significant change. Understandably, clinicians publish their success stories when writing up single case-histories. But failure rates can be depressingly high.

If you believe that behaviour is lawful then there are several possibilities:

(1) You may have got the 'story' wrong; failed to understand the key determinants of the problem; omitted key items/persons in the assessment; prescribed the wrong remedies; initiated the right remedies but with insufficient support, reinforcement for the mediator, or attention to transfer and maintenance of effects.

(2) The client is resistant to change (see Gottman and Leiblum, 1974) and you have not been sensitive enough to the signs (homework assignments not performed, lateness for appointments, criterion slippage) and therefore not tried to deal with it as a problem in its own right.

(3) The client lacks crucial skills, resources (help, health, energy, incentives) to see the programme through to the end.

(4) The behavioural approach is not a panacea; it may simply not accommodate the particular problem or suit the persons you are dealing with.

Countering failure

Before giving up, you might emulate Gottman and Leiblum (1974) who, when all else fails, try the 'force field analysis' — a problem-solving approach which assumes that things are 'stuck' because there is an equilibrium between the forces facilitating change and those that are opposing and restraining (p. 216). What you do is:

(1) List facilitative forces for change;
(2) List restraining forces for change;
(3) List alternative intervention strategies for:
　(a) strengthening facilitative forces;
　(b) adding new facilitative forces;
　(c) weakening or removing restraining forces;
(4) List the advantages and disadvantages (including costs) of each intervention.

Step 18a   FADE OUT THE PROGRAMME
             GRADUALLY

Consider carefully the problem of temporal generalization.

An abrupt transition from a rich reinforcement schedule, in a behaviour modification programme, to a lean one following treatment (or indeed, one in which *no* provision is made for the administration of reinforcers), is often the equivalent of placing the desired target behaviour on an extinction schedule. A gradual modulation is possible using *fading procedures* or other scheduling techniques.

Technique: Gradually increase the delay between reinforcement and the target behaviour — in order to maintain improvements (temporal generalization).

Fading procedures change the environmental stimuli so that they approximate more closely those natural conditions that are likely to prevail following the end of formal treatment. Reinforcement schedule transitions have to be introduced *gradually over a period of time.*

Preventing the child's behaviour from reverting to pre-treatment patterns soon after the cessation of treatment is one of the most intractable problems associated with behaviour modification programmes. Gelfand and Hartmann (1975) point out that if such a reversion occurs, the child will have benefitted only briefly from the programme; he and his family might become unduly fatalistic and disillusioned about the possibility of his ever improving. In other words, in some instances an untimely relapse might worsen an already distressing situation.

It is possible to reinforce behaviour in ways which are likely to facilitate its persistence. An intermittent schedule of reinforcement might be used, as behaviour which has been reinforced in this way requires fewer reinforcements to maintain it and it takes longer to extinguish after the cessation of reinforcement. Similarly, we have seen how artificial reinforcers in treatment such as tokens or material rewards are gradually replaced by others like social attention and approval which are more likely to apply after treatment ends.

Gelfand and Hartmann (1975, p. 251) offer advice on how to proceed in order to maintain the level of behaviour achieved during the therapeutic intervention at that critical termination juncture:

The wise therapist incorporates increasing intermittency of reinforcement into the treatment whenever circumstances permit. . . . If you have been applying a fixed-interval or fixed-ratio prior to termination introduce a less predictable variable schedule prior to termination. The variable schedule more nearly matches most naturally occurring schedules and so blends well into the child's everyday routine. If you have applied a variable schedule since the inception of treatment, increase its intermittency until the natural environment's schedule is closely approximated. . . . It is advisable to thin the schedule gradually. Sometimes the process of thinning the reinforcement schedule produces a performance loss. This problem is relatively easily remedied, however. Should the target behaviour decrease appreciably in rate following an increase in performance requirements to earn each reinforcer, you must revert to the immediately preceding schedule, restabilize this behaviour, and then introduce a less dramatic schedule change. (Note that this procedure is similar to that employed whenever introduction of a new performance requirement disrupts the process of shaping.) Insofar as possible, avoid large magnitude and sudden reductions in the frequency of reinforcement of the desired.behaviour.

In another approach the therapist fades out special and perhaps artificial discriminative stimuli used in the behavioural programme so that the targeted behaviour is evoked in situations where the control is exerted through appropriate and natural cues. These should be present in the child's day-to-day environment.

Where treatment has been conducted in the clinic, it may be possible to promote stimulus and response generalization by making the treatment setting as similar as possible to the child's natural environment. This involves stimulus generalization; similar situations tend to elicit the same behaviour, and the more parallel the situations can be made, the greater is this tendency. With regard to the response side, it has been shown that a situation which elicits one response is likely to evoke similar responses. There is a gradient of response generalization according to the degree of similarity between responses. One way to programme response maintenance and transfer of training is to develop the target behaviour in a variety of situations and in the presence of several individuals. If the response is associated with a range of places, individuals, situations and other cues, it is less likely to extinguish when the settings vary. (See Jones and Kazdin, 1975; Wildman and Wildman, 1975.)

It is not always necessary to arrange special measures for the purpose of prolonging treatment effects; the intervention may strengthen skills or remove inhibitions so that the client gains access to existing sources of reinforcement, or it might reduce the aversiveness of his behaviour for himself or others and thus entail reinforcing consequences. This sounds easy but is extremely difficult to do in practice—especially with the volatile, highly coercive children, who are so quick to seize the 'main chance' and who make up such a large proportion of a clinical population. The fading out programme can so easily degenerate into a haphazard pattern which approximates the original unhappy situation. At the Centre we have made use of *overlearning* as a protection against relapse; it involves erring on the side of plentiful (and redundant) practice well beyond the point at which the child has acquired new behaviours and skills.

Self-direction

A promising approach to the generalization problem is represented by attempts to provide the child with self-regulating strategies which can be applied across a number of situations. The goal of treatment increasingly incorporates the development of a child's cognitive as well as his instrumental repertoire in an effort to establish the foundations for self-sufficiency and further growth. At the highest level of functioning, mature individuals regulate their own behaviour by self-evaluative and other self-administered consequences. A further dimension concerns the *attribution* of any favourable changes that have been brought about. If a client perceives himself as mainly responsible for his improvement during treatment, he is more likely to maintain these advances.

Early manifestations of self-control are encouraged during childhood training by many parents. The common disciplinary and other child-rearing methods for developing resistance to temptation have been reviewed by the author (Herbert, 1974, 1987). The profusion of research and theory into the mechanisms of socialization reflects the centrality of this issue for understanding the transition of the infant from an impulsive, uncontrolled organism into a social being who is able to exert a reasonable degree of self-restraint. Just as the development of self-regulation has been viewed consistently as one of the most important objectives of the socialization process, therapeutic procedures which can be brought under the control of the individual himself are most beneficial.

Technique: Tangible, self-reinforcement and symbolic rewards can be used to maintain new patterns of behaviour until they become a source of personal satisfaction. While this may be a desideratum of treatment, especially with more mature individuals, the behaviour of children is very much under the control of external contingencies and the relative generality of responses (implicit in self-regulation) is the exception rather than the rule.

SECTION 5

Family-Orientated Behavioural Work

Therapeutic change depends upon:

(1) Persuasion, which rests on practical knowledge or practice wisdom. It offers reasons why the client should change his beliefs and or behaviour. This manual does not eschew the arts of persuasion. Subject to the ethical constraints discussed below, and the process of negotiating goals with clients, it is an important component of therapy to voice clear opinions based upon valid information and knowledge of the developmental literature and of hard-gained practice wisdom and experience.

(2) Teaching, which entails the offering of information and training in skills of acting. The client may not be able to act without instruction, training and monitoring. Because some actions (e.g. child-training techniques) are so ingrained in parents' repertoires (being anchored by ideology or habit, or constrained by lack of skill), it is not usually good enough to simply *advise* parents to change. Demonstrations, rehearsals, instructions and practice may be required in order to provide clients with the equipment for change.

(3) Providing explanatory 'stories' (cognitive restructuring), which help clients to re-order their beliefs about the nature of their problems. Attempting to change a person's beliefs, desires and actions is a commonplace activity in ordinary life. The therapist is particularly interested in providing helpful explanations ('stories') or changing existing belief systems which he or she considers to generate distressing, self-defeating actions on the part of the client. Insight, then, is not rejected as a faciliative therapeutic agent. Yelloly (1972, p. 147) says:

> Awareness may operate in a number of ways. The sheer provision of accurate information may correct a false and erroneous belief and bring about considerable change in behaviour. Prejudice, for instance, may be diminished by new information which challenges the prejudiced belief. And in human beings (pre-eminently capable of rational and purposive action) comprehension of a situation, knowledge of cause and effect sequences and of one's own behaviour and its consequences, may have a dramatic effect on manifest behaviour. Thus to ignore the role of insight is just as mistaken as to restrict attention wholly to it. It would seem that the relative neglect of insight by behaviour therapists until recently has

116

occurred partly in reaction to the over-emphasis on it in traditional psychotherapy, and partly because of their pre-occupation with directly observable behaviour, particularly in laboratory studies of animals. The potential of symbolic factors for therapeutic change has not been fully exploited although classical behaviour therapy procedures rely heavily on cognitively-produced effects; for example, symbolic rehearsal of behaviour in imagination forms part of systematic desensitization and of some aversive techniques. Such imaginative rehearsal or fantasy is surely evidence of the powerful effects of symbolic arousal on manifest behaviour.

The teaching component mentioned above predominates in this section. Almost all of the methods to be described in Section 6 and the principles underlying their application, require some training input. Those seeking to provide behavioural parent training have an abundance of parent training research to turn to (Horton, 1982). What is not so readily available are clear guidelines with regard to such practical issues as content, structure and formats for training. While different therapists inevitably have different points of emphasis there does appear to be some agreement about the most significant components: first, many approaches are increasingly offering a common core of training content; second, modelling of appropriate behaviours for parents is a very helpful way of teaching them; and third, since many studies have shown little difference in the outcome measures achieved by individualized training and by group training, there is a strong case to be made for group training in that it is more cost-effective in terms of time.

There are also implications for the cooperation and commitment you can expect from adult 'learners'—the parents—who will be taking part in tiring, emotionally demanding training programmes.

Client commitment

One of the most critical problems to overcome in implementing a successful therapeutic programme is stimulation and maintenance of the parents' interest and motivation to participate in joint work. There are some important *specific* and so-called '*non-specific*' factors to take into account, while carrying out your intervention.

(a) Perceived self-efficacy

Bandura (1977b) is of the opinion that human behaviour is subject to two major categories of influence: efficacy expectations and outcome expectations, represented in schematic form (Fig. 17).

These are the constituent parts of Bandura's notion of *perceived self-efficacy*. They are distinguished because (say) a mother may believe that a particular course of action (for example, a behavioural programme) will

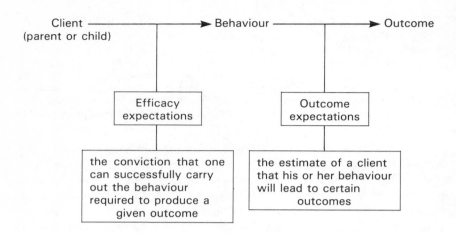

FIG. 17

produce certain outcomes — an improvement in her child's behaviour. However, she may have serious misgivings as to whether she has the wherewithal (for example, patience and consistency) to bring about such a desirable outcome. According to Bandura all psychological procedures designed to bring about change, whatever their type, are mediated through this system of beliefs about the level of skill required to bring about an outcome and the likely end result of a course of action. Efficacy expectations are thought to be the most important component. The main effect on outcome expectations is through the strengthening of efficacy expectations ('I am able to do it'). Successful treatment thus depends — in this view — on the degree to which the therapy creates or strengthens the client's expectations of personal efficacy.

Now verbal persuasion has only relatively weak and short-lived effects on such expectations; *performance accomplishments*, on the other hand, are very potent hence the success of techniques like behaviour rehearsal.

It has to be admitted that the usefulness of self-efficacy (like others such as self-esteem and ego-strength) are open to criticism (e.g. Hudson and Macdonald, 1986).

Remember: A practical consideration with regard to your clients: their conceptual and verbal abilities. If these are underdeveloped they are more likely to benefit from behavioural demonstrations than from verbal modelling (Bandura, 1977b).

(b) Motivation

The most popular scapegoat label in Clinical and Social Work must surely be 'unmotivated'. It provides the ideal exculpation for the failure of a client's treatment. Like other 'trait' labels, motivation is situation specific; a client may appear apathetic and resigned in one setting because of learned helplessness, while showing energy and resourcefulness in another.

Do analyse and 'unravel' any apparent lack of motivation. Are there strong disincentives that you could help minimize? Are there too few incentives for the client? If so, you might remember the maxim: 'Always reinforce the reinforcer'.

(c) Therapist variables

Variables which have a therapeutic influence are:
(a) Attitude to the client (e.g. interest, empathy, warmth, sympathy, liking, friendliness; or their opposites).
(b) Attitude to therapy (e.g. enthusiasm, conviction, commitment, interest, belief, faith, optimism; or their opposites).
(c) Attitude toward results. Experimenters (and therapists) may 'obtain' the results they want or expect.

(d) Non-confirming experiences

Many clients have non-adaptive beliefs about the world. These beliefs often play a critical role in creating the problems that bring the individual for help. Since all forms of psychotherapy seem to involve changes in belief systems, a powerful tool in therapy is the provision of non-confirming experiences, as a result of which non-adaptive beliefs can be replaced by more effective ones. Behaviour modification—especially in its deployment of real-life role play—makes use of this therapeutic principle.

(e) Personality of the therapist

The factors which play a part in the social influence of therapists are their:
Credibility: This depends upon perceived
(a) expertness;
(b) reliability (dependability, predictability, consistency);
(c) motives and intentions;
(d) expressions of warmth and friendliness;
(e) dynamism of the communicator (confident, forceful, active);
(f) opinion of the majority of other people concerning the expertness and trustworthiness of the person.
Attractiveness: This depends upon perceived
(a) cooperativeness and goal facilitation;
(b) physical appearance;

(c) liking;
(d) similarity;
(e) competence;
(f) warmth;
(g) familiarity and propinquity ('to know them is to like them').

Parent training

Of course the rationale of the desire to train parents to a competent level is the belief that the parents' ongoing contact with the child and possession of new skills might facilitate generalization of treatment effects across time. Clients learn (it is argued) not only a new model of behaviour — a construct system which emphasises the significance of behavioural consequences and environmental causality — but they assimilate new *methods* of understanding behaviour. They learn a new language for communicating about behaviour and a more precise way of specifying, defining, observing and thinking about behaviour–environment relationships.

The time span for change is necessarily, in the case of conduct problems, a long one, given the slowly evolving, complex psychological attributes (e.g. internalization of rules, resistance to temptation, empathy, self-control) we are dealing with. Parents — in real life child-rearing — do not expect to train their children (with regard to all attitudes, behaviours and skills) in one-off programmatic bursts. They expect to remind, repeat lessons, to have setbacks! There are implications here for the availability of relatively frequent, brief booster sessions.

Components of training programmes

1. Choice of format
(a) Consultation. Parents are provided with information about behavioural principles and methods. The training takes place by lectures, seminars, films, demonstrations, written material (bibliotherapy) and quizzes. Consultations occur individually or in groups.

It would be unusual for the consultant to meet the child or visit the home or supervise the implementation of what has been learned. There are many examples of the consultation format described in the literature (e.g. Hall *et al.*, 1972; Kovitz, 1976; Weathers and Liberman, 1978).

(b) Individual parent training. The therapist focuses his or her efforts on one set of parents and their children at a time. Direct training and supervision are provided and the therapist observes the parents applying the knowledge they have obtained from him or her, and from other sources (e.g. manuals,

video, films, etc.). Examples of this approach can be found in various sources (e.g. Iwaniec *et al.*, 1985; Patterson, 1982; Zeilberger *et al.*, 1968).

(c) Group training programmes. This approach combines aspects of both (a) and (b). A group of parents whose children have problem behaviours are given instruction in behavioural child management skills, using a variety of techniques. There is usually some supervised 'hands on' experience for the parents. Monitoring and evaluation of change in parents' knowledge and skill *and* the child's behaviour is common in such programmes (see O'Dell *et al.*, 1977; Walter and Gilmore, 1973).

All of these formats have been shown to work in improving parents' child management skills. The relative cost-effectiveness of the approaches remains undecided. Each type has its advantages and disadvantages. The individual model enjoys flexibility and depth and the opportunity for direct monitoring of change. It is less economical of therapist time than the group and consultation models. Parents feel less satisfied with the 'cheapest' consultation approach than the group method and less satisfied with both than the personal contact implicit in the individual approach. The group approach offers the benefit of peer support and modelling. All in all, the choice of a parent training format is a complex matter for the individual therapist and agency.

Following an extensive review, Gordon and Davidson (1981) comment favourably upon the following format:

> Parents meet for ten weekly, two-hour group sessions. In a large group format, didactic information is presented via brief lecture by the program director for no more than 20 to 30 minutes. Parents then break up into small groups of four to six with a group leader, where they develop a personalized home behaviour change project. Weekly homework assignments involve record keeping, as well as actually implementing the various techniques presented through lectures and role-playing. The structure of large and small groups, combined with numerous parent trainers, is both efficient and highly effective . . .

They also conclude that a particularly efficacious approach to training is the programme used by Patterson and his colleagues (Patterson, 1975). They provide parents with progressively more direct intervention until success is achieved. They begin with verbal methods such as texts, verbal rehearsal, and sometimes audiotape modelling, then continue treatment by means of frequent phone contacts. They report that only one-fifth of the parents require additional training; those who do receive home visits with live modelling and behavioural rehearsal.

2. Choice of content of training programmes
(a) Should parents rehearse or practise the skills they learn? In principle practice of child management skills would seem highly desirable, but there

is no evidence to suggest that actual practice is a *necessary* or *sufficient* condition for helping parents develop such skills.

(b) Should parent training focus on specific target problems or develop their knowledge of general behavioural principles? It does seem that the latter is more cost-efficient as it facilitates implementation and generalization of newly acquired child management skills in *non-training* situations (Ollendick and Cerny, 1982).

(c) Should parent training programmes begin with easy or difficult problems? There is no simple answer. According to Eyberg and Johnson (1974) problems are easy if:

(i)   they occur under conditions that permit ready observation by parents;
(ii)   they occur with relatively high frequency;
(iii) they are maintained by stimuli from parents rather than others;
(iv)   they occur naturally at a specified time (i.e. mealtime, bedtime, and so on).

One might expect early reinforcement arising from success with easy problems would increase co-operation. However, beginning treatment with more or less difficult behaviour problems does not seem to affect parental co-operation (Eyberg and Johnson, 1974), but there is still some doubt about this issue.

It may, however, increase parents' sense of self-efficacy. Ollendick and Cerny (1982) are of the opinion that parents will maintain their enthusiasm and interest for the programme as long as they perceive some progress in managing their offspring's actions, regardless of how difficult these behaviours are to deal with, in the therapist's opinion.

(d) The choice of concepts to be taught. There is a measure of agreement among authors on the subject of parent training on a number of core concepts and skills to be taught. Nevertheless, different trainers emphasize different principles or topics. Gordon and Davidson (1981) comment that some trainers open their series of sessions with parents with teaching on the clarification and enforcement of household rules. Patterson (1975) prefers to begin with the concept of 'social reinforcers'.

Gordon and Davidson acknowledge these differences, but are still able to find a common core to behavioural parent training courses:

Session I   Learning to define and measure behaviour
Session II   Graphing behaviours
Session III   Using consequences to change behaviour
Session IV   How to apply reinforcement to behaviour
Session V   Using good teaching procedures
Session VI   Response punishment: how to decrease undesired behaviour
Session VII   What to do regarding specific behaviours
Session VIII How to maintain a responsive parent image

3. Choice of procedure in parent training programmes

(a) Are written instructional materials (bibliotherapy) effective? The answer is that they are generally useful rather than wholly effective (of themselves) in parent training. They do generally increase parents' knowledge of behaviour child management but parents trained only with written materials have substantially more difficulty implementing the knowledge gained from their reading than do parents trained by other techniques (Christensen *et al.*, 1980).

Parents trained by means of written presentations tend to perform poorly in real-life situations (Flanagan *et al.*, 1979).

(b) What other methods of instruction are available? A variety of techniques that cue parents to behave in this or that way at appropriate times (e.g. headphones, signals, walkie-talkies) have proved useful, as have teaching aids such as role play, behaviour rehearsal, live modelling, symbolic modelling, lectures and discussions. Modelling is particularly effective (whether live or symbolic) as a training method. Film and video aids are useful media for teaching skills. Reliance on written materials alone should be avoided (see Flanagan *et al.*, 1979; O'Dell *et al.*, 1979).

(c) Are contingency contracts worth using? The answer is yes. They tend to engage the parents, facilitate their involvement in programmes and secure co-operation (e.g. completing assignments) (see Eyberg and Johnson, 1974; Fleischmann, 1979). The use of monetary deposits, 'parenting salaries', and so on, are somewhat alien to British practice. Some therapists build in 'treats' for parents (outings, buying oneself or one's partner a present, etc.) and of course, more extensive use of verbal reinforcement. Client/therapist contracts need not be over-complicated.

There is a 'working' contract between client and therapist on p. 124.

(d) The number and duration of sessions. These appear to vary considerably according to whether parents are seen individually or in a group. The variety of arrangements which has been used is surprisingly large. For example, those parents who met with Rose (1972) attended between seven and ten sessions of one and a half hours, which included formal instruction and modelling and role play by all concerned. Those who worked with Lehrer *et al.* (1973) however, attended ten two-hour sessions in which the first hour was devoted to instruction attended by parents from ten different families, and the second hour was devoted to small group discussion with two or three sets of parents and a trainer. By contrast, Rinn *et al.* (1975) reported a training programme in which over a thousand parents attended five, once weekly, two-hour sessions at a community mental health centre. Groups ranged in size from 16 to 90 with a mean of 41.

Sadler and Seyden (1976) have published a helpful guide for teaching child management to parents. They enumerate several basic course concepts:

Centre for Behavioural Work with Families,
Department of Psychology,
University of Leicester.

Agreement to work together

This agreement is drawn up between . . . .
for the Centre for Behavioural Work with Families, and . . . .
. . . .
parent(s) of . . . .

In keeping with the wishes of those concerned to arrive at a happier
family situation, an agreement was made by both parties to keep
to the following general arrangements:

On your part	On our part
1. To keep appointments arranged.	1. To keep appointments arranged.
2. To keep records concerning the child's behaviour.	2. To provide charts or other means of recording the child's behaviour.
3. To read the booklets which will be provided.	3. To explain the principles of the behavioural approach.

Renegotiation clause

The above agreement is open to renegotiation at any time by the
parties involved at the request of any party.

Signed . . . .
Signed . . . .
Signed . . . .
Date . . . .   Signed . . . .

(1) More learning occurs when people feel comfortable, relaxed and in friendly supportive surroundings.
(2) It is best to remove as much social anxiety as possible.
(3) A fun-filled atmosphere heightens the interest and excitement of the workshop.
(4) People learn better by actually doing rather than talking about something.

(5) Parents' reluctance to take tests can be overcome with innovative quizzes.
(6) It is helpful to work on parental attitudes as well as behaviours.
(7) Some simple exposure to and practice in communication skills is useful to many parents.
(8) It is somewhat destructive to self-esteem when parents see this kind of training only as remedial therapy for 'problem' parents and children.
(9) Parents make major contributions to the course itself. Telephone contact and carefully-timed home visits also increase parents' co-operation (Horne and Patterson, 1979; Iwaniec et al., 1985).

Ayllon and Azrin (1968) propose a guideline: 'Teach only those behaviours which will continue to be reinforced after training'. The therapist's aim in using behaviour modification procedures is to introduce the child to behaviours which are either intrinsically reinforcing or which make reinforcements available to him which he was not previously experiencing. In a sense there are two therapeutic objectives in working with children:

(1) To enhance a child's responses to the controlling factors in his environment without deliberately altering the latter. Assuming a family environment to be essentially satisfactory, one might attempt to adjust a child to it.
(2) To change the controlling factors in an unsatisfactory learning environment as a means of modifying problem behaviour. Where the latter strategy is predominant the therapeutic objective is to programme the environment so that it sustains the child's (and parents') 'improvement' after the formal programme is terminated. The long-term purpose of this phase of therapy is to help parents to become more systematic in their own behaviour, so as to be more effective in managing their children.

CASE STUDY: Treatment of conduct disorder (Ted, age 5)

(a) The referral

The family was referred to the Centre by a social worker. She had been called in to make a family assessment at the dermatology clinic which Ted attended because of his severe eczema. She noted Ted's severe behaviour problems and the fact that his mother was depressed and obviously in need of assistance. At this stage Ted's problems were listed as temper-tantrums (screaming, kicking, banging, stamping and scratching his eczema whenever he did not get his own way); extensive non-compliance; defaecating in the street; and refusing to go to bed in the evenings without his parents (he slept in their bed). The family comprised of Ted, his mother, father, a half-sister Susan (aged 9 years) and a younger brother Robert (aged 3 years). They lived in a small council house on a large pre-war estate on the outskirts of the city — an area stigmatized for its general air of delapidation and the presence of many so-called 'problem families'.

(b) Behavioural assessment (FIND and ABC)

The first task (as it is conceptualized) in the assessment phase is to 'find' out precisely *what* the problems are, specifying them in terms of their frequency, intensity, number and duration. The next task is to identify those environmental stimuli which are instigating and maintaining the child's maladaptive behaviour. Attention is paid to the ABC sequence. An analysis is also made of setting events — environmental conditions (and organismic factors) leading up to and immediately preceding the occurrence of the problem behaviour; also those that follow the performance of such behaviour. In other words, the therapist is on the look-out for antecedent stimuli and consequences which may serve to instigate and maintain problem behaviours because of their eliciting, discriminative and reinforcing value. He or she also tries to make *sense* of the problem behaviours, the purposes they serve, from the child's point of view. This involves finding out what the *child's perception* of his situation is, in terms of how he reacts to it and what he says about it.

(c) Behavioural analysis

A close and detailed account of Ted's problem behaviours was sought by means of interview in order to identify these factors. In order to tease-out family interactions and target behaviours, the 'typical day' in the life of the child and family was worked through in *minute* behavioural detail, pinpointing the precise happenings in those areas which caused confrontations and concern. In addition to these verbal reports, direct observations were made (at home and at school) of the problem behaviours. During the assessment period of 6 weeks (much longer than usual), twice-weekly home visits were made. Because Mrs C. was frequently distressed, following marital conflict or after particularly trying behaviour on the part of Ted, some interviews could not focus upon the behavioural assessment. During these sessions discussions of a supportive and advisory kind took place concerning the mother's personal problems.

The analysis of the target problems (which follows) classifies them into 'demanding' and 'oppositional' behaviours. Such a classification is to some extent arbitrary, but it facilitated the recording and identification of ABC sequences.

(i) Demanding behaviours

These originated with a demand made by Ted and were usually directed towards his mother.

Demanding his tea in the morning. The antecedent conditions here only involved the mother as the father left for work at 5.00 a.m. and Ted's brother and sister were still in bed. What would typically occur was as follows: Ted's mother got out of bed at 7.15 and would go downstairs; if Ted did not wake by 7.30 his mother went upstairs and carried him down. Trouble occurred only when Ted woke between 7.15 and 7.30. When this happened he would go to the upstairs landing and shout to his mother that he wanted his bottle. He would continue to shout louder and louder and if his mother did not respond immediately the shouting turned into screaming. Next, he would shuffle about making a noise with his feet, bang his head on the wall and scratch his eczema (the ultimate and most effective coercive strategy in his repertoire). Mrs C.'s reaction was to come to the foot of the stairs, show Ted his bottle of tea, and ask him to come down and get it. Ted invariably refused and the tantrum at the top of the stairs continued until his mother went to fetch him, carrying him downstairs and putting him in the living room in front of the fire, where he would lie quietly with his bottle. His mother's reaction to this situation was always the same: no verbal reprimands were made and no punishment was given. What varied was the time she took to 'obey' his commands.

Demanding behaviour while outside the home. These demands were made whenever Ted was out with his mother and they passed a sweet shop, toy shop, ice cream van, etc. If Ted's demands were not met then his response might consist of refusing to walk any further or resisting his mother's attempts to get hold of his hand so as to drag him away. Ted would also scream on these occasions. Invariably he got his own way. The most notable long-term consequence of this sequence was that Mrs C. took pre-emptive action to prevent confrontations. This she did by taking Ted his favourite sweet when she collected him from school in the afternoon. If for some reason she failed to bring these sweets then Ted was allowed to buy something from the local shop. Finally, his mother avoided possible conflict situations by no longer taking him into shops where she might not be able to meet his demands (e.g. toy shops). The tantrums, thus, were only escalated when his mother found it impossible to meet Ted's requests (e.g. she might have no money with her). On these occasions she had to take him by the hand and drag him home. His screaming and resisting behaviours continued for the entire journey, but no punishment was used at the time of the misbehaviour. The tantrums would often continue after they had reached home. Mrs C. would not punish Ted in the street but did do so (and then only occasionally) when they reached home — by smacking him perfunctorily. The child's response then was to kick or spit at his mother and throw things at her. Sometimes he would go out and defaecate in the street. At this point Mrs C. lost control of herself and she would throw things and shout. Ted seemed to recognize that he had gone too far and terminated his disruptive behaviour. However, after 10 minutes or so, he would return to the *original* request — the point where all the trouble began — and his mother now usually complied. They would make a journey to buy the object at the shop.

Demanding behaviour within the home. It was this range of problem behaviours which afforded the best opportunity for direct observation within the home and the following account is based largely upon such observations.

As with the two previous problem situations the discriminative stimulus for surplus behaviour seemed to be the presence and actions of his mother. It did not seem to matter whether the father or anyone else was present, but both parents reported that the problem behaviour was not manifested if Ted was alone with his father.

During the observation period, Mrs C. and the therapist were talking. Ted, his brother, and sister were also present. During their discussion Ted approached his mother and began tugging at her arm, making it obvious by his actions (no request) that he wanted to sit on her knee. Her first response was to say 'No' and tell him that he must not interrupt when she was talking. She suggested that he went and played with his toys as his brother and sister were doing. Ted took no notice of this request and, still standing by his mother, he began to whimper, continuing to tug at her arm. A verbal threat was given of future punishment but Ted again took no notice; eventually Mrs C. picked him up and put him on a chair by himself. Ted remained in this position for about 30 seconds and then went across the room and picked up a large hammer which was lying on the ground. His mother told him to put it down but he took no notice, and a threat of punishment was made. Ted still refused to comply with his mother's request and moved threateningly towards the window and then the television set. As he did this his mother took the hammer from him. For the next 10 minutes his disruptive behaviours included switching the television set on and off repeatedly, turning the volume up to maximum and jumping up and down on the television stand. His mother, during this period, gave numerous commands that Ted stop, made frequent threats of punishment, and often dared Ted to do something, promising that punishment would ensue if he did so. No sanctions, however, were applied during a prolonged period and the end result of the sequence was that the mother picked up Ted and put him on her knee.

This observation was *representative* of many other incidents within the home during the period of assessment; Mrs C. also reported that similar sequences of behaviour often occurred. The most frequent demands made by Ted were for attention and physical proximity, especially when others had the 'limelight' or when Mrs C. was attending to other persons. The ultimate consequence was invariably that Ted's original demand was met and no unfavourable consequences for his unreasonable demands* occurred, apart from verbal reprimands and an occasional, mild, almost cursory slap on the head, neither of which Ted seemed to notice.

Demanding behaviour during the night. Ted always slept in his parents' bed and was a very poor sleeper, sometimes staying awake for most of the night. Ted was asthmatic and in addition suffered at night with his eczema—scratching away, particularly when he was going through a phase of sleeping restlessly. If Ted was scratching his mother would smack his hand softly and occasionally he would begin to cry. On these occasions Ted would usually demand that his empty bottle be filled. Initially, his mother tried to ignore this, but gradually the frequency and intensity of Ted's demands and the crying and scratching reached a level of intensity at which his mother felt compelled to accede to his request. This resolution could take place after a conflict of some hours. Once he had his bottle Ted invariably fell into a deep sleep.

(ii) Oppositional behaviour

These were defined as behaviours Ted displayed in order to obstruct attempts made by his mother to make him do something.

Refusal to dress or undress. These problems occurred when Mrs C. attempted to dress Ted for school in the mornings or undress him in the evenings. They were not experienced at weekends or during the holidays; indeed, the problems had originated when Ted started school. Mrs C. would attempt to dress Ted while he was sitting on her knee. His brother was usually present at this time, but his sister would still be in bed. If Ted did not wish to be dressed or undressed he would struggle to get away from his mother, make himself stiff, and be generally obstructive. This involved removing the clothes that his mother had just put on him. In the evenings he would remove his pyjamas and put on his clothes again. The consequences of such behaviour was that Mrs C. made frequent unfulfilled threats to smack Ted. On the rare occasions that she did smack, Ted seemed quite unconcerned. In the morning this

---

*Ted's monopolizing of his mother's attention (and money) meant that his siblings failed to get a fair share and Mrs C. had no time to attend to herself. Sadly, the attention was misdirected to negative behaviour.

sequence was usually terminated by a lengthy struggle, Mrs C. only managing to put on Ted's coat as it was time to leave for school. The sequence might last for up to half an hour, with Ted having to be dressed about three times. In the evening, after Ted had removed his pyjamas on two or three occasions, his mother allowed him to remain in his clothes and eventually cajoled him into putting on his pyjamas much later on.

Refusal to walk to school. Ted was taken to school in the morning by his mother, accompanied by his brother. Usually there were other parents and children present, but on some occasions Ted's mother took responsibility for the other children. Ted, however, was never taken by the other parents. Usually Ted would walk beside his mother, but on some occasions he might lag behind and hide from his mother. When his mother turned and asked him to hurry up he would say 'No'. She then threatened to smack him, but this rarely had any effect. He was most likely to sit on the ground or grab hold of some railings, and when his mother went back to collect him he resisted her efforts to try and lift him by going stiff. She was obliged either to pick him up or drag him by the hand, and by now Ted was likely to be screaming. As usual, verbal threats of punishment were not carried out. The oppositional behaviour invariably terminated in sight of the school gates, when his mother threatened to tell Ted's teacher about his behaviour. (His behaviour at school was reasonable.)

Refusal to go to bed in the evening. Ted had always been a poor sleeper and a situation had now developed in which his mother rarely attempted to put him to bed before she herself went because she realized that there would be considerable disruption if she put him to bed against his wishes. On occasions in the past when she had attempted to put Ted to bed she had to sit with him until he was asleep. When leaving the room Ted invariably woke up and began to cry. If the crying was not answered then it turned to screaming, and his mother had to go back and at his request she lay down beside him. The significant outcome of this pattern of behaviour was that Ted's mother rarely attempted to take him to bed before she herself went at 10.00 p.m.; the exceptions were when he fell asleep downstairs. If that occurred and he was taken to bed, then either he awoke soon afterwards and came downstairs or he began to cry until his mother went up to him and lay with him. If he came downstairs no punishment, threat of punishment, or even encouragement to go back to bed was given, and it was accepted that Ted would remain downstairs.

(d) Towards a clinical formulation

Another stage of the behavioural analysis is to formulate hypotheses about the possible antecedent and consequent stimuli which appear to be instigating and maintaining the problem behaviour and to examine other situations in which the child's behaviour differed from that in the problem situations (e.g. evidence of prosocial behaviour and the settings in which it occurs).

Clearly, Ted's mother was unwittingly reinforcing his maladaptive behaviour. Ted's demands, without exception, for drinks, sweets, attention, etc. were acceded to, following his display of tantrums and disruptive behaviours. The invariable outcome in the case of the oppositional behaviours was to increase the interaction between Ted and his mother. The resulting attention was reinforcing these non-compliant actions. It was quite straightforward to identify favourable consequences in the example of his being allowed to stay downstairs in the evening. Conversely, in all examples of misbehaviour, there were no really aversive contingent consequences which might serve to extinguish them.

With regard to discriminative stimuli for the performance of problem behaviours, the most significant of these were the presence and actions of Mrs C. The currency of her commands and threats had been debased. Ted did not trust her words. He had learnt that in her presence his wishes (for her undivided attention and for 'goodies') were likely to be met if he persisted long enough or escalated his coercive behaviours. Under normal conditions of socialization it would be expected that defiance of prohibitions given by his parents would be linked in the child's mind with unfavourable sanctions; but in Ted's case ignoring or opposing mother's threats and commands had almost no aversive consequences.

As Mrs C. appeared to bear the brunt of most of Ted's misbehaviour, it might be concluded that his father was able to exercise control over him. This was not so, in fact. Mr C.'s small part in this analysis of the problem situation reflects the little contact he had with Ted. Parental roles were sharply defined within the home (mother brings up the children); in addition, the father worked extremely long hours and spent most evenings and weekends at the local club. The only regular contact Ted had with his father was in the early evening. On the rare occasions when both parents were together in the evening Ted's behaviour was problematic, but his demands and oppositional behaviour were always directed towards his mother and his father did not attempt to intervene.

Situations in which neither parent was present were considered. Babysitters encountered situations comparable with those experienced by Mrs C. — constant demands followed by temper-tantrums when they were not met. Also, they were unable to put Ted to bed before his parents returned home. Not surprisingly, Mrs C. found it almost impossible to find babysitters. The other major period of absence from his parents was during school time. During a school visit, his teacher stated that after a difficult start (in which he showed defiant, disruptive and hyperactive behaviour) he was now prepared to sit and work, and to sit and listen at story time. She said that Ted did not stand out in class as a particularly difficult child; he mixed well with other children. Significantly his teacher had noticed (during his early days at school) that he rarely responded immediately to verbal instructions but needed to be told to stop doing something five or six times before he complied; even then he might return to the prohibited behaviour soon afterwards. This was consistent with his current failure to respond appropriately to verbal instructions at home. However, the general improvement in Ted's behaviour at school demonstrated that given an appropriate reinforcement regime (a structured and consistent environment—firm but friendly—had been provided) significant behavioural changes could be brought about.

(e) Somatic factors

Having attempted to identify the here-and-now conditions controlling the problem behaviour, the next task was to try to explain their origins. The importance of this in a behavioural approach is not so much to help the client achieve insight (although awareness may facilitate change) but rather to discover to what extent the original 'causal' factors continue to influence the current controlling conditions.

Ted's developmental history was analysed in order to seek any possible contributions to the problem by somatic or other factors. Physical conditions might produce problem behaviour directly or might contribute to it indirectly through the reaction of the child and/or his parents to any disability. Ted was born at term at home; there were no obstetric complications which might be suggestive of minimal cerebral dysfunction. Developmental milestones such as sitting, walking, talking, etc. were all within normal limits. However, Ted had inherited an allergic diathesis and suffered severe bronchial asthma and a chronic skin condition. There was strong evidence that Ted displayed early temperamental (and physical) attributes which had a considerable effect upon his relationship with his mother and thus on the development of his problem behaviours.

(f) Previous learning experiences

In Ted's case it was considered that his temperamental and physical attributes had influenced the quality of his early learning in the sense that they made it difficult for his mother to develop effective control, and thus a socializing ethos for her child. Mrs C. herself, and the immediate family, identified the cause of the problem behaviours as being due to her inadequacies as a mother. The family GP told Mrs C. that the cause of the problem was that she told him off too often. Her own mother said she was too 'soft'. No one took account of the effect of characteristics exhibited by Ted himself which had affected the situation; Ted's problems *seemed* to reflect poor care. But what looks like bad mothering often shows up, after careful investigation, to be the mother's confused reaction to a difficult child rather than a primary cause of the child's problems. This was the case here. Ted had been one of those infants who displayed marked irregularity of biological functioning from birth; it showed itself particularly in poor sleeping patterns; he appeared to sleep better during the day than at night and (in absolute terms) appeared to need less sleep than would normally be expected by a child of his age. Children with poor sleep records often develop behaviour problems and this seemed to apply in this case. Demanding behaviours which Ted manifested during the night may well have arisen out of his mother's early reinforcement of crying during these hours. In babies a night feed is usual, but this is soon discontinued as the child sleeps through the night. Ted never developed this lengthy period of sleep and consequently his mother had felt compelled to respond to his crying. (He still demanded his bottle in the middle of the night with tea in it.) Additionally, as Ted did not fall asleep when put to bed, crying, screaming, and coming downstairs had resulted in the child being allowed to stay up until his mother went to bed. The habit of having Ted in the double bed had arisen out of her taking him into bed with her when he had asthma attacks. Now he demanded to be there every night and Mrs C. colluded here because it gave her an excuse not to have sexual relationships with her husband. (When Mr C. finally abandoned the family, this situation was one of the reasons he gave for leaving.)

Poor sleeping had another indirect effect upon the problem situation: the period in which aversive interactions occurred was extended in time and Mrs C. had little rest and no time to relax. Consequently, her ability to deal appropriately with problems was hindered by her frequently exhausted or tense state. This led her eventually to take the line of least resistance, providing reinforcing consequences despite having initially threatened aversive consequences. The result of all this was that mother's words were devalued. Ted's asthma and his eczema provided the checkmate situation in bringing about his mother's capitulation to his demands. If she made an effort to resist his screaming and tantrums then Ted began to scratch his eczema until it bled, and because this was particularly upsetting for her it was invariably effective. Ted was fully aware of the relationship between scratching and the satisfaction of his demands. He now actually threatened verbally to scratch if his mother did not give in to his demands. Ted also had the 'ability' to manifest physical symptoms in order to control his mother. An example of this occurred when his mother attempted to dress him. If she put clothes on him which were not to his liking he would develop a heaving cough, complain that he was going to be sick, lose his facial colour, and have difficulty in breathing. All of these resulted in his mother hurriedly dealing with the unpleasant situation by complying with his demands. In general, Mrs C. was afraid to confront Ted, because 'excitement' might bring on his asthma. There was also an ideological reason for her avoidance of 'discipline'. She had been brought up by brutally strict parents and had vowed never to be like them with her own children. Indeed, she had swung to the opposite extreme of 'laissez-faire' parenting. Not surprisingly the other two children were not without their problems. These were, however, not of the same order as Ted's. The mother's management of Ted can only be assessed accurately when account is taken of the influence that his physical constitution had had upon their early relationship. Mrs C. admitted that Ted had always been a 'special' child — perhaps because she had two miscarriages prior to his birth and because of his 'handicap'. What this meant in practical terms was that she never really punished Ted, but merely tried to prevent him from doing things. Ted's attention-seeking behaviour seems to have increased markedly when he was 18 months old at the time when Robert was born; on occasions he was seen to strike Robert while he was in the cot. His mother remembered quite clearly that her usual response to this and to his screaming (which also increased considerably at that time) was to pick him up.

The social situation of the family may also have reduced the ability of Mrs C. to cope with Ted. The large council estate in which the family lived had a widely-held reputation for child abuse and poor standards of child care, and Mrs C. was extremely sensitive about this. She was determined not to be labelled a 'bad mother'. She herself equated poor mothering with the commonly used control techniques of smacking and depriving children of privileges — hence another reason for her refusal to smack Ted in the street, despite extreme provocation and embarrassment, and hence her concentration upon the use of verbal reprimands and threats which proved to be ineffectual in his case. During initial discussions, time out techniques were mentioned and it was explained that this might involve keeping Ted in his bedroom for short periods of time. His mother was adamant that she would not consider using such a method because to her this would be cruel and it might further damage her reputation in the neighbourhood. The stigma of being incapable of controlling her child, which she felt she suffered from at present, was seen as preferable to the possibility of being known as an uncaring, insensitive mother should she adopt more physical techniques of control.

During the initial assessment interview, Mr C. seemed reluctant to enter any discussions about Ted. When pressed he insisted that he had few problems with his son and that the problem was essentially his wife's. As the assessment progressed it became evident that considerable tension existed between the couple and Mrs C. expected that a separation would occur in the near future. The major problems in the marriage, from Mrs C.'s point of view, were her husband's violence towards her when he came home after drinking and her resentment because he went out to the club or pub almost every evening and left her to cope with the children. A closer examination of the problem revealed that Mr C. was also in a difficult situation. Susan was his step-daughter and some resentment existed between them. Mrs C. forbad her husband to exercise any restraint over her, insisting that he left disciplinary and other matters to her. She allowed him to deal only with his own children. However, when Mr C. did try to control the children she complained that he only did so when it was in his interest (e.g. when he wished to watch television). She threw in his face the fact that he spent relatively little time at home. The situation had double-bind qualities; on the one hand, the father was criticized for going out too often and not giving sufficient support to his wife, but when he did attempt to intervene in family situations he was also criticized by his wife. Faced with this situation Mr C. opted out of his parental role and it was not unusual for him to come home from work at 5.30 p.m., be confronted with a distraught and accusing wife, and so repair immediately to the pub without waiting for his food. There appeared to be little that was positive left in the marriage and Mrs C. had partially resigned herself to bringing up the children without the support of her husband.

(g) The clinical (causal) formulation

The attempt to formulate reasonably precise hypotheses with a view to planning treatment, derives from all the information available. The data upon which they are based are also used in deciding whether a behavioural treatment programme is appropriate. This case was postulated to be one largely of inappropriate stimulus control. As a result of discrimination learning, certain stimuli had come to signify the likelihood of particular reinforcement consequences, thus influencing the probability of Ted's deviant response being performed. Mrs C.'s words of command and denial, for example, were functioning as inappropriate discriminative stimuli—cues for verbal disputations and other forms of attention (not to mention getting his own way) which were reinforcing his oppositional behaviour. There was also an almost complete absence of sanctions contingent upon such behaviour. It might be said that Ted was on a continuous schedule of reinforcement for inappropriate behaviour.

Ted appeared to be a child who had displayed a range of 'surplus' behaviours almost from birth; these have been shown to be closely linked with the development of maladaptive behaviours at a later age. In addition, his mother's ability to cope had been considerably reduced in a number of ways. First, Mrs C. had been handicapped by her fear of being labelled an inadequate, uncaring mother. This (together with a philosophy of child rearing which was a reaction to her parents' methods) had considerably limited her choice of disciplinary procedures at her disposal. Second, because of miscarriages preceding Ted's birth and the baby's allergies, he acquired a 'special' status in his mother's eyes which led to particularly inappropriate methods of socializing the boy—even more so than his siblings. Finally, because of the marital tensions, his mother had ended up coping alone with a particularly difficult child, deprived of the help and support of a husband.

(h) Resources for treatment

In the classroom situation it had been demonstrated that Ted was able to learn to behave reasonably—a good sign that the child *could* modulate his presentation of himself within a context of clear rules and predictable consequences.

There were likely to be difficulties with his mother. She had *learned*, being reinforced negatively to 'give way'. Although help could not be expected from Mr C., Mrs C. was highly motivated to carry out a programme. A therapeutic intervention imposes great strain upon parents because it requires that they keep rigorously to a prearranged plan and are consistent in their approach to problem situations. In this case Mr C. rarely dealt with the children and thus it was not expected that he would hinder the programme by reinforcing problem behaviour. A potential source of difficulty might be that Mrs C. was so volatile (despite the tranquillizers she took regularly) and could become so distraught that it might seriously affect her ability to be consistent in managing the programme. As a counter to these reservations was the co-operation and dedication of the mother throughout the lengthy assessment period. Although she did object to sending Ted to his room she continually stressed her willingness to attempt any other methods of control suggested. At the time that the final assessment was being made the parents separated, for Mrs C. told her husband that he must leave after one of his frequent threats to do so. The effect of the separation was to increase her determination to overcome Ted's problems and to some extent it facilitated treatment by removing an additional tension from the situation, allowing the mother to concentrate upon the therapy.

(i) Treatment decision

It seemed obvious from an early stage in our contact with the family, that the extent and severity of the problem would necessitate some intervention in order to aid Mrs C. and a palpably unhappy child. The interactions between Ted and his mother and siblings were predominantly negative ones; tension was a common feature of the mother–child relationship. Ethical considerations at this stage seemed to depend upon whether the mother's expectations of Ted were reasonable. It was felt that Ted's behaviour was not acceptable in a 5-year-old who, by normal standards, should have begun to show some self-restraint. By discussion with his mother, criteria of what could be considered to be appropriate behaviour in a child of this age were agreed. It was hoped that therapy would provide a basis for a more productive relationship between Ted and his mother — and thereby facilitate his learning in other areas. It was also felt that if Mrs C. could be helped to overcome the necessity of succumbing to Ted's demands then this would enable her to give more attention to Susan and Robert.

The approach of the Centre is (*inter alia*) to attend to parents' self-perceptions, in particular their often damaged sense of self-efficacy, by discussion. There has to be an honest endeavour to be open with them, to provide them with all available information and to share one's thinking with them. Parents have their own expertise and skills which should be assessed and utilized.

There is a practical (as well as ethical) imperative here. Considerations such as these turn out to be among the main factors which minimize dropping out of treatment (see Backeland and Lundwall, 1975). It is only reasonable to propose that those who have the responsibility for a job should have access to the best available technical information relevant to that task. And parents have the awesome responsibility for guiding the behavioural development of their offspring. Because behavioural principles can be clearly and simply explained the therapy (or educational process) minimizes the air of mystification that surrounds some treatment methods and objectives.

It will have been noted that in the case of Mrs C. there were several problems other than those displayed by Ted. A bonding of traditional therapeutic/casework skills (such as clarification of problems, support-giving, sympathetic listening, acceptance and resource mobilization) to the behavioural approach, has been required of us at the Centre.

(j) Treatment plan

It was possible to overcome one of Ted's problem behaviours simply by asking his mother to wake him at 7.15 a.m. and take him downstairs with her, thus removing the possibility of disobedience and temper-tantrums occurring following his demand for tea. His mother agreed to do this and found that when she took him downstairs no further problems were encountered. (Change was from 9 tantrums in a 13-day baseline period to a zero rate). The development of a programme to achieve a set bedtime for Ted illustrates the need to take into account the abilities and wishes of the parents. The common behavioural approach to bedtime problems is to take the child to bed, settle him down, and leave him in his room, paying no attention should crying occur and, if necessary, returning him if the child persists in coming downstairs. It was felt that Ted would almost certainly come downstairs, and as we were not prepared to lock him in his room an alternative treatment programme had to be devised. There was no need to obtain a baseline record for this as Ted was never put to bed in the evenings. The programme required the mother to put Ted to bed at 9.00 p.m. and if he came downstairs he was to be taken back to bed immediately. If he cried and screamed upstairs his mother was not to go to him. As Ted was expected to come downstairs, a reward system was to be used in which he was to be given a star, considerable praise and a tea card for staying in the bedroom after being taken upstairs. Also an attempt was to be made to compensate Ted for the loss of attention he received by being taken to bed early; Mrs C. was asked to read him a story for 15 minutes when he was in bed. An ultimate treatment goal was set of developing a regular bedtime for Ted of 8.00 p.m. and to get him to sleep in his own bed. It was felt, however, that a gradual approach would reduce the burden upon Mrs C. and therefore Ted's bedtime was originally set at 9.00 p.m. and he was to be allowed to continue sleeping with his mother at first. The major effect of this gradual approach would be to reduce the time period in which Ted would be able to come downstairs before his mother's usual bedtime of 10.00 p.m. An important antecedent condition which was altered in this case was that the mother was asked to prevent Ted from falling asleep downstairs in the early evening so that he might be more tired at 9.00 p.m.

Although the results of the programme were extremely encouraging, these occurred despite the mother's failure to adhere strictly to the treatment programme. During 3 out of the first 4 days Ted came downstairs on a number of occasions and was eventually allowed to stay, thus reinforcing his behaviour. Also during the first week his mother went to bed early on two occasions because Ted was crying and screaming upstairs. Mrs C. was reminded of the terms of the contract and the *notes* detailing the programme were consulted again. The frequency and intensity of the screaming decreased as treatment progressed, because the mother was more successful in ignoring it. The crucial factor in the success of the programme appeared to be Ted's extremely high motivation to obtain stars. Observation of the family situation throws light on this; Mrs C. and the rest of the immediate family all gave enthusiastic praise when Ted obtained a star. During visits by the therapist he had now become the central figure in the family, not because of his maladaptive behaviour as in the past but because of his having succeeded in going to bed at 9.00 p.m. without coming downstairs. Ted's schoolteacher was told of the programme by his mother and she also praised him for obtaining a star. It was felt in this case that the use of stars had a significant effect other than simply reinforcing Ted. The frequency of Ted's maladaptive led to a situation in which almost all his mother's interactions with him were negative and Ted rarely experienced positive attention. The giving of the stars acted as a reminder to his mother that this was the appropriate time to give praise. Further evidence as to the importance of the token system was shown by the fact that although Ted was taken to bed at 9.00 p.m. he was invariably awake when his mother went to bed and it must be assumed there had been a conscious decision by him not to go downstairs. The ultimate treatment goals of achieving an 8.00 p.m. bedtime and getting Ted to sleep in a bed of his own were successfully accomplished, by similar means, in a matter of weeks.

The target behaviours of refusing to dress and refusing to walk to school reduced during baseline recording. (Direct observations corroborated Mrs C.'s recording and indicated that she was less tense and growing in confidence.) As so often happens, change does not await the formal initiation of a programme but shows itself from the first contact with the family. Experience with families suggests a reactive effect for parental tracking and recording; for some problems and for some children this procedure in itself can produce a treatment effect. Several speculative explanations for this change suggest themselves. First, it may be that the extra but more detached interest that the mother showed in Ted's problem behaviours for the purpose of recording, brought about the change. Ted was certainly aware that his mother was recording and she often remarked to him that she was keeping a record of his 'naughty' behaviour. Second, it is evident that the discussion of problem situations has had a considerable effect upon Mrs C.'s management of Ted. It has been observed in many cases at the Centre that during the assessment stage parents seem to pay more attention to the relationship between behaviour and its consequences and relate this to their own situation. Some experience an access of self-confidence (perceived self-efficacy) and they are sometimes difficult to restrain through the baseline period, wishing to get started on a programme of their own. With Mrs C. such a change in her behaviour did occur; during the recording of temper-tantrums following Ted's demands for his bottle she began refusing to give it to him until at least 5 minutes after his temper-tantrum ceased. Mrs C. was certainly aware of this change in her behaviour and gave a further example: previously she took sweets to school in the afternoon to prevent the occurrence of a temper-tantrum, but she made a decision to stop doing this and instead have something waiting for Ted when he reached home. He was told, however, that he would only receive this if he walked home without exhibiting any of his problem behaviours. On the first two afternoons Ted displayed serious tantrums and did not receive his reward, but after that, no such problems arose.

What appears to have happened is that Mrs C. developed for herself effective ways of coping with the various problem situations that arose — untidy from the standpoint of research and evaluation but excellent from her point of view and the service aspect of the Centre's work. She reported that there was an overall improvement in Ted's behaviour in many areas. A follow-up of 3 months revealed a maintenance of the improvements in non-compliant behaviour. The formal programme in connection with bedtime problems was discontinued in the meantime. Mrs C. reported at follow-up visits that she felt that Ted was much improved and that she had the situation under control. Ted still displayed occasional temper-tantrums but these were much less frequent. The most striking feature of this case was undoubtedly the almost complete collapse of Ted's problem behaviour in so short a time. This can perhaps be explained by re-examining his reinforcement history. In behavioural terms Ted was on a continuous reinforcement schedule in which almost every deviant response was followed by a reward. The extinction of deviant responses was probably facilitated by this pattern.

Patterson (1975) notes that the failures that occur in his work tend to be obtained with father-absent families and families in the lower socioeconomic classes. It was his clinical impression that many disruptions in the performance of parenting skills were associated with marital conflict, separations and divorce.

We have observed in many of the parents attending the Centre — and this, as well as theoretical considerations, has been our rationale for giving the therapeutic task back to *them* — that their lives seem minimally satisfying. These clients usually suffer from painfully low self-esteem, experience feelings of inadequacy and failure as parents. Feelings of hopelessness and despair prevail about their ability to improve their offsprings' behaviour and to improve their own lives. This extreme sense of futility and incompetence seriously damages the parent–child relationship. People whose inner resources are so depleted often have few pleasurable activities. They are isolated and demoralized and need as much help and understanding as their difficult children. At the point of referral we often see the members of the family as being trapped in a vicious circle — a downward spiral of mutually unrewarding aversive interactions. Some of the parents appear to be at a point of marital and nervous breakdown. We came to the conclusion that simply applying behavioural casework to ameliorate the children's problems would not be sufficient. There was a great need for community support for the parents. Initially, the parents need exclusive individual attention and help in a therapeutic partnership to enable them to overcome interactional and emotional difficulties, not only connected with the child's behaviour, but also with their own anxiety, fears, hurt and guilt. They need encouragement to face life again, and a way of analysing and applying flexible strategies to cope with fraught situations. However, in the later stages, when life becomes a little easier, because of general improvement in the home and in the child's behaviour — when a sense of achievement is dawning — support from a larger group becomes desirable. This is the time and place when a *self-help parents' group* might prove very beneficial.

CASE STUDY: Treatment of emotional disorder (Tessa, age 5, suffering from an animal phobia)

Tessa was referred to us by her GP because of her intense fear of animals. She had first become fearful of dogs at the age of 3 and this fear intensified and generalized over the years, to all animals, birds and insects. She was now reluctant to go out and play in case of a chance encounter with an animal or insect. If this occurred she would become hysterical, screaming uncontrollably. She nearly suffered a serious accident when she ran across the road, panic stricken, to avoid a dog. The therapist (Berry, 1986) following an assessment of the parameters of the phobia conducted the behaviour therapy programme as follows:

Preparation

The treatment plan was fully discussed and negotiated with Tessa and her mother. The therapist and Mrs W. were jointly (and separately) to be the mediators of the therapy (mother reinforcing the *in vivo* outside events with home-based tasks). Between sessions the mother's tasks were discussed and modelled. Parents were reassured that the pace of the exposure training (symbolic and *in vivo* graduated desensitization) would never be too quick or overwhelming for Tessa.

Therapy

The programme consisted of two stages:
(1) The therapist engaged Tessa in story-reading and telling, drawing, colouring and cutting out pictures of animals, birds and insects, also playing with hand animal puppets, etc. These exercises were graduated so as to make Tessa more familiar with the non-harmful and pleasant side of animals while feeling confident and relaxed. They also helped the therapist (during her contribution) to establish a relationship of trust with the child. These home-based sessions enabled the mother to observe the therapist and to learn various ways of reducing anxiety provoking situations by using play; reassuring words; distraction. Eventually she took over a major part of the work of symbolic desensitization.

(2) The second phase consisted of gradual exposure (*in vivo*) to animals, birds and insects away from home, and initially, in the company of the therapist.

Session 1, 2, 3

Tessa was asked to draw pictures to illustrate stories that the therapist read or made up about animals. She coloured pictures of insects and animals drawn by the therapist and cut them out and then displayed them proudly in her room. She enjoyed these activities after a little initial apprehension; throughout the sessions the useful, friendly and helpful aspects of animals and insects were emphasized and illustrated, e.g. hens laying eggs, sheep dog helping the farmer gather in the sheep, the dog guiding the blind person, an army dog helping soldiers to find explosives, the dog being a companion for an elderly, lonely person, bees making honey, etc. (Flies are difficult to accommodate!) Between sessions, Tessa's mother was asked to read or tell stories to Tessa that had animal characters in them. She also brought up the subject of animals whenever the opportunity arose; she was *not* to continue if Tessa became tense and anxious.

By the end of the third session, Tessa appeared to be quite at ease with the therapist and she did not, by now, show any anxiety or apprehension with symbolic material — visual, verbal or tactile. By now it was felt that she was ready to begin the second stage of treatment.

Session 4

Tessa was taken by the therapist for a walk along the canal. The therapist brought a camera so Tessa could take photographs of geese and birds from a distance. She next observed, and then fed the geese from a gradually shorter distance. She enjoyed these activities and showed little fear. On the way back they stopped at the pet shop and peeped through the window for a few minutes. Tessa saw some rabbits and birds. When she was asked to take a photograph of the first dog she might see on the street, she became subdued and anxious. The suggestion was therefore not pursued further.

Session 5

This session involved play with a dog hand-puppet at home and then a trip to the park for further contact with animals. Tessa took some photographs of dogs at a short distance and seemed to be at ease. She remained close to the therapist. While on the swing she saw a spider and immediately alighted; she didn't want to talk about the episode so the matter was dropped. No fuss was made on either side.

Session 6

The first part of the session took place at home, drawing spiders on cardboard, colouring them and then cutting them out. The cut-out spiders were put on string and hung up in her bedroom. During these activities the therapist talked to her about spiders (where they live, how they spin webs and the fact that they don't interfere with or hurt people). The therapist then took Tessa to the RSPCA to look around the kennels and to talk about the plight of the animals there. Tessa became very interested and concerned, stopping at many cages and asking questions about abandoned or ill-treated dogs. She paid little attention to the continuous barking of dogs. However, when the therapist stopped to touch and play with some very appealing puppies and tried to encourage her to touch them she refused and kept her distance.

Session 7

The therapist brought her dog (a very friendly one) and asked Tessa to walk him on a lead in the park with her. She enjoyed this, making remarks about how good he was. She was still reluctant to pat him. Later she helped the therapist to clean a bird's cage and spent several minutes talking to the bird. On the way back home, they stopped once again at the pet shop. This time they walked into the shop and Tessa took some photographs of rabbits and birds. She appeared to be quite relaxed in close proximity with the animals and moved freely around the shop.

Session 8

Tessa was taken for a long walk along the canal to feed the ducks and later to the park to see various dogs and also to walk the therapist's dog. Tessa remained calm and comfortable despite being in quite close contact with dogs in the park.

It was felt that Tessa had become noticeably less fearful of animals and insects (even dogs) and that further encouragement (enabling Tessa to see animals) should be left to the parents. Throughout the treatment Tessa's parents had been extremely supportive of the ideas and methods used and mother played an important role of co-therapist. Both parents stated that family friends and neighbours had noticed a marked change in Tessa's attitudes to animals; Tessa had reached a stage of getting pleasure from seeing some animals and birds like ducks, geese, rabbits, cats. She became tolerant of insects. Flies and bees no longer bothered her. She helped mother to remove a spider from the bath and showed interest in ants while playing in the garden. She was gentle and calm when a ladybird landed on her dress; she began to play freely in the garden and was now asking mother to take her to see geese and animals in the pet shop. The loss of fear with regards to flies and ants was a result of generalization rather than specific therapeutic input on these species.

The parents were advised to get in touch with us if they needed any advice or assistance.

9 Months follow-up
A 9 months follow-up revealed that the progress had been maintained and that they had already 'forgotten' that Tessa had been so acutely fearful of animals, insects and birds.

It will be noted that our agreed goal with the child and her parents was tolerance of the proximity of animals and insects. No effort was made to force the issue of her actually touching (stroking) a dog, any more than it was thought necessary to touch a spider. We took her to what was thought to be a functional level of interacting with animals.

CASE STUDY: Treatment of child abuse (Wayne, age 2, suffering from failure to thrive)

To see the twins, Jimmy and Wayne Grant,* together—on one of our home visits—is to understand something of what the paediatric term 'failure to thrive' means. Jimmy is a chubby, rosy-cheeked, boisterous 2-year-old. He appears to be a happy, mischievous boy, running, playing, talking and laughing. He comes to his mother for help and comfort and cuddles up to her spontaneously. He responds readily to her attention and affection. She smiles at him, picks him up, sits him on her lap, plays with him, answers his questions, watches his movements, warns him when he is in danger.

On the edge of the room, like a stranger, stands Wayne—posture rigid, staring fixedly at us. He is a sad, lethargic looking child, very small and extremely thin. His pale face throws into relief the dark shadows under his eyes. He remains in one spot, as if at attention. Later he gazes unswervingly at his mother. She takes no notice of him. When asked to call Wayne over to her she looks in his direction; as she does so her face hardens and her eyes are angry. She addresses him with a dry command; when he hesitates she shouts at him.

Our observations of his interactions with his mother (several visits over four weeks) which gave us baseline data, indicated that she *never* smiled at him, *never* picked him up, *never* sat him on her knee, *never* played or read to him. The only physical contact came about when she fed, bathed or dressed him, and at such times, her handling was rough and silent. When she

*These names are purely fictitious. The case is described by Herbert and Iwaniec (1980) in the *Australian Journal of Child and Family Welfare*, and is reprinted with permission.

Child's reactive and proactive behaviour	Often	Seldom	Never
1. Playing freely			
2. Laughing/Smiling			
3. Running			
4. Talking freely			
5. Comes for help			
6. Comes for comfort			
7. Cuddles up to Mother			
8. Responds to affection			
9. Responds to attention			
10. At ease when she is near him/her			
11. Joins in the activity with other Children			
12. Is not frightened when approached by Mother, or corrected			
13. Eats more quickly			
14. Eats wider variety of food			
15. Asks for food — indicates hunger			
16. Seems to be at ease during meal time			
17. Vomiting			
18. Heaving			
19. Diarrhoea			
20. Puts on weight steadily			

Mother's reactive and proactive behaviour	Often	Seldom	Never
1. Talking to the child			
2. Looking at the child			
3. Smiling at the child			
4. Eye contact (loving)			
5. Touching (gently)			
6. Holding (closely, lovingly)			
7. Playing			
8. Cuddling			
9. Kissing			
10. Sitting him/her on her lap			
11. Handling him/her in a gentle way			
12. Giving requests (as opposed to commands)			
13. Helping him/her if in difficulties			
14. Encouraging him/her to participate in play and other activities			
15. Being concerned about him/her			
16. Picking him/her up when he/she cries or when hurt			
17. Answering his/her questions			
18. Ignoring his/her presence			
19. Emotionally treats him/her the same as other children			

approached him he appeared to be frightened and occasionally burst into tears (see above for the check list we use with our observations at various times and in various situations).

He would never come to her for comfort or help and she never approached him except to carry out the bare essentials of care and control. The children were both meticulously clean and well-dressed.

Home-based observations allowed us to see that when the father returned from work, Wayne brightened a little, he became somewhat more alert and lively, especially when mother was out of sight. When she entered the room he stiffened up. Jimmy and Wayne don't play together. Jimmy frequently pushed his brother and smacked him. Wayne's cries were largely ignored by his mother.

Looking at Wayne and Jimmy it is hard to believe that they are twins who were of the same weight at birth. Wayne's small stature was now reflected in a height and weight that were below the third percentile curves of normal growth. Wayne had been hospitalized several times because of his failure to gain weight. During the latest hospitalization Wayne's mother refused to visit him and requested his reception into care; she appeared to be very depressed and said that she could no longer cope with trying to feed him (he would refuse food, or spit it out screaming loudly). She added that she could no longer tolerate his behaviour ('defiance', whining and crying) and her hostile feelings towards him. At the stage of our entry into the case Wayne had to be fed by a combination of the health visitor, father or a neighbour. Wayne showed, on several occasions, severe bruising. The health visitor had placed him on the 'at risk' register.

Wayne was hospitalized five times during his 2 years and 3 months of life. Altogether he had spent 68 days in hospital. The first admission was at the age of 4 weeks. He had been a difficult baby to feed from the start. He vomited frequently and seemed to cry or scream incessantly for the first few weeks of life. He was suffering from pyloric stenosis. After the operation he improved a little. His sucking became more vigorous although he took a long time to feed. The situation deteriorated when solids were introduced at the age of five months. He persistently refused to take them and gradually stopped taking liquids as well. From that time onwards, feeding time became a battle.

Wayne was 14 months old (weight 6 kg, height 69 cm) when his mother finally found it impossible to cope with his reluctance to eat. She screamed at him, smacked him, shook him, getting angrier and angrier. When she forced him to eat, he screamed, vomited immediately and then had diarrhoea. Soon Wayne began to scream at the sight of his mother. She could not touch him or come near him. In anger and helpless despair she would take him upstairs and leave him there for hours. Wayne took some food from his father and nextdoor neighbours and was fed only when they were available. Because he was losing weight rapidly, he was admitted to hospital for investigation. In hospital, Wayne cried a lot, was at first unresponsive to nurses and movements around him. when not crying he looked blank and lethargic. Gradually he began to take food and became more alert and lively, doing well enough in the end to be discharged. This pattern was to be repeated several times. All of this increased his mother's feelings of hostility and rejection towards the child, not to mention her feelings of inadequacy as a mother. He seemed better all round when he was in different places with different people. In the end she refused to have Wayne back home from the hospital. The Grant family — now in acute crisis — were referred to us for assessment.

In order to be able to institute a full programme of assessment and treatment, we had to teach Mrs Grant to relax and to structure small, manageable daily tasks to counter her tension and her inertia and apathy. We diagnosed her depression as learned helplessness (see Seligman, 1975). So as not to exacerbate her feelings of helplessness and demoralization, we underlined the point that we were not there as 'experts' to take over the burden of the child's problem from the parents, but that we would be partners in a co-operative venture with a major part of the responsibility rightfully in their hands. A period of counselling and support-giving and relaxation-training was embarked upon and covered seven weeks. We arranged for full-time attendance by the twins at a day nursery.

Looking at the history we took at this time, it seems likely that the child learned (on a classical cum operant basis) to avoid food by associating feeding with painful experiences, e.g. forcing, hurrying, shaking, smacking, scolding and throwing. Finally, mother's person became a stimulus to evoke fear which (in proximity) brought physical symptoms like vomiting and diarrhoea, if she was angry. He screamed sometimes even at the sight of his mother approaching him. Given a history of social isolation and a paucity of stimulation, it is not surprising that Wayne manifested serious developmental delay in speech. His brother was more generally advanced but also showed speech retardation.

Treatment programme

A variety of methods is used in the provision of services at the molar level. This provision of methods and resources falls into two categories.

(i) Immediate

A variety of methods play their part. During the early stages of the Centre's involvement, attention is paid to immediate needs (crisis intervention) of the child and family. This has involved, in general:

(a) ensuring that the child was safe, fed and stimulated
(b) arranging attendance at a day nursery (in part a safety measure). This allowed us to monitor the child for a substantial part of the day. It provided mother with a 'break' and the space to work on her problem with the social worker. It also gave the child some much needed social stimulation.
(c) arranging for health visitors, home-start volunteers and neighbours to assist mothers with feeding and child-care and to provide moral support
(d) assisting parents with problems of housing, finances, welfare rights, etc. where and when appropriate
(e) providing supervision by regular visits and phone calls (also emotional support)
(f) placing children in the 'at risk' register because of extreme rejection and/or abuse (failure to thrive)
(g) beginning and supporting self-help parents groups (earlier clients) which parents could attend.
(This intervention is discussed elsewhere.)
(h) Desensitizing (where necessary) the mother's tension, anger and resentment when in the child's company. It was almost always necessary for the mothers of these children to learn to control and resolve feelings of anger and resentment and to deal with high levels of anxiety. This was sometimes achieved (before any formal feeding programme could be initiated) by training in relaxation, stress management and self-control.

(ii) Longer term
After the attention to the immediate safety and needs of child and family, the intervention focuses on critical issues such as the mothers' relationship with her infant, her ability to feed her child and his to receive (and benefit from) sustenance, the depression and or anxiety she so often suffers from, the parents' relationship, and so on.

During this phase the treatment of failure to thrive cases consists of a 'package' of psychosocial methods ranging from 'talking' (personal and developmental counselling) to behaviour modification. This family-oriented approach combines behavioural methods of assessment and modification with family casework methods (including discussion, clarification of problems, task-setting and support giving). It is carried out in the home with both parents (generally speaking) and the child, but mother–child transactions become the main focus of therapy because of the acute crisis we meet in most cases. This *was* the case for Mrs Grant and Wayne.

Example of intervention strategies

Phase 1

This was tackled in a highly structured (and thus, directive) manner. Mealtimes had to be made more relaxed. She agreed (albeit reluctantly and sceptically) to desist from screaming, shouting and threatening the child over his meals. The period of eating was made quiet and calm. Mrs Grant was asked to talk soothingly and pleasantly to him. This was extremely difficult for her to achieve. (The social worker joined the family for a few meals, helping to reassure Wayne, prompting the mother to help him eat in a gentle manner when he was in difficulties.) Mrs Grant was encouraged to look at him, smile, and occasionally touch him. If Wayne refused his food she was to leave him if she couldn't encourage or coax him by play or soft words. The food was arranged decoratively to look attractive.

This aspect of the programme (lasting several weeks) was purely 'instrumental' or 'symptomatic' in the sense of encouraging the child to eat by creating less fraught circumstances. As long as the mother kept to this schedule, Wayne would eat (not much, but a life-supporting amount). If she broke the rules because she was moody or unstable, Wayne would not sit in his high chair. We added another rule (on the basis of this observation), that she never fed the twins when feeling acutely angry or tense. There should be a period of quiet relaxation (using the relaxation tape and the training we had given her) if this was difficult to achieve.

Phase II

This phase (as with earlier stages of treatment) was discussed in detail—rationale and method—with both parents. A contract was drawn up specifying the mutual obligations and rules for the family and ourselves. *Objectives.*

(1) To deliberately, and in planned fashion, increase positive interactions and decrease negative interactions between mother and child;
(2) To desensitize Wayne's anxieties with regard to mother's caregiving (and other) activities;
(3) To desensitize mother's tension, anger and resentment when in Wayne's company;
(4) To increase and make more general the intra-familial interactions (e.g. as a group, between Wayne and his brother etc.).

Methods. Mrs Grant agreed to play exclusively with Wayne every evening after her husband returned from work, for 10 minutes during the first week, 15 minutes during the second week, 20 minutes during the third week and 25 minutes during the fourth and subsequent weeks. The father took Jimmy for a walk, or to another room, while Wayne had this period of play. Afterwards they would join in for a family play session. The mother was asked to play with Wayne on the floor — this was demonstrated and rehearsed — and she was encouraged to talk to him in a soft reassuring manner, encouraging him to participate in the play.

She was also instructed to smile at Wayne, look at him, touch him, briefly, or praise him for each positive response she detected from him. (His tentative approaches towards her were 'shaped' by just such a series of successive approximations.) After a period of weeks she was guided to seek proximity to him by hugging him briefly and then holding him on her lap for increasing intervals of time, eventually holding him close, but gently, while reading him a story.

There is no doubt that Mrs Grant found all this difficult, and, at times, distasteful, but they became gradually less so as time passed and especially as Wayne began to seek her out shyly and to smile and chat to her. We had to provide a good deal of support and encouragement to both parents during frequent visits or by phone calls. (Reinforcing the reinforcer is critical in this work!!). Three months were occupied by this stage of the intervention.

Phase III
The final phase took two weeks and deliberately involved an intensification of Mrs Grant's interactions (now much improved) with Wayne.

(1) She was to take him almost everywhere she went, whatever she was doing from morning till night. She was instructed to chat as much as possible to him in a soft measured way, smiling and cuddling him at appropriate times. (These had to be discussed as Mrs Grant frequently put Wayne in a double-bind by giving contradictory verbal and non-verbal cues.)

(2) She was asked to read to him and Jimmy, encourage them to play together, and read to them both at bedtime. *Their* positive interactions were to be reinforced socially.

The formal programme was faded out gradually (over a period of several weeks) after discussing with parents the importance of a stimulating environment and a rich reinforcement schedule for the maintenance of the improvements they both detected in the family interactions, and mother's feelings and attitudes (these were monitored for us by herself). Our perceptions of Wayne's improved health, weight and height (and indeed his general psychological well-being) were confirmed by the assessments of the paediatrician, the nutrition consultant, and a health visitor. Mrs Grant's sense of attachment to Wayne had returned. What is of interest is that although we discussed her feelings and attitudes with her they were not the primary focus of treatment. She found it difficult and, in the end, refused to discuss them. We hoped that old feelings of affection and nurturance would return if we countered the avoidance situations (and sense of helplessness) which stood in the way of her learning to love him again. Feelings (and insights) *followed* actions!

SECTION 6

Methods of Treatment

The categories of behavioural methods fall broadly into three categories:
(a) Strengthening/developing patterns of behaviour. The methods include (*inter alia*) positive reinforcement, negative reinforcement, shaping, modelling, skills training, etc.
(b) Providing the correct context for behaviours. The methods include discrimination training, prompting, cueing, modelling.
(c) Reducing or eliminating inappropriate behaviour. The methods include (*inter alia*) satiation, extinction, time out from positive reinforcement, overcorrection, response-cost, promotion of alternative/incompatible actions, problem-solving, etc.

Table VII Methods for increasing behaviour

Procedure	Method
1. Positive reinforcement	Present a positive stimulus (a rewarding event or object) following the desired behaviour.
2. Negative reinforcement	Remove a stimulus (an aversive or noxious event) following the desired behaviour.
(1 + 2) Contingency management in the token economy.	
3. Differential reinforcement (including discrimination training and method of successive approximations).	Reinforce appropriate behaviours in the presence of the S^D. leave them unreinforced in the setting of inappropriate circumstances, S^δ.
4. Provide an appropriate model.	Get someone suitable to model the desired behaviour
5. Skills training	Various approaches
6. Remove interfering conditions (e.g. aversive stimuli).	Remove stimuli that are incompatible (interfere) with the desired behaviour.

151

1. Positive reinforcement

> Procedure 1   **POSITIVE REINFORCEMENT**
> *Arrange matters so that an immediate reward follows the performance of the desired behaviour.*

Applications
Choose positive reinforcement as a method of change when:
(a) a new behaviour is to be incorporated in the child's repertoire:
(b) when the strength of an already acquired behaviour pattern is to be increased; and
(c) when by increasing the strength of a particular behaviour the effect will be to cause an undesirable incompatible response to diminish in strength.

Method
Positive reinforcement involves the presentation of a stimulus (a rewarding event or object) following the required act; thus it embodies the principle that the likelihood that behaviour will recur depends on its consequences. Circumstances are arranged so that the correct performance of an act (or an approximation of it) is followed closely in time by what are thought to be reinforcing (i.e. rewarding) consequences.

Reinforcers
There are, broadly speaking, four classes of reinforcer:
Those provided by others:
(a) Tangible — material reinforcers (treats, privileges, sweets, money, crisps etc.).
(b) Intangible (social) reinforcers (hugs, smiles, encouragement, etc.).
Those provided by oneself from 'within':
(c) Tangible reinforcers (leisure activities, treats to oneself).
(d) Intangible reinforcers (self-praise, self-appreciation).

   Adult attention is a powerful acquired secondary reinforcer for the child who has built up an association between adult attention and the provision of primary reinforcers, such as food, comfort, security. Children reinforce adults too. As was stated before, happy adult–child relationships result from mutually reinforcing interactions.

   In the case of behaviours which are complex and difficult to perform, it is essential to reward the child for *trying* as well as for success. Reward often. Do not mix criticism with praise. You arrange for only the better approximations to the correct (desired) actions to be reinforced — as the child becomes more adept (see Procedure 3b). When the child becomes successful, reward for accomplishment rather than mere obedience. It is the approved behaviour that is being praised rather than the whole child; identify specifically (i.e. cognitively structure) what is being rewarded. To give a simple example: mother might say 'Thank you for letting your brother share your game' rather than 'You are a good boy'.

Contingencies
Let the child know what the contingencies are. Work out an agreement with the child by word of mouth (or one written down) and make clear parental expectations of the child and the reciprocal obligations to him or her.

A contingency is a *rule* which stipulates that a particular consequence (reward *or* punishment) follows the performance of a particular kind of behaviour.

Ask yourself:
        (a) Are the rules clear?
        (b) Are the rules simple?
        (c) Does the child understand the rules?
        (d) Does the parent interpret and implement the rules fairly and
            consistently?

Children should be encouraged to think about the reasons for having rules so they have standards for judging their own behaviour, and learn to reason things out for themselves. Socialization is particularly effective when training is presented in terms of a few well-defined principles. The use of inductive methods — explanations and reasons — especially when they elucidate a few clearly defined principles, seems to enhance moral awareness and resistance to temptation. Conformity of behaviour to specific norms in particular situations is more likely to depend on sanctions attached to those particular situations than on the general parent–child relationships.

Remember: Four important points:
        (1) Do not assume that parents (or teachers) have a repertoire
            of effective phrases for giving praise or, indeed, give praise
            with the right degree of warmth, enthusiasm and eye contact.
            Check on this!
        (2) A child may become satiated to a reinforcer. It loses 'reward'
            value.
        (3) Reinforce the reinforcer (build in treats and encouragements
            for the person/s mediating the child's behaviour, e.g. the
            caregiver).

(4) Ultimately the child should learn to reinforce himself, i.e. become self-directed (this is a major objective in child-rearing).

Procedure 1a	DIFFERENTIAL ATTENTION
	Combine attention (praise and approval) and ignoring.

Applications

The differential use of .... advocated as the first step in behavioural i[n] .... ,chool settings. It is particularly pertiner .... ıg enough positive reinforcement (atten .... .ppropriate times.

Forehand and Mc .... ion rule': a child will work for attention f .... ıe attention can either be positive (e.g. pr .... riticism) in nature. If the child is not rec .... ıe will work to receive negative attention. .... d: 'I'd rather have bad publicity than no .... e children are not very responsive — inde[e] .... ⁄hat adults think of as positive attention

Method

A prerequisite f[r] .... thought, by many, to be an assurance th[a] .... , positive attention to the child, in a man .... ıng inappropriate actions.

Tactics such as attending, g..... ...... ; (praise) and an extinction procedure (ignoring) are taught; the emphasis is on social rather than material reinforcers. In essence, this is a planned praising and planned (judicious) ignoring strategy. It is the first phase (often) in a further intervention to tackle specific problems such as non-compliance.

Note: *For the 'praise–ignore' formula to work, certain conditions are essential (Birnbrauer, 1985): (1) Parental attention must be capable of reinforcing the child's behaviour; (2) The parent is capable of giving attention of the right kind at the right times; (3) Attention, and not other consequences, is maintaining the inappropriate behaviour; (4) Ignoring is aversive or non-reinforcing; (5) Non-reinforcement alone is an effective means of eliminating unwanted behaviour; (6) continuation of the unwanted behaviour will not be harmful to the child or others; (7) Parental reactions are controlled by child-appropriate and inappropriate behaviour with some consistency. That is, it appears that the parents have reasonably consistent expectations from day to day and the child could learn the definitions of appropriate and inappropriate from changes in contingencies.*

Birnbrauer analyses the reasons why this approach does not always live up to expectations in terms of problems connected with the items above. For example, it is not simply that the parent praises and attends and also gives opportunities for outings, hugs and cuddles, provides comfort and interesting exchanges, listens and amuses, but rather that these opportunities are contingently paired with appropriate behaviour and with parental approval. That is, (a) child appropriate behaviour is followed by attention is followed by a variety of other positive events on an intermittent schedule, and (b) child inappropriate behaviour is not followed by attention (is followed by another signal) and not positive reinforcers but instead loss of other positive reinforcers as well.

If an assessment fails to reveal any meaningful relationship between parental approval and parental giving (taking other forms) then it may not be appropriate to recommend the praise–ignore formula. The focus might rather be upon strengthening the reinforcement value of parental attention through increasing pleasant events within the family, contracts and token systems. Patterson (1982) refers to the 'first–then' rule: *first* you do your homework and *then* you may go out and play. This should be extended according to Birnbrauer to the following formula: *first* you do your homework, *then* I will be pleased *and* you can go out and play. If you do not do your homework first, then I will be displeased and you will not be able to watch TV later.

Where families are characterized by coercive exchanges (Patterson, 1982) and their relationships have deteriorated seriously, positive attention will be difficult for the parents to provide. Some parents will have to learn to do so for the first time; praise will not come easily to many of them. If the mother is depressed, anxious about other matters, oppressed by other demands of running the household and relationships with her husband and offspring, then her attention may be in short supply.

Timing of reinforcement
Timing of the reinforcers is crucial. Reinforcers should not be given before the child has begun to improve his behaviour. Immediate, rather than delayed reinforcement is generally more effective in establishing a conditioned response. Prompt reinforcement is essential to obtain *new* or improved behaviour patterns. In real life rewards are not always awarded immediately. Ways of tapering off the reinforcement to prepare the youngster

Procedure 1b   SUBSTITUTION
When a reward is ineffectual, present it to the child just before (or as close in time to) the moment in which a more effective reward is presented.
REINFORCING EVENT MENU
Offer a variety of reinforcing stimuli so as to avoid reinforcer satiation; some therapists make use of the 'reinforcing event menu' which allows children to make a choice of reinforcers.
DEPRIVATION
A little judicious responding to temporary states of deprivation may have the desired effect, increasing the potency of the reinforcement. (The thirsty child is more interested in doing a task for a glass of lemonade than the child who has just had a drink.)
PRAISING IN FRONT OF OTHERS
This adds to the value of reinforcers. The teacher tells the mother in front of the child how well he is doing.

for real life — learning patience and long-term commitment — are discussed in Step 8.

Schedules of reinforcement
Responses that are reinforced on a partial or intermittent basis (the regime under which most of us learn in the natural environment) prove to be most enduring, in other words, resistant to extinction. Different rates of reinforcement produce varying results in conditioning procedures. In order to establish new behaviour as promptly as possible, it is crucial — initially — to reinforce immediately and often. When reinforcement follows each correct response, the schedule of reinforcement is referred to as *continuous*. In order to encourage a child to continue performing an established pattern with few or no rewards, ensure that the frequency with which the correct behaviour is reinforced, is gradually and intermittently decreased.
Reinforcement schedules may be categorized in terms of:
(1) the interval between reinforcements (determined either by time elapsed or the number of responses); and

(2) the regularity or irregularity of the intervals.

This classification gives four basic schedules:

(a) Variable-interval schedule: a programme used in which the individual is reinforced after an interval of time which varies around a specified average.

(b) Variable-ratio schedule: here the individual is reinforced after a number of reponses which varies randomly around a specified average.

(c) Fixed-interval schedule: a schedule of partial reinforcement in which a response made after a certain interval of time is reinforced.

(d) Fixed-ratio schedule: a schedule of partial reinforcement in which every nth response is reinforced.

Variable schedules result in stable response rates which are difficult to extinguish.

Note: *Don't let people convince you that reinforcement is a simple matter of giving children smarties or stars. It requires a great deal of thought and planning.*

Informative function of reinforcement

The effectiveness of a reward depends partly on the child's expectations of success in a particular undertaking. During the course of learning, the child not only performs responses, but he also observes the variations in consequences that flow from his actions. On the basis of this informative feedback, he develops hypotheses about the types of action most likely to succeed. These hypotheses (expectancies) then serve as guides for future actions. We need to know about the child's reinforcement history and achievement in order to select effective reinforcers. Children vary in their interpretation as to whether rewards follow from, and are contingent upon, their own behaviour ('internals') or are controlled by forces—luck, fate—outside themselves ('externals').

Attribution problems

Some children are difficult to work with in terms of reinforcement programmes, be they externally or self-administered. They may have been habitually lavished with 'rewards' which have no link to their actions (non-contingent reinforcement); consequently they fail to recognize and attribute a causal connection—in the programme—between acceptable behaviour and rewards.

If the child has a low expectation of passing an arithmetic test, yet is successful, the value of the reinforcement occasioned by the triumph may be great. Criticism or failure may serve as an excellent motivating device for the bright and able child yet discourage and handicap the child who is already doing poorly. Although reward does not do very much 'extra' for the bright and successful, it motivates the unsuccessful child highly. After all, the bright child expects to succeed, hence success and praise do not surprise him or raise him to new levels of performance. He does not expect to fail or be criticized; hence, when such things happen to him, the effect is great. The punishment, as it were, is so severe that he redoubles his efforts to avoid encountering it again. The failing child expects failure and criticism, hence it has little effect on him except to confirm his beliefs and reduce his effort. But an experience or praise or reward is so striking and sweet that he works doubly hard to encounter such a state of affairs again.

The effects of feelings of failure are somewhat more unpredictable than those of success. If a child does not achieve what he has expected to achieve but accepts failure in a realistic manner, he will lower his expectation for the next performance. Sometimes, however, a child will react to failure by raising his expectations. He may simply blame his failure on some external obstacle. The expectations of people important to the child also play a part in the way he reacts to failure. If there is pressure on him, he may continue to base his expectations at a level far above what is realistic. There are children who are unable to attain their own goals, or the goals set by their parents, because they are dominated by a fear of failure, and therefore avoid, at all costs, achievement situations.

Assessment implications
This matter of the child's own expectations of success or failure is important in determining his performance. You cannot make facile assumptions about reinforcement. You need to know about the youngster's subjective expectations of his future achievements and his likelihood of success in different situations; and you have to find out what they are by talking to him.

Summary of our guidelines
In planning to apply reinforcers, be precise; responses that occur just prior to the reinforced (to-be-learned) response will also be strengthened. Those nearest in time are strengthened more than those further away (this is the gradient of reinforcement). On the other hand, responses nearer to the point of occurrence of reinforcement tend to occur before their original time in the response sequence and crowd out earlier, useless behaviours. (This is the development of anticipatory responses.) Select your reinforcers carefully. They vary in potency according to the individual's tastes and his reinforcement history. Use a variety of reinforcers and arrange for there to be more than one *source* of reinforcement (e.g. mother, father, older siblings, relatives, teachers). Try to ensure that they are consistent, that they only reward after the correct response and then, promptly.

2. Negative reinforcement

> Procedure 2 NEGATIVE REINFORCEMENT
> *Arrange for the child to terminate
> immediately a mildly aversive situation, by
> changing his behaviour in the desired
> direction.*

Applications

To get a child to behave in a certain (desirable) way, and conversely, to stop him from acting in another unwanted manner, the removal of an aversive stimulus is made contingent upon a required behaviour; this procedure is known as negative reinforcement. Like the application of positive reinforcement in operant conditioning, it tends to increase the required behaviour. Thus the mother says: 'If you don't say "please" when you ask for something, I'll turn off the TV'. If the rate of saying please on appropriate occasions increases, the television switch-off (that is to say the avoidance of it) has acted as a negative reinforcer.

Contingency management (rearranging consequences)

This is the generic title given to programmes involving the manipulation of reinforcement, positive (Procedure 1) and negative (Procedure 2). Flow chart 5 provides you with a step-by-step guide.

Note: *Although positive and negative reinforcement are distinctive procedures, they serve to maintain, strengthen or increase the likelihood that a behaviour will be emitted. Positive and negative reinforcement procedures generate four training methods: reward training, privation training, escape training and avoidance training. The procedures (all of which strengthen behaviour) involve the following characteristic statements:*
(a) Reward training: 'If you make the response, I will present a reward'; (b) Privation training: 'If you don't make the response I will withdraw a reward'; (c) Escape training: 'If you make the response I will withdraw a punishment'; (d) Avoidance training: 'If you don't make the response I will present a punishment'.

Self-reinforcement

Self-administered reinforcement is effective in maintaining various kinds of behaviour (see Procedure 20).

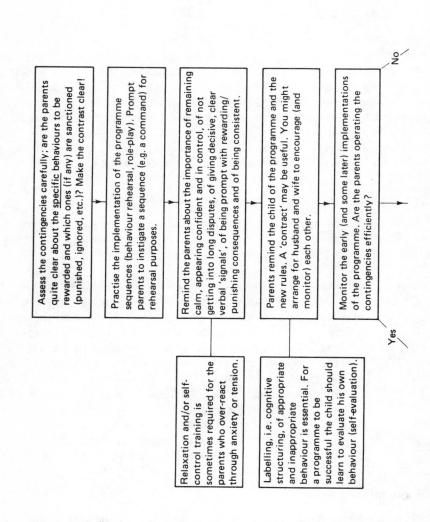

FLOW CHART 5   Step-by-step contingency management.

Yes

Praise and encourage the parents. Remember to reinforce the reinforcers.

No

Assess what is going wrong.
1. Discuss the sequences.
2. Sit in and cue the parents.
3. Rehearse the parents again.
Common problems:
1. There is a criterion slippage — the behaviour loses its precise definition.
2. The child argues the merits of the case leading to long and futile debates.
3. The parents warn too often.
4. The parents use the programme as a threat.
5. The reinforcers are ineffectual.
6. Timing is not prompt enough.
7. Prosocial behaviour needs rehearsing after continuing infringements.
8. There is insufficient consistency.
   Parents are taking the line of least resistance or disagree.
9. Parents make too many demands.
10. They are still ambiguous or vague.
11. Parents don't keep to the contingencies/rules.

As the programme progresses ensure that:
1. Parents generalize their new skills across the situations; get them to put them into effect in various places. (Supermarkets and friends' homes pose special problems and require pre-planning.) Anxiety may stop them transferring their skill.
2. Parents generalize their skills across behaviours. They should learn how to assess and deal with novel problems, not only the target behaviour.

Pay due attention to the phasing out of the contingency programme.
Move toward a differential schedule of reinforcement for prosocial/skill behaviour.
Move toward 'natural' rewards, e.g. social ones like smiles, praise.
Move toward self-reinforcement.

FIG. 18   From Herbert (1985) with permission.

Token economies

Figures 18 and 19 illustrate typical home-made reward charts.

The token economy is, in a sense, a work-payment incentive system in which the participants receive tokens when they display appropriate behaviour. At some specified time, the tokens are exchanged at an agreed tariff for a variety of back-up reinforcers — items and activities. Kazdin and Bootzin (1972) list the following advantages:

(a) They allow the consequences of any response to be applied at any time.

(b) They bridge the delay between target responses and back-up reinforcers.

(c) They can maintain performance over extended periods of time when the back-up reinforcers cannot be administered.

(d) They allow sequences of responses to be reinforced without interruption.

(e) The reinforcing effects of tokens are relatively independent of the physiological state of the individual and less subject to satiation effects.

(f) They permit the use of the same reinforcers for individuals with preferences for different back-up reinforcers.

Applications

Token reinforcement procedures are not applied in isolation; they are usually supplemented simultaneously by rules, extinction, praise and response-cost. They have shown their usefulness in school classrooms and in specialized classrooms for disadvantaged, hyperactive, retarded, and emotionally

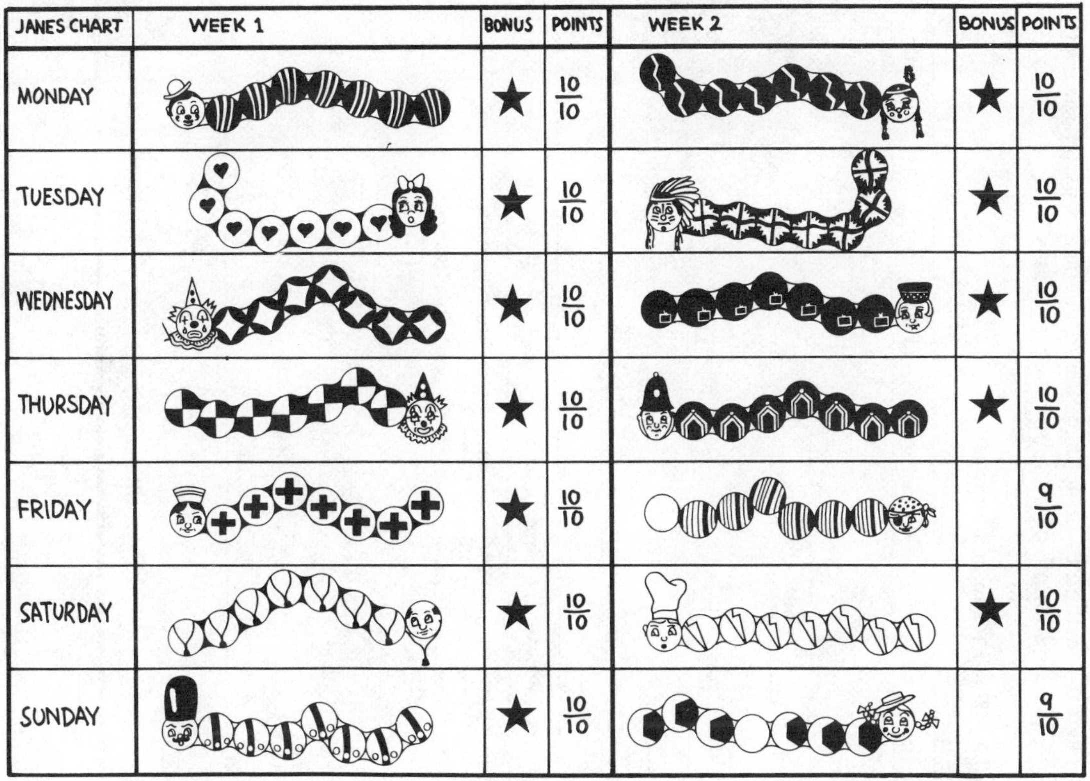

JANES CHART	WEEK 1	BONUS	POINTS	WEEK 2	BONUS	POINTS
MONDAY		★	0/0		★	0/0
TUESDAY		★	0/0		★	0/0
WEDNESDAY		★	0/0		★	0/0
THURSDAY		★	0/0		★	0/0
FRIDAY		★	0/0			9/0
SATURDAY		★	0/0		★	0/0
SUNDAY		★	0/0			9/0

FIG. 19   A typical home-made reward chart.

disturbed children. There are many ways—witting and unwitting—to make a token system fail. Kuypers *et al.* (1968) suggest important procedures for pre-empting the things that go wrong. As they remark: 'A token system is not a "magical" method to be applied in a mechanical way.' Tables VIIIa and b provide an example of a home token economy.

Table VIIIa   Home token economy chart
Name: _____   Dates: _____   Recorder: _____

	Points earned	Points lost	Comments
Monday			
Tuesday			
Wednesday			
Thursday			
Friday			
Saturday			
Sunday			
TOTAL:			

Table VIIIb

Behaviours that earn points	Points	Behaviours that lose points	Points
Good report note from teacher (as detailed in contract)	4	Hitting other children (as defined)	5
Leaves for school without complaint	2	Non-compliance (as defined)	3
Gets dressed himself without argument	2	Swearing/tantrums	2
Stays at dining table until meal ends	1		

Back-up reinforcers: 10 points: Mother reads extra long story (half-hour), *or* allowed to stay up an extra half-hour; 8–9 points: special treat at dessert; 5–7 points: Father has game of Ludo with him; 1–4 points: no TV; 0 points: goes to bed early 8 p.m.; Minus: extra early 7 p.m.

Illustration 1

Group setting

McLaughlin and Malaby (1972) describe a token programme in a primary school class designed to enhance the academic performance of 25–29 pupils with regard to completing assignments in maths, spelling, language and handwriting.

Table IX indicates the 'earnings' and 'costs' of particular behaviours. Variations in points are related to variations in the performance, e.g. the number of items on a test. The pupils were encouraged to join in the selection of privileges, the choice determined by reinforcers natually available in the classroom.

Table IX   Behaviours and the number of points that they earned or lost

Behaviours that earned points	Points:
(1) Items correct	6 to 12
(2) Study behaviour 8 : 50–9 : 15	5 per day
(3) Bring food for animals	1 to 10
(4) Bring sawdust for animals	1 to 10
(5) Art	1 to 4
(6) Listening points	1 to 2 per lesson
(7) Extra credit	Assigned value
(8) Neatness	1 to 2
(9) Taking home assignments	5
(10) Taking notes	1 to 3
(11) Quiet in lunch time	2
(12) Quiet in cafeteria	2
(13) Appropriate noon hour behaviour	3

Behaviours that lost points	Points:
(1) Assignments incomplete	Amount squared
(2) Gum and candy	100
(3) Inappropriate verbal behaviour	15
(4) Inappropriate motor behaviour	15
(5) Fighting	100
(6) Cheating	100

Source: McLaughlin and Malaby (1972, p. 264).

3. Differential reinforcement

Procedure 3a   DISCRIMINATION TRAINING
Reinforce, in the presence of the S^D, appropriate behavioural responses. Never reinforce actions in inappropriate circumstances (S^Δ). In this way you help to bring about stimulus control over behaviour.

Applications
When we wish to teach a young child to act in a particular way under one set of circumstances but not another (in other words, to develop new behaviour), we help him to identify the cues that differentiate the circumstances. This involves clear signals as to what is expected of the child and it presupposes unambiguous rules. The application of differential reinforcement can be used (especially with mentally handicapped children) to make — eventually — very fine discriminations.

Method
Make the appropriate situations (S^D) and the inappropriate ones (S^Δ) as different from each other as possible — at first.

Procedure 3b	SUCCESSIVE APPROXIMATIONS *Reinforce approximations to the correct act. The successive steps to the final behaviour are reinforced according to an increasingly rigorous criterion. Only better and better approximations are reinforced, until eventually only the correct action is rewarded. Begin with a clear definition of what the child has to learn to do; then begin by reinforcing something he does that in some way resembles it.*

Applications
Successive approximations (or, shaping, as they are called) make possible the building-up of a new response.

Method
Shaping involves the use of differential reinforcement and a shifting criterion of reinforcement. In order to encourage a child to act in a way in which he has seldom or never before behaved, the therapist works out the successive steps the child must and can make so as to approximate more and more closely to the desired final outcome. This last element, called 'shaping' or the principle of 'successive approximations', involves taking mini-steps towards the final goal. The therapist starts by reinforcing very small changes in behaviour which are in the right direction even if somewhat far removed from the final desired outcome. No reinforcement is given for behaviour in the 'wrong' direction. Gradually the criteria of the individual's approximation to the desired goal are made more rigorous.

Remember: A slavish reliance on shaping procedures alone for teaching new ways of behaving, or novel skills, might well lead to frustrating delays. The apt provision of a model for the child to imitate could lead to a quicker solution, depending on the nature of the problem and the potential of the child.

4. Exposure to appropriate models

Procedure 4	MODELLING
	Give the child the opportunity to observe a person who is interesting or significant to him performing the new and desired pattern of behaviour. 'Watch how he does it.' 'Do it like this'. Indicate that it is rewarding to behave like this..

Applications

Modelling can be used to change a wide variety of behaviours — in at least three situations:

(a) acquiring new patterns of behaviour;

(b) strengthening or weakening responses already present in the child's behavioural repertoire, by observing high status models demonstrating the appropriate behaviour;

(c) inhibiting learned fears, such as phobias of dogs, by observing a fearless model in the presence of the fear-object.

If the child never, or only very rarely, emits some desired behaviour and if this low rate is due to a deficit in the child's repertoire rather than inadequate incentives, then combinations of modelling, cueing, prompting, instruction and putting through (sometimes called passive shaping) should be used. You ensure that the behaviour can occur and then reinforce it.

There is evidence that children learn *complex* acts through cognitive processes based on observation rather than through being trained by external reinforcements administered by the parent. This does not mean that the reward and punishment of specific components of behaviour play *no* role in social learning; it does mean that that role is defined in a context provided by the very special reactions that people have to people.

Children learn many of their actions and skills, either deliberately or inadvertently, through the influence of example. This provides you with a potent therapeutic tool.

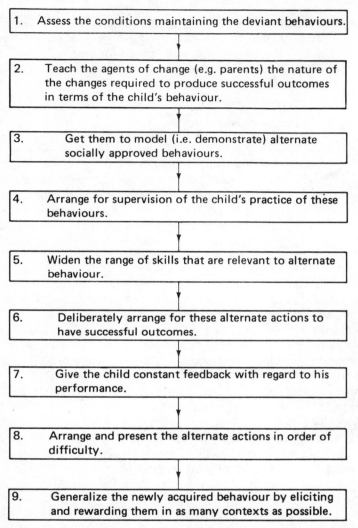

1. Assess the conditions maintaining the deviant behaviours.

2. Teach the agents of change (e.g. parents) the nature of the changes required to produce successful outcomes in terms of the child's behaviour.

3. Get them to model (i.e. demonstrate) alternate socially approved behaviours.

4. Arrange for supervision of the child's practice of these behaviours.

5. Widen the range of skills that are relevant to alternate behaviour.

6. Deliberately arrange for these alternate actions to have successful outcomes.

7. Give the child constant feedback with regard to his performance.

8. Arrange and present the alternate actions in order of difficulty.

9. Generalize the newly acquired behaviour by eliciting and rewarding them in as many contexts as possible.

FLOW CHART 6   Step-by-step modelling. Bandura (1973) provides these useful principles (put into step form by the author) as a guide to the acquisition, by modelling, of alternative behaviours.

Method
See Flow Chart 6.

Note: *Some exemplars (models) exert more influence over a child than others. It is usually possible to identify individuals in the child's peer group (or adults) of significance to him. Their behaviour is likely to be initiated because of the* prestige *they have, either for the youngster alone or for the entire group with whom he interacts (e.g. the popular child at school).* Similarity *is another important factor. There is evidence that student observers who perceive — or are told — that they have some characteristics or qualities similar to the model (e.g. sex, age and physical attributes) are more likely to imitate the responses of the model, than students who do not identify such similarities. Therapists can facilitate imitation by pointing out areas in common between the model and the client; a behaviour is more likely to be modelled if its complexity is not too great or too rapidly presented for assimilation, and if the child perceives that it has some components which he has already mastered.*

An important influence on the extent to which children will imitate a model is the consequence of that model's actions. Is the outcome of the person's behaviour rewarding, pleasant and successful, or disastrous?

Three variations of modelling — filmed modelling, live modelling and participant modelling — tend to be used (Ross *et al.*, 1971). In fear-provoking situations (including social settings) participant modelling has proved to be most effective, reducing fears in nearly 80% of cases.

5. Skills training (e.g. behaviour rehearsal, social skills training)

Procedure 5a	BEHAVIOUR REHEARSAL *Simulate real-life situations in which skills are to be developed.* *(1) Prepare the child.* *(2) Select the target situations (e.g. social skills to be learned).* *(3) Rehearse the behaviour in the security of the consulting room/child's home.* *(4) Get the child to try out the new behaviours in real-life situations — as 'homework' exercises.*

Applications
Some children, for a wide variety of reasons, lack skills which are essential in order to cope with growing up in a satisfactory manner. Physically handicapped children, for example, are massively overrepresented in the

population of youngsters with behaviour problems. If such children behave dysfunctionally in response to a variety of stresses, frustrations and humiliations, it is hardly surprising. They can be helped to become more competent and thus have less need of what proves to be counterproductive problem behaviours.

Methods
During rehearsal:
(1) Demonstrate the skill.
(2) Ask the child to practise the skill. (Use role play. Provide a model if necessary.)
(3) Provide feedback as to the accuracy/inaccuracy of the child's performance. (If possible, it is advantageous for the youngster — and video equipment is most useful here — to evaluate the effectiveness of his own performance.)
(4) Give homework assignments, e.g. real-life planned practice or the try-out at home of skills. Not only does behaviour rehearsal provide for acquiring new skills but it also allows their practice at a controlled pace and in a safe environment, and in this way minimizes distress. With increasing client skill in self-monitoring (sensitivity and accuracy of self-perception), the therapist hands over increasingly the evaluation and corrective actions to the youngster himself.

The technical details of social skills training are too multitudinous to include in a general manual such as this. However, there seem to be two basic attitudes which should be enhanced if friendships and other social relations are going to come with reasonable ease.

(a) Other people are perceived primarily as sources of satisfaction rather than deprivation.
(b) The child has opportunities for social interactions that reward and make enjoyable the giving, as well as the receiving, of affection.

Obviously, there are many strategies described in these pages which have a bearing on these attitudes. Careful assessment is required to determine whether skills are absent; to identify relevant situations; to determine whether there are discrimination problems in relation to when behaviours can most profitably be displayed; and to determine whether negative thoughts and irrational anticipations interfere with the display of effective behaviours. A variety of routes may be employed to gather assessment information, including self-report, role-playing and observation in the natural environment. And a variety of paths, including relationship enhancement and attitude modification might be chosen for the mitigation of social deficits (Kanfer and Goldstein, 1986).

Procedure 5b	SOCIAL SKILLS TRAINING (SST)
	Coach the child so he calls on a new and more socially acceptable repertoire of skills, which will enable him to influence his environment sufficiently to attain basic personal goals (see Combs and Slaby, 1978).

Applications

The subjects (and by implication, problems) covered in the manuals and programmes on social skills training typically include such topics as: improving powers of observation and accurate judgement; basic conversation skills such as listening, asking questions and talking; expressive skills such as the use of body language; social techniques for special situations, assertive training etc. These, and other skills, break down essentially into the three groups shown in Table X.

Table X

Observational skills	Performance skills	Cognitive skills
Getting information	Listening skills	Planning
Reading social signals	Speaking skills	Problem solving
Asking questions	Non-verbal expression	
	Greetings and partings	
	Initiating conversations	
	Rewarding skills	
	Assertive skills	

Methods

(1) Assessment

Baseline (pretreatment) *assessment* is commonly derived from the child's performance of social behaviours on behavioural role play tests, direct observation in naturalistic settings (see Herbert, 1986) sociometric devices, and a variety of self-report instruments.

Analogue strategies have been adopted, making use of role play tests. For example, an adult role model delivers a prompt to a child starting a brief scene—a social interaction of one kind or another. Another approach involves contrived encounters (which allow direct observation in a natural setting of a problematic social situation).

Note: *A fundamental problem in the assessment of social skills is the absence of agreement on a clear definition of social competence.*

This means that there are no precise, generally accepted external criteria against which to validate and cross-validate the plethora of assessment methods. The agreement between measures of socially withdrawn/isolate behaviour, to take but one example, based upon direct observation in the natural environment, sociometric ratings and test measures, is questionable.

Remember: *To make use of a* variety of methods *in order to arrive at more generalizable conclusions about the child's social skills (see Hops and Greenwood, 1981).*

The conditions in which social skills are evaluated rarely attempt to identify whether the children *actually* have deficits, i.e. whether the requisite responses are in their repertoires but not being elicited (Kazdin *et al.*, 1982). Under standardized assessment conditions, attempts are not always made to maximize performance to see if the skills are actually present.

(2) Goal setting
Treatment goals in the social skill area are based upon value judgements of what are socially appropriate behaviours. The literature (Herbert, 1974; Mussen, 1970) suggests some specific notions about what makes a child socially successful or unsuccessful:
(i)   Children who are highly acceptable to their peers tend also to show sensitivity, responsiveness and generosity in their interactions with their peers. They nurture (help) others often, they give attention, approval and affection often to others, they give and receive friendly overtures and respond positively to the dependent behaviour of their peers, and they are sensitive to the social overtures of other children.
(ii) Children who are not much liked by others, but are not particularly disliked tend to be withdrawn, passive, fearful of social contact.
(iii) Children who are actively disliked by others tend to be aggressive. They seem to get locked in a cycle whereby they learn that to get what they want they should be aggressive; this often succeeds in the short term (e.g. they gain a toy by using threats) but fails in the long term in that other children avoid and reject them. In this way, the aggressive children never learn alternatives to their actions, and become more and more reliant on aggression as their only social 'skill'.
(iv) Children who are well liked are better at seeing things from the point of view of another child; disliked children tend to be poor at this.
(v)   The most effective, most socially competent individuals are particularly sensitive to *non-verbal* communications. Popular children are socially sensitive, as can be gauged from the rich, complex and highly-organized descriptions they give of other children.

Many other things determine how successful a child will be in a social setting—for instance, how attractive he or she is, how bright, good at sports, amusing, etc.

Researchers have consistently identified a *sociability* dimension in children. Those at one extreme are described commonly as withdrawn, shy, isolated, having few friends, being loath to engage in interactive behaviour with peers (Herbert, 1974).

Social withdrawal has been estimated to be a major presenting problem in 15% or more cases referred for psychological treatment. There is evidence that such an independent personality factor is stable over time. A pattern of withdrawn behaviour may be established as early as 3 years of age and prove to be predictable through childhood and even into adolescence. Personality problems would require attention in any remedial programme. Studies of well-liked persons have shown that they were co-operative, even-tempered, showed initiative, and were willing at times to accept subordinate roles (Herbert, 1974). Those not chosen as friends were characterized as quarrelsome, irritable, nagging, nervous, aggressive, inclined to interrupt group activity, resentful of being criticized, attention-demanding and praise-seeking.

In the current enthusiasm for SST as a 'package' it is important to remember the need for a functional analysis and comprehensive assessment in each childhood case of 'problematic' behaviour. 'Cookery book' application of SST without such assessments are likely to fail, mainly because of the multi-determined nature of children's problems. McFall (1982) is at pains to caution against an over-emphasis on the situational nature of skilfulness or a polarized view of the all-importance of social traits— attributes that reside within the child.

(3) Training
The following steps may facilitate the development of social behaviour and skills if parents (or significant others) learn to:

(1) Teach the child to see the other's point of view (not necessarily at the expense of her own). Role-taking—the mental placing of oneself in the other person's position—is central to all forms of human communication. There is evidence that children engage in rudimentary forms of role-taking very early in life. Nevertheless, when children are confronted with perspectives that are different from their own, they often assume similarity where there is none. This leads to misunderstanding—mutual and at times painful.
(2) Praise the child for initiating social behaviour.
(3) Model social behaviour to a child; physically demonstrate the various ways of interacting socially with others. Demonstrate how she might make

positive comments about another child; also show her how to play constructively.

(4) Ask her to demonstrate something to another (e.g. how to work the fizzy machine); direct her to help, or seek help, of another.

(5) Coach the child in social behaviour — encourage her in social activity and describe or explain ways of interacting socially (e.g. when she is with children parents have invited home). Here are some suggestions for parents:

(a) Encourage the child to adopt a sociable perspective (e.g. 'Let's talk about some ways to have fun with other kids when you play games'; 'One way to make a game fun for everyone is to take turns . . . when you take turns in a game other kids will have fun too and will want to play with you again').

(b) Clarify what 'taking turns' means (e.g. 'During a game, taking turns means giving everyone a chance to play').

(c) Encourage the child to identify some good and bad examples (e.g. 'Yes, waiting until others have finished before you begin would be taking turns': 'Always trying to have first go or stopping others from having a try would not be taking turns').

(d) Get the child to rehearse verbally some examples of sociable actions and then to recall them.

(e) Give the child feedback about the way she has learned (and later, hopefully, performs) the social skill.

Procedure 5c   ASSERTION TRAINING
Make use of modelling, rehearsal and reinforcement, to help clients stand up for themselves without being aggressive.

Applications

Children often feel (realistically, and also unrealistically) weak and powerless. Their parents (and particularly their mothers) may feel demoralized and ineffectual (Herbert, 1980). Much exploitation (e.g. bullying, 'taking advantage') depends upon the exploiter's expectation that he or she will be successful — that the exploitee will be a 'pushover'.

Assertion training can be carried out with individuals and groups to mitigate a wide variety of interpersonal problems.

Methods

Assertion training is usually an amalgam of:

(a) Discrimination training: teaching the client to distinguish accurately between aggression, assertiveness and slavish conformity/deference;

(b) Modelling/rehearsing, on a graduated basis, of assertive behaviour, in different situations;
(c) Reinforcing/shaping assertive actions and reactions;
(d) Desensitizing fear and anger responses that inhibit modulated assertive behaviour;
(e) Generalizing gains in assertive behaviour to different situations and 'real-life' settings.

Lange and Jakubowski (1976) suggest the sort of feedback to give young people practising their role in a situation fraught with the potential for hostile conflict or humiliating retreat.

1. Start off with the strengths of the performance. Specify exactly which behaviours were positive.

Verbal behaviours
Was the statement direct and to the point?
Was the statement firm but not hostile?
Did the statement show some consideration, respect, or recognition of the other person?
Did the statement accurately reflect the speaker's goals?
Did the statement leave room for escalation?
If the statement included an explanation, was it short rather than a series of excuses?
Did the statement include sarcasm, pleading, or whining?
Did the statement blame the other person for the speaker's feelings?

Non-verbal behaviours
Was eye contact present?
Was the speaker's voice level appropriately loud?
Was the statement filled with pauses?
Did the speaker look confident or were nervous gestures or inappropriate laughter present?
Was the statement flat or expressive?

2. After all positive feedback has been given, offer feedback suggestions. Describe the behaviour, rather than give a label. Be objective rather than judgemental. Offer a possible way of improvement. This should be expressed in a tentative rather than absolute manner. Do not impose a suggestion. Ask the group member for a reaction to the suggestions, allowing the member to accept, refuse, or modify the suggestion.

Assertive training (like social skills training) is complex and requires a manual in its own right. Guides to the literature are provided in the section Further Reading.

6. Remove interfering conditions

Procedure 6	*Remove or reduce aversive stimuli associated with the problem behaviour; such a strategy may lead to an increase in desirable behaviour (and conversely a reduction in the undesired behaviour) — granted, a proposal easier to make on paper than to meet in practice.*

Applications
A large variety of aversive stimuli can set the stage for the development of problem behaviours—for example, bullying and teasing of a painful, threatening, or humiliating nature; deprivation of the child's proper nurturance, rights and opportunities.

Method
A helpful technique therefore involves the defusing of aversive stimuli by diminishing their power to arouse anger in the child. This may be achieved (to take one example) by densensitization procedures. However, the harsh realities and constraints of the lives of many children and adolescents preclude the remedies which lie in reducing or removing misery, stress and temptation.

Methods for Producing Appropriate Stimulus Control

Table XI Methods for correcting the context of actions

Procedure	Method
7. Stimulus control and change (including cueing and prompting)	Determine (or develop) appropriate discriminative stimuli for the desired behaviour

7. Stimulus control

Stimulus control refers to the extent to which an antecedent stimulus determines the probability of a response being manifested. Some 'triggering' stimuli are referred to as eliciting stimuli; on the other hand, discriminative stimuli (see Appendix III) mark a time or place of reinforcement—positive or negative—being presented or removed. In other words, discriminative stimuli are markers as to when an operant will have reinforcing consequences.

Applications

A frequent complaint from parents is that their child 'won't listen' or 'knows what to do but just won't do it!' These are examples of faulty stimulus control. The child has a behaviour in his repertoire but will not perform it when the would-be directing stimulus is presented (i.e. at the appropriate time). The therapist and parents have to reinstate stimulus control. It is worth looking at the parents' requests or commands. They may be weak and ambiguous signals.

Method

A basic condition for correcting faulty stimulus control, as for establishing initial stimulus control, is to get the behaviour (or some approximation to it) performed while the child is attending to the stimulus which is to control it. There are ways to reinstate the discriminative stimulus, e.g. *cueing*.

Procedure 7a   CUEING
Encourage the child to respond to cues for the correct performance just before the action is expected, rather than after he has performed incorrectly — in order to train him to act at a specific time.

Applications

Drives can act as responses (and become elicited by certain cues, and strengthened by reinforcement). This principle can be applied to remedy the poorly motivated, underachieving child's performance.

Method
(a) Cues are among the most important behaviours used by the classroom teacher to control behaviour. A cue can be defined as anything used as a stimulus with the intent of evoking a response. The teacher cues (e.g. instructs, encourages) as a means of informing the pupils about the responses they should make (e.g. concentrating on the task to hand). To be effective, cues should serve to elicit a response which it is within the pupil's capacity to make. By presenting cues and withdrawing others (fading) the teacher can become an effective contingency manager, attaining stimulus control over certain crucial classroom behaviours. The association between a cue and a response is strengthened each time the response is followed by reinforcement. These preliminaries make up the stage of

acquisition. Once a specific cue-response habit has been acquired, another cue which is similar in some way to the original cue, can also elicit the learned response (a phenomenon called 'stimulus generalization'). The teacher may give only the briefest signal for work to begin.

(b) There are internal (intrinsic) cues as well as external cues. Drives can act as cues and elicit specific learned responses; thus a child with hostile impulses is helped to respond to signals from his incipient 'feelings' by training him to identify them and the situations in which they occur. You then take him through self-control procedures rather than letting him know he has gone wrong after he has lashed out at another child.

(c) In the case of those complex behaviours which are made up of a series of simple responses linked together in a behaviour chain (e.g. tying up shoelaces) you reinforce *combinations of simple behaviours.*

Procedure 7b	CHAINING *Make reinforcement dependent (contingent) upon the emission of more than one behaviour in succession and then gradually require more behaviours in the chain to be emitted before providing reinforcement.*

Applications
Chaining is often used when the client can perform the simple responses (or these can be taught by shaping) but does not combine them together.

Method
(1) Describe the steps to be followed clearly and minutely.
(2) Try to forge the chain from actions which already form part of the client's repertoire.
(3) Use differential reinforcement to increase the number of behavioural links in the chain.
(4) Backward chaining, beginning from the final link in the chain, is sometimes more effective than the reverse direction.

It may sometimes be necessary to use prompts in training the child, in the sense of giving a child special cues that direct his attention towards the task the adult is trying to teach him.

In teaching a mentally handicapped child to speak it may be useful at the beginning of training to utter a word loudly while encouraging him to observe. This verbal prompt would eventually be faded (i.e. gradually removed) as

---

Procedure 7c   PROMPTING

Coach the client — using verbal and/or non-verbal cues — to perform the required behaviour. Present a cue prior to the desired behaviour in a way which increases the probability that the behaviour will occur. It may sometimes be necessary to show him what to do or say.

---

the child becomes proficient in speaking. To take another example of prompting, the observant mother or teacher may notice that the child is fidgeting and draws his attention to the bladder signals, reminding him to go to the toilet. She may be required to help the child physically through the behaviour by prompts or verbal instruction.

Remember: *Attention is crucial to the establishment of stimulus control. A child will neither learn, nor have stimulus control, if he does not pay attention to the cues being used to direct his behaviour. Having established stimulus control, a special procedure is still required to maintain stimulus control under changing stimulus conditions. Fading is a procedure for slowly decreasing dependence on 'artificial' stimulus control—it involves the gradual removal of discriminative stimuli (S^Ds) such as cues and prompts in the child's environment.*

Fading Out Cues: If cues are withdrawn (e.g. prompting the child less and less) the procedure is called 'fading out'.

Fading In Cues: If new cues are gradually introduced this is called 'fading in'.

Applications

Some children, notably those who are mentally handicapped, find it difficult to make fine discriminations. Discrimination learning is basic to all learning; to say that an organism has learned to discriminate simply means that it has learned to respond differently to different stimuli.

A behavioural deficit of any form may be described in at least three different ways. It may result from

(a) an inability to perceive the stimulus (S) or discriminate it from others, a problem notably of sensorily handicapped individuals (e.g. blind and deaf children);

(b) a specific inability to make the appropriate response (R) as with physically handicapped children; and

(c) a specific inability to form an association between a particular S and R — not a general inability to associate events, but a specific stimulus control deficit (i.e. a difficulty in establishing appropriate control of responses by stimuli).

If, as is suggested, the errors of mentally handicapped children on discrimination tasks are due to responses to irrelevant stimuli, it follows that if we can obtain greater control over the discriminative stimuli and thereby prevent errors. We should be able to improve their performance on discrimination tasks, and thus on other skills which depend on the ability to discriminate between essential and non-essential elements.

A typical method of establishing a discrimination is to present two stimuli, either simultaneously or alternately: a positive stimulus (S +) and a negative stimulus (S −). Responding in the presence of the S + is reinforced while responding in the presence of the S − is not reinforced. The establishment of a discrimination has been viewed as the outcome of two antagonistic mechanisms: conditioning (the reinforcement of responses to S +) and extinction (the non-reinforcement of responses to the S −).

Traditionally it was assumed that responding to the S − is a necessary condition for discrimination learning; however several studies have indicated that a discrimination can be learned without responding to the S −. Interest has grown in 'errorless' procedures as tools for teaching discrimination to those who fail to learn under normal trial-and-error conditions.

Stimulus fading

This procedure involves the gradual shifting of control from some dominant stimulus element to a different and criterion stimulus. In fading an element of a stimulus gradually changes to a point where discrimination is based on *another* dimension, usually one that is more difficult for the learner.

The correct choice (S +) appears at the final or criterion level from the outset of training, and it is the distractors (S −) that are gradually faded out until they too reach criterion level. Fading does not alter the overall configuration or topography of a stimulus.

Stimulus shaping

Stimulus shaping involves a change in the topography of the whole stimulus complex so that the stimulus first presented to the subject in the training programme bears little resemblance to the final stimulus complex. As in fading, the initial differences in a stimulus shaping programme are ones that a child *can* successfully discriminate.

Illustration

Correcting faulty stimulus control

Guthrie (1935) gives the following illustration of faulty stimulus control and the method used to stop a child being untidy. The behaviour of the child was used to reinstate the S^D.

The mother of a ten-year-old girl complained to a psychologist that for two years her daughter had annoyed her by a habit of tossing coat and hat on the floor as she entered the house. On a hundred occasions the mother had insisted that the girl pick up the coat and hang it in its place. These irritating ways were changed only after the mother, on advice, began to insist not that the girl pick up the fallen garments from the floor but that she put them on, return to the street, and re-enter the house, this time removing the coat and hanging it up properly. The principle at work then is that the child must be made to perform the required act while she is attending to the stimulus which is to control it. In the example, the mother had been getting the response out in the presence of the wrong stimuli. The stimuli which were meant to control the response were those present *immediately* after the child entered the house. What was going wrong was that the 'tidy' response was being repeatedly and merely evoked in the presence of a stimulus — essentially an inappropriate one (an S^Δ) — the mother saying 'Please pick up your coat'.

A basic objective in training, education and therapy is to encourage behaviour that is emitted spontaneously rather than as a response to a prompt or cue. Bear in mind the role of the parent in ineffectual stimulus control! So often the problem is an interactional one — between the adult and the child. It may be necessary to train the parent to give more assertive, unambiguous verbal signals (e.g. commands). A parent (or teacher) may be ineffectual because he or she over-reacts to certain situations. A mother may feel depressed, hostile or anxious. You might ask her to record her own responses along with the child's (see Fig. 10). Relaxation or self-control training could help her to remain calm and competent in these circumstances.

Remember: The teacher's role in ineffectual stimulus control! There exists within a classroom, as within any social setting, a substantial array of stimulus variables which can cue behaviour (discriminative stimuli), reinforce behaviour (reinforcing stimuli) or produce no effect on behaviour (neutral stimuli). It is the aim of a behavioural programme to manipulate these stimuli in order to modify behaviour. It may be possible to manipulate conditions already present in the situation, and/or introduce additional conditions into the existing arrangements.

Rules

Among the critical antecedents to behaviour — especially when considering non-compliant, rebellious children — are the rules (implicit and explicit) enforced at home and at school. The particular rules which are set and the specific disciplinary techniques which are used, are probably much less important than the establishment of some principles and guidelines which are both clearly recognizable and accepted as unambigous and fair. For all that, thoughtful rules are crucial. The pupil needs to attend to the consequences of his academic and social performance in order to make progress. One of the most important of these consequences is the *feedback* he receives from the teacher as to whether the academic answer he gives is correct or incorrect and in the case of behaviour, appropriate or inappropriate.

Guidelines to stimulus control in the classroom

A closer examination of the teacher's sequencing of classroom antecedents and consequences may help you diagnose problems in classroom performance and management.

Altering stimulus conditions in classroom settings may take the form of posting rules or instructions as prompts for desired behaviours. Cues (rules) inform the pupils about what is required of them.

(1) Negotiate rules. Discuss the rules and the reasons for them with children who are old enough to participate in such a process. Rules are more likely to be obeyed if they are perceived as fair and seem to have a purpose. It may be possible to engage pupils in the formulation of *their* classroom rules. Negotiate a set of classroom objectives and clarify the function of rules in facilitating these objectives.
(2) To be effective rules should elicit responses which the pupils are capable of making.
(3) Emphasize rules that offer beneficial outcomes for appropriate actions.
(4) Select a few essential rules only — ones that can be enforced, and reinforced.
(5) Praise pupils who follow the rules, identifying the precise grounds for the praise. Rules alone are unlikely to be effective. Group reinforcers (privileges) might be built into a programme.

Some teachers arrange a competitive points system: one half of the class (say) competing with another for points and an eventual prize or bonus. Such 'team' endeavours can be highly successful but they carry the danger of group coercion against the individual.

There are other useful types of cueing behaviour such as modelling, prompting (physical or verbal), fading, chaining, successive approximations and using instructions.

Methods for reducing behaviour

Table XII   Methods for reducing behaviour

Procedure	Method
8. Extinction	Withold reinforcement following inappropriate behaviour.
9. Stimulus change	Change discriminative stimuli (remove or change controlling antecedent stimuli).
10. Punishment	Present mildly aversive/noxious stimuli contingent upon (following) inappropriate behaviour.
11. Time out from positive reinforcement (TO)	Withdraw reinforcement for X minutes following inappropriate behaviour.
12. Response-cost (RC)	Withdraw X quantity of reinforcers following inappropriate behaviour.
13. Overcorrection	Client make restitution plus . . .
14. Positive reinforcement: (a) Reinforcing incompatible behaviour (RIB) (b) Differential reinforcement of other behaviours (DRO)	Reinforce behaviour that is incompatible with the unwanted one. Reinforce behaviour other than the undesired one on a regular schedule.
15. Gradual exposure to aversive stimuli (e.g. desensitization)	Expose child gradually to feared situation while secure and relaxed.
16. Avoidance (e.g. covert sensitization)	Present (*in vivo* or in imagination) to-be-avoided object with aversive stimulus.
17. Modelling	Demonstrate behaviour for child to copy.
18. Role-playing	Script a role so client can rehearse behaviour and/or a situation.
19. Cognitive control (cognitive restructuring including problem solving)	Teach alternative ways of perceiving, controlling, solving problems.
20. Self-control training	Various approaches.
21. Verbal agreements/written contracts.	

When a particular behaviour occurs at a high rate (with excessive frequency) or with surplus intensity and magnitude, or where a response is emitted under inappropriate conditions, the therapeutic task is to bring the behaviour within a range that is more socially acceptable. Unlike the child with a behaviour deficit, who has to learn a response that is not in his repertoire, the child with excess behaviour has to learn to modify existing responses.

To facilitate this, the therapist has a choice among a variety of techniques which he can use singly or in combination — but, as always, in a clinically sensitive and imaginative fashion.

8. Extinction

Procedure 8a	EXTINCTION (e.g. Planned Ignoring) *Arrange conditions so that the child receives no rewards following undesired acts; in other words, withold reinforcements such as approval, attention, and the like, which have previously and inappropriately been contingent on the production of inappropriate responses.*

Applications
Successful extinction brings about the relatively permanent *unlearning* of a behaviour (the elimination of a behaviour from a person's repertoire). It refers to a procedure by which reinforcement that has previously followed an operant behaviour is discontinued. For example, to stop a child from acting in an attention-seeking manner which is antisocial in its effects, conditions are arranged so that he receives no reinforcement (attention) following the maladaptive action.

Method
See Flow Chart 7.
Carefully analyse the contingencies operating currently to maintain problematic behaviour and plan the elimination of such contingent reinforcement. Often these contingencies involve social reinforcement. Ask the reinforcing agents (parents, teachers) to offer their attention, responsiveness, praise and smiles contingently upon behaviours *other* than the undesirable one and to 'grit their teeth' (turn their back, look away, leave the room, or divert their attention to something or someone else) when the maladaptive behaviour occurs. In withdrawing reinforcement, be specific in defining the behaviours to be extinguished.

Remember: The child may 'work hard' to regain the lost reinforcement and thus may get 'worse' before he gets 'better'. Warn parents of this distinct possibility or they may become disillusioned, and will not persevere with the programme long enough to obtain results.

The reinforcement history of the child is important in determining how much patience the therapist and parents are going to require. If the problem behaviour has been continuously reinforced in the past then extinction should be swift; after all it is much easier for the youngster to recognize that he has lost reinforcers than it is for the child on intermittent reinforcement. In the latter case, extinction tends to be slow.

Remember: The association between a cue and a response is weakened each time the response occurs and is not followed by reinforcement. Thus disuse alone does not lead to extinction. It is essential that the behaviour should occur in order for extinction to take place; for only then are the internal motivating factors truly weakened. So no restraint is put upon the child (see by contrast Procedure 10, Punishment). For this reason alone (there are others) give careful consideration to this procedure as in Flow Chart 7. Problem actions may provide intrinsic satisfaction and pleasure (self-approbation) over and above the external reinforcement inherent in the adult paying anxious attention to them. If a child plays up in the classroom the child may still obtain reinforcement from his peers although the teacher ignores his behaviour.

Involving others

Some behaviour is so dangerous, unacceptable, or disruptive of others, that it just cannot be ignored in isolation — in the hope that it will eventually extinguish. In some cases it has proved necessary to supplement extinction by procedures designed to short-circuit these difficulties; in other cases the help of sympathetic people has been enlisted. The teacher could reinforce classmates for ignoring certain aspects of the client's behaviour, or reinforce the child's peers contingent upon her improvement. It is often a good idea (given parental permission) to explain to friends and family (and sometimes neighbours) what is happening so that they do not unwittingly subvert the programme. Siblings can prove helpful in the furtherance of therapeutic objectives.

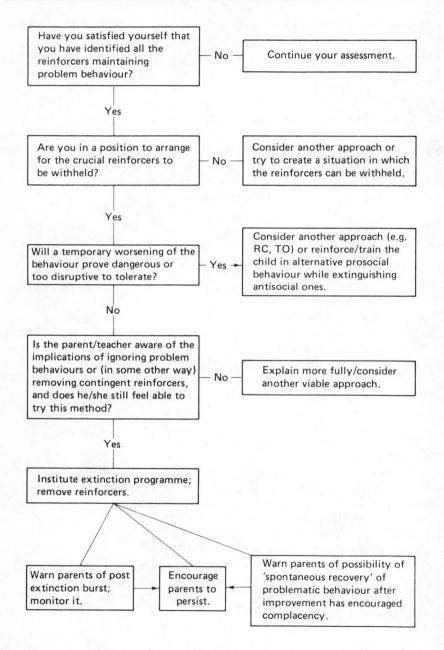

FLOW CHART 7   Extinction programme (e.g. ignoring).

Avoid: Complacency. Sometimes the unwanted behaviour—which has apparently been successfully extinguished—returns after a period . . . to everyone's dismay. This may occur when the child returns (say) to his classroom after a holiday. In learning terms this is referred to (paradoxically, for the parent and therapist) as 'spontaneous recovery'.

For reasons like these, extinction procedures are most suitable for the reduction of behaviours whose temporary continuance and (possibly) exacerbation before extinction can be tolerated. This would exclude high-intensity acts of assault and self-injury. Another consideration is the possibility of imitation by other children. If this is a major concern then extinction alone is probably not an appropriate choice of treatment procedure.

Try to facilitate the extinction process by combining the procedure with reinforcement for alternative actions. The possibility of obtaining reinforcement by other means may hasten the renunciation of deviant behaviour.

Note: *Don't underestimate the difficulty of ignoring problematic behaviour, especially if it is disruptive and especially if one is teaching (and don't forget that extinction does not invariably work). Not surprisingly teachers are likely to attend to pupils when they are difficult and rowdy. Walker and Buckley (1974), for example, found that 18% of a teacher's attention to 'non-problem' children was for inappropriate behaviour while 89% of her attention to 'problem' children was for undesirable classroom behaviour. Furthermore, 77% of the attention given to all the observed children was bestowed on the disruptive children.*

It is true, too, that parents provide attention, interest, approval, and positive physical contact as a consequence of behaviour such as shouting, hitting, and non-compliance in deviant children. The same pattern is seen in institutions for the mentally subnormal, where a child exhibits some form of undesirable (say self-injurious) behaviour and attendants terminate the behaviour by restraining the child. Such attention—a commodity which is very precious in an institution where stimulation, affection, and self-esteem are sometimes in short supply—may reinforce the self-mutilation.

In summary, to withhold reinforcers appears easy in principle. However, it may be difficult in practice, in the untidy and unpredictable world outside the clinic, to gain contingency control; the therapist has to assess whether she is in a position to arrange for the crucial reinforcers to be withheld.

Sadly, some children do appear to get worse rather than better when their parents ignore deviant behaviour and attend to more appropriate behaviour. Why should this be? We examined some of the reasons on p. 154. Other explanations have been put forward. It may not be certain that attention by caretakers was definitely the reinforcer for the disruptive behaviour of the child observed. Thus it is feasible that removal of the parent's or teacher's attention following the deviant behaviour does not really constitute extinction. Even where it is considered unnecessary to introduce additional procedures in order to maximize therapeutic control over reinforcement, it is likely that residual minor sources of reinforcement for deviant behaviour may go unnoticed after witholding the more powerful reinforcers. These left-over low-potential reinforcers continue to subvert attempts to extinguish behaviours.

Birnbrauer (1985) asks the question: 'Can attention, without other benefits, maintain inappropriate behaviour?' He is sceptical, concluding that this condition rarely can be met. He can find no examples in which the child's aversive or inappropriate behaviour does not also produce other positive reinforcers on some schedule, and/or delay punishment. Parental attention will prolong coercive exchanges, arguments and whinging, because as long as the parent is talking (no matter how angrily or loudly) there is a chance of succeeding. Thus, this negative attention is discriminative for positive reinforcement. Silence would be an effective means of eliminating the delaying behaviour; also teaching parents to cease 'nattering'. Relinquishing ineffective dialogues, (chatter, idle threats and discussion) will be necessary if punishment is to be implemented effectively. Birnbrauer (1985) questions whether ignoring is aversive or non-reinforcing. He is of the opinion that the answer depends on whether or not a 'no response' has been paired with positive or aversive consequences. It is, of course, not uncommon in our society for no comment to mean okay. Several studies with university students and children have found that the combination of reactions, 'right' for correct answers and no comment about incorrect answers is much less effective (indeed ineffective with many subjects) than no reaction to correct answers and 'wrong' for incorrect responses. This combination was as effective as 'right' and 'wrong'. There appears to be little justification (on this evidence) for recommending the use of ignoring alone. Birnbrauer states that research conducted with animals employing primary reinforcers and with humans using monetary and other material reinforcement has shown repeatedly that stimulus control and schedule of reinforcement control may not be obtained until non-reinforcement is replaced by time out from positive reinforcement (which is merely signalled non-reinforcement) or response cost (in the form of delaying opportunity to obtain positive reinforcement or loss of points that could be exchanged for money). In the hurly burly of social exchange, it is likely that what behaviour is being reinforced socially and what is being ignored will not be discriminated. Hence, from this line of evidence also it appears that simply ignoring behaviour will not always suffice.

A further question arises concerning planned ignoring: Can the behaviour be allowed to continue without harm to child and others? It is important to remember that the parents' conception of the likelihood of danger and definition of harmful behaviour may differ from the therapist's.

Procedure 8b   **SATIATION**
Make the child (or allow him to) continue performing the undesired act until he tires of it.

Method
Get the child who is (say) destructive to tear up piles of newspaper until she sickens of the activity; the child who uses obscene language, to use the words over and over again in your presence (deadpan) until the 'shock' value of the words are lost.

9. Stimulus change

Procedure 9   **STIMULUS CHANGE**
Remove or change the discriminative stimuli signalling reinforcement or cues signalling punishment.

Applications
Certain responses seem to occur only when specific conditions are present. Thus, by altering the antecedent controlling conditions, you may well eliminate the behaviour. Stimulus change is the process of changing the discriminative stimuli — the environmental cues — which have been present when problem behaviour has been reinforced in the past.

Method
Stimuli associated with rewarded undesirable behaviour are removed — a technique commonly practised by teachers. If a child continually talks to the student next to her, the teacher generally moves her desk away. By moving the desk, the teacher is changing the stimulus-context (proximity) in which the talking took place. Stimulus change has the short-term effect of reducing undesirable behaviour. It gives the teacher a chance to get new behaviour

going by using positive reinforcement. If the old stimulus conditions are simply reinstated (e.g. the child's desk is moved back), there is a chance the maladaptive behaviour will reappear.

10. Punishment

> Procedure 10   PUNISHMENT
> *Follow an unwanted response with a mildly aversive stimulus.*

Applications

Punishment can be effective in controlling behaviour. It all depends on how we interpret the word and deed called 'punishment'. Both *withdrawal of positive reinforcement* (known as the extinction procedure) and *contingent application of an aversive stimulus* tend to decrease target problem behaviours. Occasionally a moderately aversive stimulus (e.g. a smack) administered immediately following an inappropriate behaviour, is justifiable in terms of quick and dramatic results, and because the consequences of not doing so can result in death or injury (e.g. a very young child putting a knitting needle down his infant brother's ear, or his fingers into a power point).

The trouble is that punishment always seems to be equated with hitting or hurting. Severe punishment tends to suppress behaviour rather than extinguish it! The behaviour is only likely to be performed a very few times, perhaps only once in the instance of intense punishment, before it ceases. The prediction is that punishment will be ineffective because suppressed behaviours tend to recur, whereas extinguished ones (see Procedure 8) do not — at least in the longer term. Such theorizing has led to the present emphasis upon the encouragement in the child of alternative behaviours that are mutually exclusive of the undesirable ones which are being punished. The training of these behaviours could take place during the period of suppression that follows punishment.

Remember: Punishment is not necessarily intense or indeed physical. Parents criticise, reprimand, shout at, isolate and withdraw approval or privileges from their children. There is no evidence that occasional spanking carried out in the context of a secure and loving home environment ever scarred a child's (or subsequent adult's) psyche. There is clear evidence that persistent, intense physical punishment carried out against a background of cold, hostile and rejecting parental attitudes, causes a great amount of harm.

The popularity of punishment as a means of modifying behaviour for parents and teachers, may be due—to some extent—to the fact that it is often reinforced by the immediate (if temporary) relief brought about by the prompt (and also brief) cessation of the misdemeanour. In other words it can be habit-forming! The more general and long-term consequences of punishment can degenerate in ways that are destructive. It is likely to be administered in ways which are ill-timed, extreme, inconsistent, retaliatory and without any accompanying choices and encouragement of more acceptable substitute behaviours. It has a nasty way of escalating. Because its effects are usually short-lived the child repeats the undesirable behaviour; parents repeat the punishment, somewhat more forcefully; soon the child is back to the same misdemeanour . . . and there comes about another turn of the screw . . . harsher measures, and so on and on.

Several researchers urge caution in the use of physical punishment with children. While it is true that intense punishment is more effective at suppressing behaviour than mild punishment, there are unwanted side-effects to take into account. Aggressive behaviour on the part of an adult (as part of the punishment) could provide an undesirable modelling experience for the child; there might be maladaptive emotional sequelae such as fear, tenseness, withdrawal and frustration. Punishment alone does not direct the child towards appropriate or desirable behaviour; indeed, as we saw it, does not even eliminate inappropriate activity but rather slows it down. A person who frequently uses punishment, might lose his own reinforcing value and stimulate avoidance activities (e.g. school phobia) or escape behaviour (e.g. truancy). Becker (1971) believes that punishment, used properly and humanely, can be effective in changing behaviour. In order to be effective, punishment (a) is given promptly, (b) relies on withdrawl of reinforcers (see below), (c) provides clear steps for retrieving these reinforcers, (d) makes use of a warning signal, (e) should be given in a calm, matter-of-fact manner, (f) is accompanied by plentiful reinforcement of actions incompatible with those being punished, (g) uses procedures to ensure that unwanted behaviours do not gain reinforcement.

Methods
The clinical application of punitive/aversive procedures is controversial from the ethical point of view. It is argued by proponents that distasteful as punishment may be to the therapist who is moved by compassion and the desire to relieve suffering, these very motives should force him to contemplate their use in certain cases. Self-injurious behaviour such as mutilation, head-banging, self-biting, induced vomiting, etc., have been successfully treated by the contingent application of aversive stimulation (see Sandler, 1980). 'The ends justify the means' is, however, a problematic and much abused slogan.

The clinical application of shock or nausea-inducing drugs for addictive behaviour, sexual deviations and other problems, is felt (rightly or wrongly) to be outside the range of this manual, with its emphasis on community-orientated interventions and a naturalistic approach to life-difficulties. The more 'natural' sanctions, which are part of day-to-day child-rearing, are discussed in Procedures 11 and 12.

11. Time-out (TO) from positive reinforcement

> Procedure 11   TIME-OUT
> *Temporarily remove the child, following on the performance of the unwanted act, to a place devoid of people and objects of interest; in other words, a situation in which reinforcement is no longer available to him.*

Applications
TO provides one means of sanctioning unwanted behaviour by the withdrawal of reinforcement. Removal of reinforcers is not only more effective than physical punishment but it is free of the more undesirable side-effects. TO is a period of time during which the child is prevented from emitting the problematic behaviour (say a temper-tantrum) in the situation in which it has been positively reinforced in the past. (It has to be admitted that whatever technical definition learning theorists give to TO, children interpret it as punishment. Emphasizing potential self-control elements by referring to it as a 'cooling off' or 'think things out' period, may be useful.)

Choosing TO
TO sometimes leads to tantrums or rebellious behaviour such as crying, screaming, and physical assaults, particularly if the child has to be taken by force to a quiet room. With older, physically resistive children the method may simply not be feasible. So the procedure and its choice requires careful consideration (see Flow Chart 8). Very rarely are children destructive, but, if so, precautions have to be taken in the choice and preparation of the TO room. In some homes there just is no such room! Additional difficulties to be aware of are the possibility that the child may adapt to the TO situation by acquiring new means of obtaining reinforcement, such as self-stimulation or fantasy; and the likelihood that adults who have initial reservations about TO may use the procedure tentatively and inconsistently.

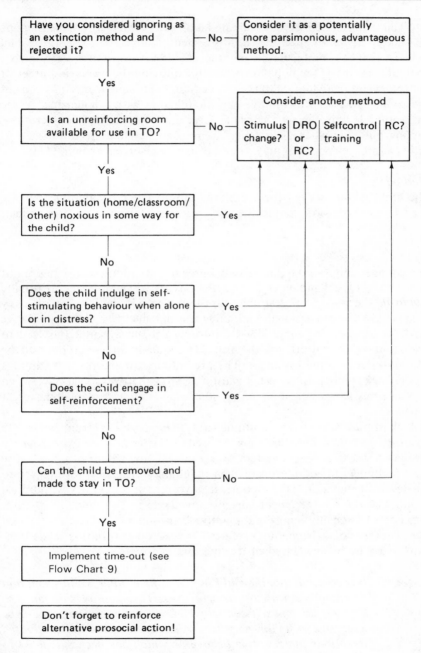

FLOW CHART 8 Some considerations in choosing time-out.

When the behaviour to be eliminated is an extraordinarily compelling one that all but *demands* attention (reinforcement) from those present, or when TO is difficult to administer because the child is a strong and protesting boy, an equivalent of TO may be instituted by removing the primary sources of reinforcement from him. So if the mother is a major source of reinforcement she could be advised to remove herself, together with a magazine, to the bathroom, locking herself in when her child's temper-tantrums erupt — coming out only when all is quiet. Removing the child from a disrupted activity (on-the-spot TO) may pre-empt her banishment (room TO).

Method
The child is warned in advance about those of her behaviours that are considered inappropriate and the consequences that will flow from them. See Flow Chart 9.

Timing
For younger children the time may be three to five minutes, for children of perhaps eight years and older, longer. Periods of 10 to 15 minutes are usually felt to be the maximum desirable duration. Ten-minute TOs are typically used in classroom situations. A stimulus associated with, and discriminative for TO, can acquire conditioned punishing properties, and thus lead to behaviour reduction. If so, the full TO sequence may not have to be administered in some instances. The presentation of the pre-TO stimulus which might consist of a verbal warning ('Stop that, or you'll have to go into time-out') a warning look, or a gesture may be enough to quell the target behaviour.

A child may or may not continue to display (say) a tantrum in the TO room; the point is that it is being ignored. *TO differs from extinction.* In the case of extinction, the reinforcers which are withdrawn are those specifically *identified* in terms of their maintaining function with regard to the deviant behaviour. TO, in contrast, involves the temporary withdrawal of *most* of the reinforcement currently available to the child. In a sense, extinction by socially ignoring disruptive behaviours constitutes a focused TO. The TO room (sometimes referred to as a quiet room) is made non-reinforcing by being cleared of its entertainment value.

Note:　　*It is essential that the child sees that the mother is consistent and timely with her use of the procedure. This method is designed to help a child gain self-control; it should not become a game or be used frivolously for 'naughty' or 'annoying' activities, as opposed to serious maladaptive behaviour which has been subjected to thoughtful analysis and discussion.*

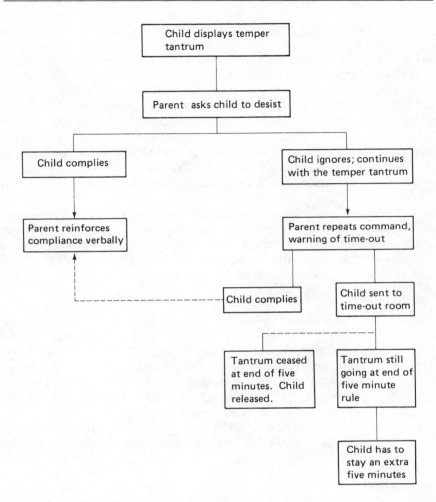

FLOW CHART 9   An example of the stages in the use of time-out.

It is important to spend time in the home supervising the programme (especially in its early stages) and, when necessary, prompting the mother.

TO in the classroom

Time-out is a familiar procedure to the teacher: it has probably been used by most teachers at one time or another. Teachers have long used the procedure of placing a child at the side of the room, at the back of a room, or in days gone by on a dunce's chair. There is disagreement as to how far it is effective in changing unacceptable behaviour. It does have the advantage of providing both the teacher and the pupil with a breathing space in which tempers can cool, thus avoiding the use of harsher methods of control. TO has a number of counterproductive effects for the child. He is in the limelight, possibly acting the buffoon and therefore still the centre of attention. Or he is getting out of doing some unwelcome scholastic task. A lightweight screen for use in the junior classroom may overcome both these difficulties. Another disadvantage of TO is that it may prove to be more attractive to the pupil than the classroom, and thus act as a reinforcer of the behaviour it is intended to punish. If this is the case the teacher should have a hard look at his teaching and/or his interactions with this child.

Behaviour modification techniques such as time-out, which are designed to eliminate inappropriate or undesirable behaviour, are unlikely to succeed unless supplemented by the reinforcement of an alternative and more appropriate behaviour pattern. Time-out used in conjunction with extinction and positive reinforcement is effective in reducing a variety of deviant patterns of behaviour (see Appendix I).

Note: *Parents almost invariably state that they have tried (and often failed) with a version of TO. Sending a child to his room for unspecified periods of time is not TO, especially when the procedure is undermined by the presence of entertaining books and toys and (most important) the absence of clear-cut contingency rules. Nor is TO the unethical practice of confining him in a dark and frightening place.*

TO should be used with caution. It is best not to use the child's own room as it could engender unpleasant connotations in his mind.

Self-control aspects

Although it was suggested that TO encourages self-control, there are procedures which allow the child to be more self-directed. By placing the subject in TO, the opportunity to make a decision is taken away from him and thus the self-control element is lessened. The mother, by placing the child in a quiet room, has made the decision for him and by the time he returns to the scene of combat, the provocative aspects of the situation are likely to have dissipated. The distinction between allowing the subject the opportunity to control his own behaviour and removing the opportunity to engage in additional unacceptable behaviour, is analogous to what is referred to as internal versus external control.

12. Response-cost (RC)

Another common punishment technique is response-cost, the contingent withdrawal of specified amounts of reinforcement. Parents often withold love, approval, and privileges when their children are 'naughty'. This is an informal use of RC.

Procedure 12   RESPONSE-COST

Withdraw specified amounts of reinforcement from the child contingent upon his displaying unwanted behaviour; these must have been specified in advance. In effect the child pays a penalty for violating the rules; the withdrawal of reinforcers constitutes the 'cost' of the maladaptive action. Response-cost can of course only be used in a context where reinforcement in measurable quantities is being regularly used, as in the case of a token economy system (e.g. in a classroom).

Applications

RC is essentially a punishment procedure which seeks to reduce the future probability of a response. The method—in the form of loss of points, grades, money, tokens, privileges, etc.—is also applied in token economy programmes. The variety of applications is immense (see Appendix I).

Method

In order to put a RC contingency into effect:
(a) Some level of positive reinforcement must be administered to the child (so that there will be something to withdraw if necessary).
(b) The value of conditioned reinforcers such as tokens, points, or money has to be established for use in the programme.

It is essential to determine the reaction of each individual child and adapt the treatment programme accordingly. As with other procedures containing a punitive element, it is necessary to make clear to the child in advance precisely the 'cost' (in the form of fines, etc.) for each unwanted behaviour. Consistency, immediacy and knowledge of results (feedback) are crucial to a RC programme. The child has to learn that his maladaptive acts will be consistently punished; this involves applying the cost immediately after the unwanted act has occurred. Feedback means ensuring that the child has information about which of his actions produced the consequence of a penalty.

Avoid: Making costs too high and the reinforcement rate too low, or vice versa, otherwise the programme is likely to fail. It is common practice for prompts to be arranged. For example, in the classroom situation a card on the child's desk is used to list the deviant behaviours and the points he will lose if he emits them. In addition, the child should receive information about his performance, i.e. consistent and immediate feedback about the consequences of his behaviour.

In the use of RC, there is no time restriction before reinforcement is available as there is with TO. For example, a child may have to pay a fine for disruptive behaviour in the classroom. Having been fined, there is no fixed period of time during which positive reinforcers are beyond the reach of the child, as is the case if he is placed in a room for 10 minutes for the same maladaptive behaviour. Another difference between the RC and TO procedures is the amount of reinforcement lost. A *specified* amount of the reinforcers is withdrawn in the case of the former, whereas *all* reinforcers are withdrawn (for a specified time) in the latter.

Remember: That response-cost is an effective way of encouraging self-management, in that awareness of the rewards and losses of certain behaviour allows the individual to participate in the contingency system. (Incidentally, it is also a convenient self-discipline for the parent, e.g. contributing to a charity box after breaking a rule about shouting at the children over trivia and so on.) As with other punitive techniques, it needs to be used in moderation in order to avoid side-effects such as anger or avoidance behaviour, and to be supplemented by other techniques designed to reinforce appropriate behaviour.

RC may well be more practicable (and have less undesirable side-effects) than TO in classroom settings. Whether at home or in the classroom, there are at least two advantages of using RC. One is that RC does not remove the subject from the opportunity to engage in desirable behaviour. From that standpoint, any time spent in TO is, in a sense, wasted time. Because RC does not remove the subject from the ongoing events it avoids this particular problem. The second advantage is that by not removing the child from the situation which is unfolding, and which involves choices about whether to behave or misbehave, the child is provided with a more realistic learning situation. He is given the opportunity either to continue to perform the behaviour and be punished, or not persist in the undesirable behaviour and experience no punishment.

As with other behavioural methods there are individual differences in the reactions of children to RC procedures. The actual aversiveness of TOs and RCs appears to be a function of the child's interactions within a particular social context, the way in which the procedures are implemented, and his reinforcemented history.

A study by McIntyre *et al.* (1968) illustrates the RC procedure in an after-school programme for elementary and junior high school boys. Each child had a counter on which a teacher could either add or subtract points. The child gained points for correct answers and lost points for disruptive behaviour. Whenever disruptive behaviour occurred, the instructor would turn on the counter associated with that student's name and allow the counter to continue to subtract points until the instructor felt that that student had corrected himself.

13. Overcorrection

A further form of response-cost or penalty is known as overcorrection. With overcorrection we have a method combining positive reinforcement and aversive control, which is used to discourage inappropriate or disruptive behaviour. This method requires a person to do something over and above that necessary to correct a situation resulting from inappropriate behaviour, or something that is incompatible with the unwanted action.

Procedure 13   (a) OVERCORRECTION (restitutional overcorrection)
Require the youth to correct the consequences of his misbehaviour. Not only must he remedy the situation he has caused, but also 'overcorrect' it to an improved or better-than-normal state. In other words, you enforce the performance of a new behaviour in the situation where you want it to become routine
(b) OVERCORRECTION (positive practice)
Get the child to practise positive behaviours which are physically incompatible with the inappropriate behaviour.

Applications
(a) A child who steals and breaks another youngster's penknife is required to save up enough money not only to replace the knife, but also to buy

a small gift betokening regret. He is praised at the completion of the act of restitution. A boy who deliberately punctures another child's bicycle tyre not only has to repair the tyre but also must oil and polish the entire vehicle.
(b) A child who indulges in self-stimulatory behaviour is required to do something which is physically incompatible with the action (e.g. walking to counter rocking). Of course, alternative sources of stimulation would have to be sought.

14. Positive reinforcement: promotion of alternative behaviour

Procedure 14a	REINFORCEMENT OF INCOMPATIBLE BEHAVIOUR (RIB) *Positively reinforce a particular class of behaviour which is inconsistent with, or which cannot be performed at the same time as, the undesired act. In other words, to stop a child from acting in a particular way, deliberately reinforce a competing action.*

Applications
To decrease a behaviour use positive reinforcement. Reinforcement, which is so crucial to the acquisition of behaviour, is also useful in eliminating unwanted responses. For example, the therapist can strengthen (by reinforcement) alternative acts that are incompatible with, or cannot be performed at the same time as, the maladaptive response (counter-conditioning). There are very few occasions, as we have stressed, in which it is desirable only to reduce a given behaviour without at the same time training the child in some alternative prosocial act.

Method
Counterconditioning involves using principles of operant conditioning to supplant problem behaviours by reinforcing and thereby strengthening socially acceptable alternatives.

The advantage of this approach is the possibility of choosing a competing behaviour of a prosocial kind to strengthen while reducing the occurrence of the unwanted behaviour. The process may occur fairly slowly, and it may be helpful to attempt to accelerate the programme with a time-out or response-cost procedure.

If sufficient reinforcement is not made available in this way for adaptive behaviours, new strategies may be adopted—and possibly undesirable behaviours — as a means of gaining reinforcement. It is probably too much to hope that the youngster will necessarily, and of his own accord, turn to socially desirable actions once the target problems are extinguished. As with punishment procedures, extinction methods on their own do not indicate to the child the kind of actions that should replace the unwanted ones. The alternatives could indeed be as problematic, including aggression or absconding.

Procedure 14b	DIFFERENTIAL REINFORCEMENT OF OTHER BEHAVIOUR (DRO) *Arrange for reinforcing stimuli to be contingent upon the occurrence of any responses other than the unwanted target behaviour.*

Applications
As in Procedure 14a, except that DRO is simpler to use, involving the reinforcement of *any behaviour* other than the target behaviour. In the literature, target behaviours include disruptive, aggressive, hyperactive, self-injurious behaviours. DRO is indicated in circumstances in which it is desirable to discontinue reinforcement for an undesirable response, but it is unwise to decrease the quantity of reinforcement the child receives.

Method
Reward the child at the end of set intervals which are free of unwanted actions.

DRO and its disadvantages
The problem with DRO methods is their 'sledgehammer' properties. The fact that *any* behaviours other than the undesired one are equally reinforceable gives rise to the possibility that unwanted behaviours may be unwittingly encouraged. For instance, the hyperactive child may fail to perform some required academic task during the specified observation period, but because he is not out of his seat, shuffling his desk, or pinching his neighbour he remains eligible for reinforcement. This complication might be avoided by putting other patterns of undesirable behaviour on a DRO regime as well as hyperactive behaviour. Hopefully there will be enough intervals which merit reinforcement to allow the programme to work. Another problem in the use of a DRO regime is the so-called *behaviour contrast* effect. If hyperactivity is being dealt with by DRO procedures in one situation (say at school) but is rewarded in another situation (at home), then while it decreases under DRO conditions it may actually increase in the rewarded circumstances.

15. Eliminating dysfunctional emotion

Emotional behaviour can be controlled by different stimulus sources. One is the emotional arousal evoked directly by conditioned aversive stimuli. To eliminate maladaptive emotional responses, repeated non-reinforced exposure to threatening events (either directly or vicariously) may be required.

Procedure 15a	GRADUAL EXPOSURE TO AVERSIVE STIMULI (variously referred to as desensitization, graded change, counter conditioning) *Expose the child gradually to the aversive (e.g. phobic) situation, using (1) graduated imaginal stimuli (a fear hierarchy presented in imagery form); or (2) graduated real-life stimuli (a fear hierarchy based on actual situations). Expose the child, when (1) he has been trained in anxiety-antagonistic responses such as relaxation or other anxiety-neutralizing conditions (e.g. while in the company of a trusted, reassuring person or while playing or eating); or (2) he is feeling comfortable, but not after special antagonistic response-training, or measures. Reinforce the child for each successful attempt.*

Applications
These methods are most useful for dealing with avoidance behaviour, e.g. fears.

The extinction of inappropriate avoidance behaviours (e.g. school phobia, animal phobia) is made difficult because the fear which is in need of extinction prevents the child coming into contact with the feared (phobic) object. This 'catch 22' stops the process of 'spontaneous remission' whereby most of our fears are extinguished or reduced. So we have to break down the phobic situation into manageable 'bits'.

Methods
Active participation procedures (so-called) emphasize the gradual approach to real anxiety-provoking cues. The emphasis here is on operant components

rather than on relaxation-training. *Passive association procedures* include those desensitization techniques that emphasize the gradual pairing of anxiety-antagonistic responses with feared stimuli.

Hatzenbuehler and Schroeder (1978) speculate that these two types of desensitization are not distinct ways of overcoming fears but are best construed as two processes on one continuum of gradual exposure to aversive stimuli.

> Procedure 15b   DESENSITIZATION — ACTIVE
> PARTICIPATION (Exposure Training)
> *Help a child to overcome his fear of a particular situation by exposing him gradually and more closely to the feared situation while he is being rewarded or is feeling comfortable or secure — perhaps in the company of a supportive person.*

This method is sometimes referred to as participant modelling or guided participation. The power of desensitization is greatly enhanced by *in vivo* (real-life) exposures. Although one lacks the flexibility of fear hierarchies constructed for imaginal presentation, the real-life exposure training can of itself be most effective, especially when graduated and combined with modelling (see Procedure 17b).

Method

The child is helped to accomplish each stage successfully with minimal or no fear before moving onto the next step. The lowest item on the fear hierarchy is presented (say, a small dog) at a distance. Slowly, it is brought closer, pausing, if the youngster signals any apprehension. Gradually more fear items are presented in turn.

Participant modelling first requires the fearful child to observe non-fearful children in the avoided situations, for example, approaching an animal.

Next the child gradually increases their own participation in stages, perhaps at one-remove, e.g. touching the therapist's hand while she strokes (say) a dog.

Rationale

If psychological treatment can boost a client's perceived self-efficacy, then the client should approach formerly dreaded situations with new confidence (Bandura, 1977b). Heightened self-efficacy leads to more vigorous, persistent and probably more successful attempts to cope with the problem. Successful resolution of problems should increase the child's perceived self-effectiveness even further. Bandura offers four major sources of self-efficacy expectations;

performance accomplishments, modelling demonstrations, verbal persuasion and emotional arousal.

The next steps consist of gradually increasing the child's degree of participation and activity while withdrawing external performance supports, culminating in direct contact with the fear-provoking stimulus.

Procedure 15c	SYSTEMATIC DESENSITIZATION — PASSIVE ASSOCIATION *A graduated approach (while physically and/or mentally relaxed) to feared objects/situations. In the procedure sometimes called 'systematic desensitization' the exposure to the feared situation (in imagined scenes) progresses in slow, gradual steps — graded by constructing 'fear hierarchies'.*

Table XIII   The fear hierarchy of an agoraphobic student (age 18). Items were rated on the subjective anxiety scale, 10–100, 100 representing extreme discomfort, 10 complete calmness.

100 Walking across the common at night (few people present)
 90 Walking across the common at night (many people present)
 80 Walking across the common at dusk (few people)
 70 Walking across the common at dusk (many people)
 50 Walking across the common in daylight (few people)
 40 Walking across the common in daylight (many people)
 10 Walking around the perimeter of the common

100 Walking from the Science Department to the Student Union (alone)
 80 Walking from the Science Department to the Student Union (with strangers)
 50 Walking from the Science Department to the Student Union (with friends)
 20 Walking from the Science Department to the Student Union (with boy friend)

100 Taking a bus journey alone (a long distance seated toward the front of the bus)
100 Taking a bus journey alone (a short distance seated toward the front of the bus)
 80 Taking a bus journey alone (a long distance seated by the door)
 60 Taking a bus journey alone (a short distance seated by the door)
 40 Taking a bus journey with boy friend (toward front of bus)
 30 Taking a bus journey with boy friend (toward back of bus)

100 Shopping at the supermarket alone (crowded away from entrance/exit)
 80 Shopping at the supermarket alone (crowded near exit)
 70 Shopping at the supermarket alone (few people, away from exit)
 60 Shopping at the supermarket alone (few people, near exit)
 40 Shopping at the supermarket (with boy friend)

Method

The most common procedure has been to arrange the anxiety-evoking stimuli in a hierarchy (see Table XIII for an example) and to present them one at a time while the person is in a state of relaxation (see method below) and at a pace at which he is able to cope with the stimulus without experiencing undue distress.

Rationale

Some theorists view this procedure as a training in coping skills — a behaviour rehearsal of what the client is eventually to do in coping with anxiety in a real-life situation. This self-control procedure involves somewhat different emphases. The gradual exposure to the fear-provoking situation can occur either in the person's fantasy (imagining himself to be in various anxiety-related situations) or it can take place in real life (*in vivo*). In the former case, if anxiety is experienced, the imagined scene is extinguished, relaxation reinstated, and then the scene imagined again repeatedly until relaxation can be maintained in its presence. In this manner the child progresses along a hierarchy of imagined aversive stimuli until the relaxation can be maintained throughout, and the desensitization is generalized from the imagined to the actual phobic situation.

It may be preferable with the child who shows intense avoidance behaviour so that his voluntary participation is inhibited, to emphasize (initially) responses (e.g. relaxation) which are antagonistic to anxiety. Subsequently, there could be more active participation of the child in approaching the feared object and less emphasis on the anxiety-neutralizing responses. With moderately avoidant children active participation is preferable because of the assured advantage of behavioural rehearsal.

An example of a relaxation training script is provided in Appendix IV.

Procedure 15d	RELAXATION
	It may be possible to teach a child how to relax as a coping skill — when he becomes frustrated, agitated or angered. Relaxation has the advantage that it can be taught like any other skill. If the relaxation exercises have been well practised and successful, the person becomes relaxed when he says to himself, 'relax' or 'remain calm'. A relaxation audio casette is helpful.

> Procedure 15e   FLOODING (sometimes called implosion) *Bring the client into contact with the most feared item on the hierarchy, and keep him in contact with it until the fear has been extinguished. Essentially there is an immediate and sustained confrontation with the strongly aversive stimulus, either in vivo or in the imagination.*

Despite growing evidence for the effectiveness of this approach where children are concerned, the ethics of using it are questionable! Children may not understand the implications of the method even when it is explained to them; they are not always voluntary recipients of treatment

16. Avoidance

> Procedure 16   AVOIDANCE/COVERT SENSITIZATION *Simultaneously present the child with the situation to be avoided (or some representation of it) and some aversive condition (or its representation).*

Applications
The purpose of this procedure is the opposite of the previous ones in the sense that you wish to reduce (not encourage) approach behaviour because the object/situation is an undesirable one. To put it another way, avoidance tendencies are being built up.

Method
Approach behaviour is associated with aversive consequences — imagined or real.

Covert sensitization is the term given to the mental (imaginary) representation of noxious outcomes. The child may be trained to imagine vomiting and feeling nauseated by inhaling cigarette smoke. The theoretical rationale for covert sensitization was derived from aversive conditioning and based upon an 'escape avoidance' paradigm. Thus, theoretically, by pairing a highly aversive event (nausea) with a stimulus which formerly elicited approach responses (a food, for example), the stimulus assumes properties which cause discomfort to the individual. When this occurs, the individual will 'escape' from the stimulus (say, cigarette smoking) and eventually will learn to avoid that stimulus. The procedure was described as 'covert' because neither the conditioned (undesirable) stimulus nor the unconditioned stimulus was actually presented, and it was called 'sensitization' because its goal was to build up avoidance responses to the undesirable stimulus.

17. Modelling

Procedure 17	MODELLING *Systematically demonstrate in actuality (or symbolically — on film) a model displaying the required behaviour: a skill, an appropriate pro-social action, a coping strategy.*

Applications
Modelling is the most frequently used and reliably effective strategy for reducing children's fears. However, it can be used in many situations including the teacher of new skills or alternative behaviours. It may have a promising preventive role in the area of stress-inoculation.

Modelling can be combined with other procedures; thus modelling combined with desensitization may be very effective in the treatment of phobias.

Method
In the case of modelling, the therapeutic intervention may be directed towards the relationship between the antecedent conditions and the deviant behaviour and/or between the problem behaviour and its consequences.

Procedure 17a	SYMBOLIC MODELLING *An excellent example of this procedure is provided by Melamed and Siegel (1975). They use symbolic modelling to prepare children psychologically for surgery. Children view a 16-minute film of an initially fearful child who gradually copes with the situation and overcomes his own fears.*

Procedure 17b	ACTUAL MODELLING *An example is the reduction of aggression by exposing youths to models who demonstrate alternative ways of handling provocative situations; these models are more likely to be imitated if the consequences for the model are rewarding, than if they are followed either by an absence of reward or by adverse consequences for the model.*

Applications

Brief symbolic modelling may be an effective aid in preparing children for dental and medical treatment (e.g. surgery) by reducing situational fears. Symbolic modelling refers (for example) to the viewing of a film.

Live modelling appears to be more effective than symbolic modelling, although there isn't much in it if one allows several therapeutic trials and several models and progressively varied fear stimuli.

Method

Modelling procedures become more powerful as additional controlled components are added to the basic technique. Thus you might use the package shown in Flow Chart 10.

As with reinforced practice and desensitization, children may or may not be trained in anxiety-neutralizing procedures and encouraged to use these self-control skills during exposure to feared situations. The severity of the anxiety may determine whether this is necessary. The more intense the anxiety, the more likely that training the child in skills for coping with anxiety will facilitate the reduction of anxiety and thus increase the probability of exposure to feared situations. Such training might also result in more generalized effects.

Lange and Jakubowski (1976, p. 180) provide some pointers for constructing modelling tapes for assertion training. (The tapes may of course be used for other purposes.)

(1) Select models (generally) of the same sex and similar in other crucial ways to the observing child (group members).

(2) Demonstrate not only assertive behaviour but that action resulting in reinforcing outcomes.

(3) Make the modelling scenes reasonably short (one to three minutes).

(4) Break down complex assertive behaviours into smaller more easily assimilable parts, capable of being remembered by the observer.

(5) Highlight key aspects of the modelled assertive behaviour, viz. simplify the modelling scenes so the key aspects are 'underlined' or include a narrative which directs the observer's attention to the salient characteristics of the model's behaviour.

(6) Include methods for helping the observer to develop codes or covert symbolic labels for the modelling sequence of behaviours (e.g. acknowledge the other person's point of view before making your own, possibly contradictory, view known).

(7) Follow the tape by individual (or group) discussion. Allow a period of practice — on personal adaptations of the modelled actions.

Procedure 17c	COVERT MODELLING *Encourage the child to imagine a model coping with the feared situation.*

In this way rehearsal of approach behaviour takes place.

18. Role-playing

Procedure 18a	ROLE-PLAYING *Role-play a problem situation (a feared event, a provocative confrontation, etc.) with the child. The adult (parent/therapist) can 'change' roles, child playing parent or vice versa. One or other can pretend to be the individual who is thought to be the source of the problem.*

Applications

Role-playing is an effective technique for helping a person to learn new skills. Initiate rehearsal of the required behaviour under the direction of a therapist. A child will be explicitly asked to perform a normal role which is not normally her own, or asked to perform a normal role but not in a setting where it is normally enacted. The method is used to teach young people very basic skills, to help them become more effective in their interactions, and to help them to become more effective when extremely anxious (e.g. through enacting scenes such as using the telephone, going to an interview with an employer or dealing with provocation).

Argyle (1984) describes four stages: (i) explanation and modelling, live or from video; (ii) role-playing with other trainees or stooges; (iii) comments from trainer and playback of videotape; (iv) repeat performance.

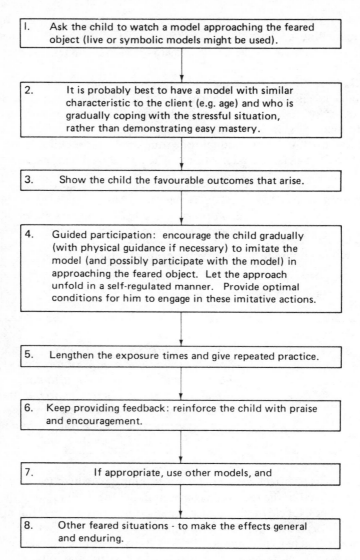

FLOW CHART 10   Modelling and reinforced practice (for fear reduction).

18b. Fixed-role therapy

This method of helping the client to test out the way he construes (and self-defeatingly miscontrues his world) is useful for youngsters who have low self-esteem, feel persecuted and socially isolated.

Procedure 18b	FIXED-ROLE THERAPY
	Encourage the youngster (or parent?) to 'try out' new behaviour patterns based upon a carefully 'scripted' role. A highly specific, fixed role is negotiated, and the client is encouraged to play this role in the expectation that by receiving new and helpful forms of feedback from the environment he will change the self-defeating constructs that control his behaviour.

Method

(1) The client is encouraged to explored (by trying out) patterns of behaviour contrasted to his own. This is based on a fixed role sketch worked out with the client and derived from a compromise between what he is 'actually' like, and what he would like to be like.

(2) He is invited to practise these patterns in everyday life.

(3) From practice he gains an experience of how the environment can differ in appearance and 'feel', and how it reacts, when *he* behaves in a different manner.

(4) Practice generates new and more effective skills, supplemented by novel experience from the feedback he receives.

The learning theorist Estes (1971) is commenting on methods such as these, in a sense, when he writes that

> For the lower animals, for very young children, and to some extent for human beings of all ages who are mentally retarded or subject to severe neurological or behaviour disorders, behaviour from moment to moment is largely describable and predictable in terms of responses to particular stimuli and the rewarding or punishing outcomes of previous stimulus–response sequences. In more mature beings, much instrumental behaviour and more especially a great part of verbal behaviour is organized into higher-order routines and is, in many instances, better understood in terms of the operation of rules, principles, strategies and the like. . . . Thus in many situations, an individual's behaviour from moment to moment may be governed by a relatively broad strategy, which, once adopted, dictates response sequences rather than by anticipated consequences of specific actions. In these situations it is the selection of strategies rather than the selection of particular reactions to stimuli which is modified by past experience with rewarding or punishing consequences (p. 23).

An example of this broader approach to therapy is the method designed to improve *social perspective-taking* in children. The young child is egocentric, seeing the world from a self-centred, personal perspective—indifferent to and unaware of the point of view of others. The development of role-taking (decentring) skills is a maturational process that results from the youngster's active involvement with his environment. Treatment methods encourage role-taking skills by means of enacted roles, discussions, observation of films, writing, debating and helping (see Further Readings).

Interestingly, behavioural procedures may be among the most powerful methods of activating cognitive processes; they are recruited for the remediation of a wide range of intra- and interpersonal problems. There is an irony about this finding. What we now find is a burgeoning literature on the cognitive aspects of behaviour modification. Kazdin (1980) believes that the major difference between cognitive and less cognitive behaviour therapists lies not so much in their therapeutic procedures, as in their rationale and selection of a given procedure in an individual case. The more cognitively orientated therapist is inclined to employ a behavioural procedure appropriate to the 'cognitive restructuring' he presumes is required. Emotional reactions — for example — may be controlled by self-generated stimuli, i.e. by symbolic activities in the form of emotion-provoking thoughts about pleasurable or frightening events. This sort of emotional arousal is susceptible to extinction through cognitive restructuring of probable response consequences.

19a Cognitive restructuring

You train the child (or adult) to re-evaluate potentially distressing events so that when they are viewed from a more realistic perspective they lose their power to upset. This involves changing his characteristic ways of organizing his experiences, and then producing alternatives. What a person tells himself about his experience affects his behaviour. For example, one youth may tend to attribute the causes of what happens to him to forces beyond his control, while another may see himself as having a major influence and say on the unfolding events of his life.

Correcting self-talk
To help children and adolescents (and, indeed, parents at times) we examine and dissect some of the faulty reasoning underlying the self-talk: the exaggerations ('No one loves me', 'There's *no* hope!'), the need to be all-competent, to show no weakness, to be acknowledged and loved *all* the time, to be for ever right. Counselling on such illogicalities, the prompting and practising of new self-talk ('I can manage . . . I'm a good mother'. 'Think first, act afterwards . . . Keep cool') may bring some relief.

Novaco (1975) provides the client with positive self-statements for dealing with anger:

1. Preparing for provocation.

This is going to upset me, but I know how to deal with it.
What is it that I have to do?
I can work out a plan to handle this.
I can manage the situation. I know how to regulate my anger.
If I find myself getting upset, I'll know what to do.
There won't be any need for an argument.
Try not to take this too seriously.
This could be a testy situation, but I believe in myself.
Time for a few deep breaths of relaxation. Feel comfortable, relaxed, and at ease.
Easy does it. Remember to keep your sense of humour.

2. Reacting during the confrontation.

Stay calm. Just continue to relax.
As long as I keep my cool, I'm in control.
Just roll with the punches; don't get bent out of shape.
Think of what you want to get out of this.
You don't need to prove yourself.
There is no point in getting mad.
Don't make more out of this than you have to.
I'm not going to let him get to me.
Look for the positives. Don't assume the worst or jump to conclusions.
It's really a shame that she has to act like this.
For someone to be that irritable, he must be awfully unhappy.
If I start to get mad, I'll just be banging my head against the wall. So I might as well just relax.
There is no need to doubt myself. What he says doesn't matter.
I'm on top of this situation and it's under control.

3. Coping with arousal.

My muscles are starting to feel tight. Time to relax and slow things down.
Getting upset won't help.
It's just not worth it to get so angry.
I'll let him make a fool of himself.
I have a right to be annoyed, but let's keep the lid on.
Time to take a deep breath.
Let's take the issue point by point.
My anger is a signal of what I need to do. Time to instruct myself.

I'm not going to get pushed around, but I'm not going haywire either.
Try to reason it out. Treat each other with respect.
Let's try a cooperative approach. Maybe we are both right.
Negatives lead to more negatives. Work constructively.
He'd probably like me to get really angry. Well I'm going to disappoint him.
I can't expect people to act the way I want them to.
Take it easy don't get pushy.

Reflecting on the experience.

a. When conflict is unresolved:
Forget about the aggravation. Thinking about it only makes you upset.
These are difficult situations, and they take time to straighten out.
Try to shake it off. Don't let it interfere with your job.
I'll get better at this as I get more practice.
Remember relaxation. It's a lot better than anger.
Can your laugh about it? It's probably not so serious.
Don't take it personally.
Take a deep breath and think positive thoughts.
b. When conflict is resolved or coping is successful:
I handled that one pretty well. It worked!
That wasn't as hard as I thought.
It could have been a lot worse.
I could have gotten more upset than it was worth.
I actually got through that without getting angry.
My pride can sure get me into trouble, but when I don't take things too
seriously, I'm better off.
I guess I've been getting upset for too long when it wasn't even necessary.
I'm doing better at this all the time.

Applications
Cognitive restructuring has been found to be effective in modifying depressive
(helpless) states, decreasing avoidance behaviour and reducing subjective
anxiety. Its usefulness is restricted to older children and adolescents.

Method
The cognitive-restructuring method (e.g. Ellis and Grieger, 1977) encourages
the individual to talk about past experiences involving (say) feared events.
Irrational ideas underlying their fears are exposed and challenged, as in
rational restructuring. In this way the client is engaged in prolonged verbal
exposure to threatening situations. You encourage him to *relabel* threatening
stimuli.

One of the features of Ellis's RET (Rational Emotive Therapy) is the notion that certain core irrational ideas are at the root of much emotional disturbance, and that these dysfunctional cognitions can be altered. Such ideas are:

—that it is easier to avoid than to face life difficulties;
—that one should be thoroughly competent, intelligent, and achieving in all posible respects;
—that one has virtually no control over one's emotions and that one cannot help feeling certain things.

The basic ABC paradigm described in this manual becomes ABC–DE in the RET model: antecedents, beliefs, consequences, disputation and effect (see Bernard and Joyce, 1984). The D for disputation (of which there are three categories: cognitive, emotional and behavioural) refers to the stage of intervention. As an example of the first type the therapist would offer an essentially rational explanation for the development of (say) the child's fear. The youngster is encouraged to attribute fear to internal cognitions rather than to external events.

As with other behavioural methods for stress reduction, there is a redistribution of the fearful behaviour away from the feared event and onto the faulty conceptualization of the distressing sequence. There are various ways in which cognitive appraisals may subvert the possibilities of mobilizing effective coping strategies. The child or mother may perceive that only in certain situations is his/her behaviour effective. Or they may credit their achievements to external factors rather than to their own ability ('external locus of control'). At the Centre we have known a mother attribute the successful treatment to 'luck' rather than to her hard earned competence *and* hard work. (Such misperception represents a failure on our part as therapists!) Indeed, the effect of successful performance on a client's sense of self-efficacy could vary, depending on whether accomplishments were attributed to ability or to effort expended.

19b. Thought stopping

Applications
Some children cannot stop themselves indulging in recurrent unconstructive ruminations. Thought stopping may help the child to control the obsessive, intrusive ideas.

216 BEHAVIOURAL TREATMENT OF CHILDREN WITH PROBLEMS

Method
The child is trained to identify negative thoughts, to tell himself (covertly) to stop them, and to focus on the task at hand or some rewarding memory or imagery. The potential of achieving control over one's thoughts can be dramatically demonstrated to clients by requesting them to verbalize their negative thoughts and by shouting at them, 'Stop!'. Typically, their speech will be interrupted. This procedure is repeated with an inquiry each time as to whether the child's thought pattern was interrupted. If it worked then there was a blocking! The child gradually assumes blocking control of himself, and learns to say, 'stop' (covertly after a few trials) when negative, self-defeating ideas and thoughts start to occur. Pleasant, positive ideas and imagery that are incompatible with anxiety are substituted for the morbid preoccupations.

19c. Problem-solving skills

Procedure 19	PROBLEM-SOLVING *Select problematic situations. Give examples (or encourage the child to do so) of various reactions to these situations, and then identify the consequences generated by these reactions.*

Problem-solving therapies
The rationale for these methods is succinctly provided by D'Zurilla and Goldfried (1971):

> Much of what we view clinically as 'abnormal behaviour' or 'emotional disturbance' may be viewed as ineffective behaviour and its consequences, in which the individual is unable to resolve certain situational problems in his life and his inadequate attempts to do so are having undesirable effects, such as anxiety, depression, and the creation of additional problems (p. 107).

Applications
Although some of the therapeutic procedures commonly used in adult cognitively-orientated work can be understood by adolescents, many of them would not be suitable for children. Nevertheless, youngsters can be taught rational thinking, stress-inoculation techniques and problem-solving strategies.

The aim of training children in problem-solving skills is to provide them with a general coping strategy for a variety of difficult situations. The method has been used to help parents, children and adolescents deal more effectively with a variety of conflict situations (e.g. arriving at mutually acceptable decisions with parents, developing cooperation with the peer group). Its prime advantage as a training method is the provision of principles so that the individual can function as his or her own 'therapist'. It is a variant of self-control training, directed towards the objective of encouraging clients to think and work things out for themselves (see Spivack *et al.*, 1976).

Method

Goldfried and Davison (1976) enumerate five stages in problem-solving:
  (a) general orientation;
  (b) problem definition and formulation;
  (c) generation of alternatives;
  (d) decision-making;
  (e) verification.

(a) *Orientation*. Encourage the client to monitor his problematic circumstances (e.g. a diary of events/feelings) but also to accept the normality of problems as a function of life and growing up. Sensitize him to the problem areas by discussion—getting him to identify fraught situations when they first occur, and to think first and act afterwards. All this presupposes the initial recognition that there is a difficulty.

To the extent that the individual has a mental set that he can cope with his problem, the greater is the likelihood that he will find a solution. The feeling of being in control (and conversely, *not* helpless) is of great significance in working through difficult situations.

(b) *Problem definition and formulation*. Encourage the client to define all aspects of the problem in operational terms, i.e. in relevant concrete terms rather than in vague, global and abstract language. This helps you to unravel what looks like a complicated problem and, perhaps to simplify it. Here is an example (an agoraphobic adolescent): 'It is a terrible effort to shop at the centre, I begin to get butterflies in my stomach when I go into the shopping centre. I feel nervous if there is a large crowd milling about. I can just about cope with small shops if I stay near the door. I really begin to panic if I have to shop in the large shops, well in or away from the door. Before long I feel paralysed, I can't move; I feel as if I might faint'. And here is an example for parents: 'I get angry with my son David. My muscles tense up. I want to lash out at him when he is cheeky. But what do I mean when I say he's cheeky? It's when I feel my dignity is threatened, especially when my friends are present, or that my authority is demeaned. It's something about his manner, dumb insolence I call it, unfriendly. And then, eventually I explode in a torrent of recrimination and abuse. Perhaps he also feels provoked by my manner. I must think about that'.

Formulation. Next you might categorize the salient features of the particular situation in a way that identifies their main *goals* and the *obstacles* that get in the way of fulfilling these goals.

In the case of the agoraphobic teenager she wishes to be able to shop normally, i.e. without anticipatory dread (her goal). To do that she will have to overcome her anxiety (the barrier). David's mother wishes to improve her relationship with her son (goal); her interpretation of his motives and manner and possibly her own attitude towards him (he says she is patronizing) may be barriers to this objective.

This is a further stage in the process of clarification. You formulate an explanation of what may be going wrong and why this is so.

(c) *Generation of alternatives.* Work out as wide a range of possible solutions as you can think of in terms of general strategies (what to do) and, later, specific tactics to implement the general strategy (how to do it). Brainstorming freely and, at first, uncritically generating as many ideas as possible, can be a help.

Brainstorming

This technique provides a creative way of generating the greatest number of ideas in the shortest possible time. It is ideally suited to group participation as well as individual application.

Method
There are three simple rules you apply to your chosen topic.
1. Accept every idea that the topic or issue gives rise to *uncritically*.
2. Aim for quantity of ideas rather than quality.
3. At this stage, do not initiate any discussion.
   List the ideas (e.g. write them on a blackboard or flip-chart).
   Set a time limit.
   Code the ideas when the brainstorming session is over.
   For example: (a) underline those that are not clear/understood.
              (b) put a cross next to those that are impossible.
              (c) put an asterisk against those that look useful and/or are worth exploring further.
   Let us look at the way David's mother put the alternatives:
(a) I could punish David more severely.
(b) I could ignore him.
(c) I could try to engage in a calm debate with him.
(d) I could turn the issue over to his father.

(e) I could penalize him (take away a proportion of his pocket money each time) without getting into an interminable debate.

(f) I could negotiate an agreement with him covering the perennial issues we argue over.

(g) I could look into my own attitudes and feelings toward him? Do *I* get *him* going as much as he does me; am I at fault in some way?

It might be useful to ask others how they would react, or imagine how others might react, if requested to solve a similar problem (e.g. how would his father, aunt or his teacher approach this problem?).

(d) *Decision making.* Work out the likely consequences of the better courses of action you have put forward. What is the utility of these consequences in resolving the problem as it has been formulated? For example, with regard to the proposed solutions:

(a) Punishment doesn't seem to work; in fact it seems to make David more intractable.

(b) He'd probably follow me around, arguing more forcibly. Like me, he can be very stubborn.

(c) Sounds good, but I find it so hard to keep cool. And we may not be able to resolve things in the heat of the particular confrontation.

(d) My husband won't thank me for that; he'll say 'It's your problem'. I have to cope in *my* way when David is disobedient.

(e) This may work but it could also generate trouble, sulking and tantrums.

(f) Sounds a possibility; David can be reasonable when he's in a good mood. The trick is to catch him at the right time.

(g) This is painful, but he may have a point when he says he wishes I could hear myself talk to him, as if he's an idiot or a baby.

(e) *Verification.* Try out the most acceptable and feasible-looking solution. Monitor your chosen course of action and its consequences. Try to match the actual outcomes against the hoped-for outcomes; if the match is satisfactory you 'exit' (to use the jargon) much relieved; if not, you continue to 'operate', which means that you return to the beginning of the sequence of problem-solving operations and start again.

Reconsider the original problem in the light of this attempt of yours at problem-solving. Do not be put off if you fail; try again. 'Experience' is based upon trial and error, and learning from one's mistakes. Work out new solutions. The phobic youngster could well be provided by the psychologist with a refinement of the problem-solving approach; a series of self-statements (a sort of script) in order to cope with her fear.

Preparing for a stressor:

What is it you have to do?

You can develop a plan to deal with it.
Just think about what you can do about it.
That's better than getting anxious.
No negative self-statements, just think rationally.
Don't worry: worry won't help anything.
Maybe what you think is anxiety is eagerness to confront the stressor.

Confronting and handling a stressor:
Just psych yourself up — you can meet this challenge.
You can convince yourself to do it. You can reason your fear away.
One step at a time; you can handle the situation.
Don't think about fear; just think about what you have to do. Stay relevant.
This anxiety is what the doctor said you would feel. It's a reminder to use your
   coping exercises.
Relax, you're in control. Take a slow deep breath.

Coping with the feeling of being overwhelmed:
When fear comes, just pause.
Keep the focus on the present; what is it you have to do?
Label your fear from 0 to 10 and watch it change. You should expect your
   fear to rise.
Don't try to eliminate fear totally; just keep it manageable.

Reinforcing self-statements:
It worked; you did it.
Wait until you tell your therapist (or group) about this.
It wasn't as bad as you expected.
Your damn ideas — that's the problem. When you control them, you control
   your fear.
It's getting better each time you use the procedures.
You can be pleased with the progress you're making.
You did it!

Source: Meichenbaum (1977).

Here is an example of a child thinking in a simple, but effective way, through
alternatives: If I attack my brother for taking my football my mother is bound
to get angry. She will punish me, and it will ruin my day. On the other hand, if
I choose to control myself and ask her to help me get my football back, the day
will continue to be good, and I can show myself how mature and patient I am.

Students (and many other teenagers) often have problems if they share
a room. Kanfer and Goldstein (1986) give this example of a young person
working out possible solutions to what had seemed an intractable problem:

Therapist: I have here a list of alternatives you suggested and I'd like you to consider which would be worthwhile pursuing. First of all, are there any not worth bothering with at all?

Client: Frankly, I don't think it would be physically possible for me to live on less sleep and still function well. I've always needed about eight hours of sleep a night and I'm in good health otherwise. I just think it's my constitution, and I doubt that it can be changed.

Therapist: Any others that you want to reject?

Client: No.

Therapist: I'd like you to think about each of these possible solutions in terms of the implications not only for you, but for others around you — friends and family. In addition, think not only of the immediate consequences, but also what the long term results may be. Why don't we think first about your trying to sleep while people are socializing in the room.

Client: I'd probably find the noise more annoying than the light so maybe I could use earplugs, or perhaps one of those machines that have a steady humming sound to blot out the noise. Actually, even if I could get to sleep it seems like a pretty awkward situation and I'm sure it would put a strain on my relationship with room-mate. Maybe I should concentrate on working out an arrangement with my room-mate where the apartment is free of guests at my bedtime.

Therapist: O.K. Let's look at that.

Client: One of the things we could do is to have people come over only on weekends. That way I could choose to be home or be out socializing on my own, without worrying how late it is getting. I'll talk to my room-mate and maybe we can come up with something like 'house rules'. Maybe I'm doing things that she doesn't like and I'd offer to change some of my ways — so it would be a compromise of sorts.

Therapist: How do you think that would affect your relationship with your room-mate?

Client: I'm not sure, but she's pretty easygoing, so somehow I think it would be all right. At least it's worth a try.

Therapist: How would you evaluate this alternative?

Client: Good, even very good.

Therapist: O.K., let's go on to some other alternatives.

Interlude

You will have noticed that some of the methods overlap with each other. Procedures are not usually exclusive to particular problems. Most treatment programmes combine elements of each of the types of learning enumerated in Appendix III. Thus, in treating a hostile, aggressive child a therapist might attempt to teach him alternative ways of interpreting 'provocative' incidents; train him to associate calm relaxation with the anger-provoking stimulus, while also modelling non-aggressive behaviour under provocation and reinforcing any exhibition of pacific behaviour by the child. It should be noted that some courses of treatment involve sophisticated extensions of basic principles, such as treatments concentrating upon self-control of behaviour. Self-control (or regulation) is a potent source of control which covers all types of learning. It has proved to be a crucial development in behaviour modification.

Procedure 20   SELF-MANAGEMENT AND SELF-CONTROL

Help the client to re-label his or her experiences and to change expectations of personal efficacy and the likely outcome. Teach your client to obtain environmental support for new responses by changing consequences.

Most self-management programmes combine techniques that involve standard-setting, self-monitoring, self-evaluation, and self-reinforcement (which also involves self-specification of contingencies and self-administration of reinforcement). Before a child can be taught to reinforce himself for a behaviour pattern, he must learn to evaluate his behaviour correctly. In order to encourage a child to evaluate his own behaviour properly, he must be taught to use some sort of standard by which he can measure his own behaviour. He also needs to attend to his own behaviour, monitoring it accurately. For example, he will have to learn to 'read' the signs of his own feelings (anger or hostility) and to label them correctly. If he hits out at another child, he will require a standard for

Continued

Continued

> *evaluating his act as antisocial and therefore as grounds for criticizing (i.e. punishing) himself. Or, if he desists from lashing out, praising himself (reinforcement) for showing self-control.*

Applications

Behaviour modifiers vary in the degree to which they plan external or self-control over the contingencies and the administration of reinforcing or punishing consequences, when it comes to the treatment of children. The field is still a very new one. Self-control refers to those actions an individual deliberately undertakes to achieve self-selected outcomes.

Rationale

Self-control techniques involve a crucial assumption—namely, that mediational processes operate in human learning and that these internal actions obey the same laws or principles as external actions do. Thus, a child can be encouraged to reward himself either covertly (by engaging in very positive self-thoughts and self-statements) or overtly (by indulging in a favourite activity). The sources of antecedent and outcome control may be in a person's own symbolic processes rather than his physiological states or external environment; the therapeutic endeavour thus becomes concerned with the manipulation of these symbolic sources of control. A person displays self-control when in the relative absence of immediate external constraints, he is able to resist a temptation—one to which he would previously have yielded.

The assumption of a correspondence between internal and external actions opens the door to a great variety of covert self-control procedures, such as (a) self-monitoring, (b) contingency management, (c) self-punishment, (d) self-reinforcement, (e) contract management, (f) self-confrontation, (g) self-administered behavioural analysis, (h) covert sensitization, and (i) altering the discriminative stimuli for the target response.

Self-monitoring provides the clinician and client with a baseline record of target behaviour for treatment purposes: in some instances the observed behaviour may actually change during monitoring in a favourable direction. Clinical practice has therefore attempted to utilize self-monitoring as a therapeutic technique.

Self-monitoring

(1) Request the youngster to keep a diary or log of events and situations (decided by both of you as pertinent) in the natural environment.
(2) Get him to note down the nature of the situation, what happened, what was said, what the child did.

(3) How comfortable—uncomfortable did he feel? (subjective rating)
(4) How satisfied was he with his actions on that occasion?
(5) What would he do differently if the event was still to come?
(6) Record any other comments: how he felt or thought.

Procedure 20a	SELF-CONTROL OF ANTECEDENT CONDITIONS *Manipulate those eliciting, reinforcing or discriminative stimuli in the youngster's symbolic processes which influence his maladaptive behaviour.*

Applications
There are several applications of self-control training (see Appendix I). One involves (as we saw) being able to resist temptation. From the therapist's point of view, the test of self-control is the ability (and inclination) of the client to minimize temptation by the early interruption of behavioural sequences which end up in the transgression of some self-imposed standard.

Rationale
Specific behaviours are performed in the presence of specific stimuli. Eventually, such an association leads to a situation in which the stimuli serve as cues for the behaviours and increase the probability that they will be emitted.

When behaviour is under maladaptive stimulus control it should be possible for a youngster to eliminate or weaken unwanted behaviour and increase desired behaviour by modifying his environment in certain ways. For example, the adolescent girl with a weight and eating problem might make a rule never to eat anywhere but at her place at the table and then at specified times; to remove herself from food stimuli wherever possible, by avoiding the kitchen, and by asking her siblings not to eat cakes and sweets in front of her.

Methods
There are several methods of stimulus control which involve building in appropriate stimulus-response connections. One such method is the technique of *cue-strengthening*. This requires that conditions be made favourable for the person to practise the response in a specific situation, where previously it was not associated strongly to any set of environmental cues.

The Schneider and Robin (1976) turtle technique for aiding self-control begins with a story to tell young children about a boy named Little Turtle. Little Turtle disliked school. In spite of his vows to stay out of trouble he always managed to find it. For example, he would get angry and rip up all his papers in class. One day when he was feeling especially bad, he met a talking tortoise. The old tortoise addressed him: 'Hey, there, I'll tell you a secret. Don't you realize you are carrying the answer to your problem around with you?' Little Turtle didn't know what he was talking about. 'Your shell—your shell' the tortoise shouted in his loud bellowing tones. 'That's why you have a shell. You can hide in your shell whenever you get that feeling inside you that tells you you are angry. When you are in your shell, you can have a moment to rest and figure out what to do about it. So next time you get angry, just go into your shell.' The story continues with an account of how the next day when he started to get upset Little Turtle remembered what the tortoise had told him so he pulled in his arms close to his body, put his head down so his chin rested against the chest, and rested for awhile, until he knew what to do. The story ends with the teacher coming over and praising him for this reaction and Little Turtle receiving a very good report card that term.

Following this story, the teacher demonstrates the turtle reaction. The children now practise it to various imagined frustrating experiences. In this way the child learns a new reaction to the cue of anger or frustration. This is combined with teaching the child relaxation skills, again employing the story of Little Turtle. The story is taken up where Little Turtle returns to the tortoise, telling him that he still has some angry feelings, even though he has used the turtle response. Starting with the stomach muscles, the children are given practice in tensing and relaxing major muscle groups of their body. Tensing and relaxation are then incorporated into the turtle response by tensing the body when assuming the turtle position, as a count is made from 1 to 10, followed by relaxation of the muscles, which is maintained for a few moments. The children are encouraged to use frustrating experiences as a cue to employ the turtle reaction.

Learning the turtle reaction is combined with teaching the child problem-solving methods (see Procedure 19). Problem-solving instruction sessions are held daily in class, during which recent problem situations are discussed. Cues are provided for the children, such as the teacher asking, 'What are your choices?'. The children are instructed to incorporate problem-solving efforts during use of the turtle technique; that is, to use this time to imagine behavioural alternatives to their frustrating situation and the consequences of each. In this way, the child learns to expand his range of alternative coping strategies. Children in the peer group are rewarded for supporting other children's efforts to employ the turtle method. They are encouraged to praise and applaud the child who is using the technique, and to cue fellow pupils to use the turtle method in situations that might lead to a fight. Peers, in turn, are reinforced by the teacher for their support. Training sessions are held for about 15 minutes each day for about three weeks and are then reduced to twice a week. Within a few weeks after introduction of the turtle technique, children start 'doing turtle in my head' without prompting and without going through the physical withdrawal reactions. It is important that children learn to discriminate when they should employ the turtle technique and when they should assert themselves.

Self-instruction

This is another method of self-control of antecedent conditions.

Applications
Children are taught to instruct themselves as a means of regulating their own behaviour. Eventually, the child's covert or inner speech comes to assume a self-governing role. A programme (Meichenbaum, 1977) was illustrated above.

Method
Instruct (say) the hyperactive, impulsive child in the concept of talking to himself. Gain the child's attention by using his natural medium of play. For example, while playing with the child, say: 'I have to land my airplane, now slowly, carefully, into the hanger'. Encourage the child to have the control tower tell the pilot to go slowly, etc. In this way help the child to build up a repertoire of self-statements to be used on a variety of tasks. Training begins on a set of tasks (games) in which the child is somewhat proficient and for which he does *not* have a history of failures and frustrations. Employ tasks that lend themselves to a self-instructional approach and which encourage the use of cognitive strategies.

The method of self-instructional training is flexible and usually follows the principle of successive approximations. Initially, the therapist models and has the child rehearse simple self-statements such as 'Stop! Think before I answer', 'Count to ten while I cool off'. Gradually the therapist models (and the child rehearses) more complex sets of self-statements.

Illustration

Here is an example of a self-instructional package which Bornstein and Quevillon (1976) used on three overactive, four-year-old, pre-school boys. Scott was described as a 'disciplinary problem because he is unable to follow directions for any extended length of time'. He could not complete ordinary tasks within the pre-school classroom setting and often manifested violent outbursts of temper for no apparent reason. Rod was described by teachers as 'being out of control in the classroom'. He displayed several problems and behavioural deficits, including short attention span, aggressiveness in response to other children and a general overactivity. Tim was reported to be highly distractible both at home and in pre-school. Most of his classroom time was spent walking around the room, staring off into space, and/or not attending to a task or instruction.

After an eight-day baseline period of observations, the children were seen individually for a massed self-instruction session lasting two hours. Each child worked with the therapist for about 50 minutes, was given a 20 minute break, then resumed work for another 50 minutes. The self-instructional training was as follows:

(1) the therapist modelled the task while talking aloud to himself;
(2) the child performed the task while the therapist instructed aloud;
(3) the child then performed the task talking aloud to himself while the therapist whispered softly;
(4) the child performed the task whispering softly while the therapist made lip movements but no sound;
(5) the child performed the task making lip movements without sound while the therapist self-instructed covertly;
(6) the child performed the task with covert self-instruction.

The verbalizations modelled were of four types:

(1) questions about the task (e.g. 'What does the teacher want me to do?');
(2) answers to questions in the form of cognitive rehearsals (e.g. 'Oh, that's right, I'm supposed to copy that picture.');
(3) self-instructions that guide through the task (e.g. 'O.K., first I draw a line here . . .');
(4) self-reinforcement (e.g. 'How about that? I really did that one well').

The entire training session was presented in a story format.

The results·of this study were measured in terms of on-task behaviour, defined as those behaviours directed towards the assigned tasks. It was expected that the child would be attentive and silent during teacher's instructions. When asked to participate during a work period (e.g. figure-drawing exercises, story-reading etc.), on-task behaviours included performing the prescribed and accepted classroom activity.

On-task behaviours increased dramatically with the introduction of the self-instructional package. The therapeutic gains were maintained 22½ weeks after the baseline was initiated.

Procedure 20b	SELF-CONTROL OF OUTCOME CONDITIONS
	Teach the youngster to rearrange contingencies that influence behaviour in such a way that he experiences long-range benefits, even though he may have to give up some satisfactions or tolerate some discomforts at first.

Methods

(1) *Self-control* involves a precise analysis of the behaviour to be controlled and (as with any other behavioural analyses) its antecedent and consequent conditions.

(2) It is necessary to identify behaviours which *enhance* appropriate responses as well as those actions which *interfere* with the desired outcome.

(3) It is necessary to identify positive and negative reinforcers which control these patterns of behaviour.

(4) Reinforcement is applied to alter the probability of the target behaviour.

There is evidence that children may be able to modify or maintain their own behaviour by administering rewards and punishments to themselves in a contingent manner. These consequences may occur in the child's environment or in his symbolic processes. The self-administered rewards and punishments may be overt or covert. Sometimes a point system is very effective in instituting a programme of self-reward. A youngster can provide himself with a point immediately after a response, and that point in turn can be exchanged for a variety of reinforcers.

Empathy is one facet of prosocial behaviour which should be of concern to social and clinical psychologists. It involves the child's capacity to control his behaviour by considering its effect on the experiences of others, particularly the potential victims of proscribed behaviour. Little is known about the development of this attribute, although presumably it has some of its antecedents in parental statements involving explanations of the effects of one's behaviour on others. The capacity for empathy requires object permanence, considerable abstract ability and represents a rather advanced state in the development of self-control and moral behaviour.

Procedure 21   VERBAL AGREEMENTS AND
                CONTRACTS
                *Negotiate an agreement with or between
                your clients, incorporating the main
                ingredients to define and produce
                mutually desired change.*

Rationale

At a time of crisis when (say) teenagers and their parents (or brothers and sisters) are at loggerheads, angry and resentful, contracts provide an opportunity for a family to take stock and to break through vicious circles of retribution and unreason.

The main assumptions underlying the use of *formal* verbal agreements or the stronger written form of contract, are as follows:

(1) The publicly endorsed, unambiguous and specific commitment to a future course of action which will prove more binding, a better guarantee of compliance, than more casual 'promises' or ephemeral statements of intention (think of those turned-over new leaves at the New Year).

(2) To obtain such results the parties concerned must not feel they have been unduly coerced into their contractual arrangements.

(3) The most potent reinforcers (rewards) available to bring about benign change in tense interpersonal situations, recede within the person experiencing the *other* side of the problem. Thus, a pre-planned and simultaneous alteration in actions from *both* parties on either side of the problem, is required to achieve a happy outcome.

Applications

Convey the following elements of contracting to the parents:

(1) Be very specific in spelling out the desired actions.

(2) Pay attention to the details of the *privileges* and *conditions* for both parties; they should be (a) important (as opposed to trivial), (b) functional (if manifested more frequently they will increase the youngster's chances of obtaining from her environment the natural kinds of rewards which most people desire and enjoy — like praise and esteem.)

(3) If parents wish their youngster to desist from certain actions and activities, encourage them to express these in terms of positive change. (For example, you would like your son to stop being so cheeky and abusive. Specify the change you wish to bring about by requiring him (say) to address people in a polite and courteous manner. This would then have to be spelled out in terms of specific *examples* of behaviour.)

(4) Get parents to sit down with their youngster to explain the purpose of the exercise — to help make family life more pleasant. Write down 5 items of behaviour (actions) you wish your son or daughter would do more often.

(5) Don't be vague (e.g. I wish she'd be more helpful). Be concrete and specific (e.g. I wish she'd help me set and clear the table).

(6) Parents may want their son to complete his homework and attend school regularly: he, on the other hand, desires more free time with his friends, or more pocket money. Encourage discussion, negotiation and compromise.

Here is a sample contract:

This Agreement is drawn up between . . . . Therapist for the Child Treatment Research Unit, and Mr and Mrs B . . . . , parents of Johnny B . . . .

In keeping with the wishes of both parents (and Johnny), to work towards the goals set out below, Mr and Mrs B. . . . . .agree with . . . . to keep the following arrangements.

General goals: for Johnny (separate agreement between Johnny and parents)
1.   Regular attendance at school.
2.   Informing mother of his whereabouts after school.
3.   Returning home by 6 p.m. for his tea.
4.   Refrain from swearing at his mother.

                    for Parents (separate agreement between parents and Johnny)
1.   Increase Johnny's pocket money to £2 per week.
2.   Allow him to go out on Saturday nights with his friends.
      (return by 11.30 p.m.)
3.   Allow him to stay up until 10.30 p.m.
4.   Refrain from criticizing Johnny's friends.
The specific plans and goals are attached.

On your part you agree to: On our part we agree to:

                              Appointments
Keep the appointments we arrange   Keep the appointments we arrange

                              Recordings
Keep records in the diaries   Explain the purpose and meaning of
and chart as arranged   assignments and graphs

Renegotiation Clause: The requirements and objectives are re-negotiable at any time on request by any party.

Signed. . . . . (Clients) Signed . . . . (Therapist).
Date . . . .

And here is another (a contract with an extremely non-compliant, hyperactive eight-year-old):

Morning arrangements for John Smith: agreed by John Smith and Mrs Smith

1. John woken by Mrs Smith.
2. John offered choice for breakfast by Mrs Smith (toast, cornflakes, etc.).
3. After a reasonable time (one minute) John makes final choice of breakfast and tells Mrs Smith. This choice cannot be changed by John or Mrs Smith.
4. John then has a bath for a reasonable time (15 minutes maximum).
5. Mrs Smith calls John out of the bath by using three minute warnings:
   a. Calls John three minutes before he is to get out.
   b. Calls John two minutes before he is to get out.
   c. Calls John one minute before he is to get out.
   d. Calls John out of the bath.
6. John has a reasonable time to dress (approximately four minutes) and then comes down to breakfast.
7. If John delays or refuses to get out of the bath and does not come down for breakfast, the breakfast to be thrown away.
8. If John comes down on time and all the stages above (1-6) are followed John is awarded one gold sticker to go on his chart (and his breakfast!).

Evening arrangements for John Smith

1. At 9.30 p.m. John is to begin to get ready for bed.
2. John is to have supper.
   get undressed
   go to the toilet before 9.45 p.m.
3. At 9.45 p.m. he is to go to his bedroom.
4. John may watch television, read, knit, if he wishes before sleeping — once he is in his bedroom.
5. John may not:
   a. Shout, demand, scream to his parents downstairs .
   b. Come downstairs again after 9.45 p.m.
   c. Disturb Sally in her bedroom.
   d. Disturb his parents in their bedroom.
6. Mrs Smith is to buy John a 'night light' for his bedroom.
7. These arrangements are for Monday, Tuesday, Wednesday, Thursday, Sunday. On Friday and Saturday, John may go later to bed — Mr and Mrs Smith to decide a reasonable time (always at least half an hour after Sally).

Signed. . . . . (John)
Signed. . . . . (Mrs Smith)
Signed. . . . . (Social Worker Witness)

Date . . . .

---

(7) Those actions chosen for the youngster to fulfil (and the parents) must be readily observable and clearly specified. For example: 'Anne must be less thoughtless' is refined to 'Anne could let us know about her movements when she goes out at night'. This could be specified as:
(a) telling parents where she is and with whom;
(b) letting parents know when she'll be home.
(If parents or teachers are unable to discern whether an obligation has been met, they cannot grant a privilege).

(8) The contract should impose sanctions for a failure to fulfil the agreement. (The youngster should know precisely what the penalties are for breaking the contract.) The sanctions are agreed to *in advance*, are decided by both sides, and are applied *consistently*.

(9) There can be no arbitrary, unilateral tinkering with the terms of the contract after the signing. Changes must be negotiated and agreed to by both sides.

(10) A contract can provide a bonus clause so that extra privileges, special activities, etc. are available for consistent performance over a long time.

(11) There should be a built-in scheme for monitoring the amount of positive reinforcement given and received. The records are kept (a chart or notebook) to inform each participant of the progress, or lack of it, of the agreement.

Procedure 22	SELF CONFRONTATION *Make use of video feedback (but with care and great sensitivity) to show clients how they appear to others and to reveal small details of actions and interactions.*

Applications
Self-image or self-confrontation techniques have been used with various clients, adults and children, since the 1950s. Therapists have used photographs, motion pictures, or videotape for self-image confrontation.

Repetitive self-observation by videotape playback (carefully planned, sometime edited, playbacks) may occasion changes in self-concept and can certainly induce intense affective reactions. For the latter reason video feedback requires careful and sensitive care. Video-based or video-augmented interventions are used to treat a wide range of psychological and behavioural problems (Berger, 1978; Dowrick and Biggs, 1983).

Rationale
Self-confrontation by video feedback allows a stepping outside of and viewing oneself as self-as-object, a means to achieving objective self-awareness.

Video feedback is not distorted by the biases, inaccurate memory, or prejudices of the feedback which comes from people (social feedback) but is reproduced exactly as it was observed from the camera's vantage point. Self-objectification entails a comparison process, not between the self and others, but rather between experienced behaviour (self-perception) and observed performance (video feedback).

Illustration

Webster-Stratton (1981) has presented guidelines for developing and using videotape modelling programmes as a method of parent education:

(1) In order for parents in the programme to relate positively to the models, they are told that the parent models in the videotapes are not actors but actual parents who have, in fact, attended a parenting course similar to the one they are taking. In addition the models selected for the videotapes are representative of white and black families, in all social classes, and include fathers as well as mothers. Parent models also have children of the same age as do the parents attending the programme.

(2) The parent models in the videotapes are frequently shown receiving praise from the therapist for appropriate parenting behaviours. In addition, the parent model is considered to have been rewarded when he or she is able to get from their child appropriate and pleasurable behaviours or a reduction in a child's misbehaviours.

(3) In order to be sure parents watching the videotapes do not get distracted, their attention is directed to the model's behaviours in the following way. They are shown vignettes of parent models interacting with their children in appropriate and inappropriate ways. After each presentation of a particular parent–child vignette, the videotape is stopped and the parents are given a chance to report their observations and to 'discover' the appropriate behaviours. If any disagreement occurs among the parents or if parents miss a crucial feature of the incident, the scene is replayed for further discussion. This contrast between the parental interactions presumed appropriate and those judged inappropriate serves to clarify and emphasize the desired behaviours.

(4) The parents attending the videotape programme do not have the opportunity to directly practise under supervision what they observe on videotapes and therefore they receive no direct reinforcement or feedback from the educator. However, parents are given a homework

assignment to play for 10 minutes a day with their child in order to practise the skills they have learned in the programme. The play periods are designed to minimize the possibility of negative exchanges and maximize the possibility of positive exchanges between parent and child. It is felt that parents are reinforced in these play periods by seeing improvements in their children's behaviours. In addition, because these parents are watching the programme in groups, the resulting expressions of support and enthusiasm by other parents act as powerful reinforcements.

(5) Finally, in order to further generalization of the effects of the videotape programme to home settings, the educator helps the parent groups discuss how the techniques demonstrated by the model on the videotape might apply to their own situations. This results in the parents becoming active participants in the educational process, thus facilitating learning. The group process cannot be minimized; the group is a source of extensive ideas and abundant social reinforcement for every parent's achievements.

APPENDIX I

Guide to the Application of Procedures

Method (Procedure No. on left)	Problems successfully dealt with
1 Graduated Reinforced Practice	Fears and avoidance behaviours Isolated behaviour
1/2 Incentive Systems (e.g. operant programmes — contingency management procedures, token economies, contingency contracts, self-reinforcement)	Language deficits Hyperactivity Bizarre behaviour Interpersonal conflict Non-compliance/negativism School phobia/truancy Various habit disorders (including toileting deficits: enuresis, encopresis, eating problems, etc.) Attentional deficits Academic skills/performance deficits Conduct disorders Delinquency Learning disabilities
3 Shaping	Skill/behavioural deficits
4/17 Modelling	Fears and avoidance behaviours Isolate behaviour Social skill deficits Conduct problems Learning disorders
Symbolic Modelling	Preventive work; preparing children for dental and medical treatment
5/6/8 Stimulus Control and Change	Inappropriate behaviour Over-eating Non-compliance
Provision of rules and response strategies	Attentional deficits

Method (Procedure No. on left)	Problems successfully dealt with
7 Extinction (withdrawal of reinforcement)	Inappropriate classroom behaviour Temper tantrums Attention-seeking disruptive behaviours Screaming Aggression Excessive crying
Satiation	Fire-setting
9/12 Overcorrection	Disruptiveness
11 Time-out from Positive Reinforcement	Non-attending classroom behaviour Assaultive behaviour Disruptiveness Tantrums Aggression
12 Response-Cost	Stealing Aggression Out of seat behaviour in the classroom Pestering Delinquency Intractable behaviour Disruptiveness Fire-setting
13 Promotion of Alternative Behaviour (Differential Reinforcement, DRO, RIB)	Inappropriate gender behaviour Disruptive behaviour Aggression Self-injurious behaviour Hyperactivity Norm-violating behaviour
14 Skill Training Interpersonal skill training (e.g. behaviour rehearsal, assertion training, social skills training)	Social skill deficits (see note on social skills below*) Interpersonal conflict Inappropriate gender behaviour Norm-violating behaviour
Self-care/vocational/academic and other skill training Guided Rehearsal	Delinquency Learning disabilities Toileting skills deficits
15 Graded Exposure to Aversive Stimuli Desensitization	Fears and avoidance behaviours Hostility

	Method (Procedure No. on left)	Problems successfully dealt with
18	Role-playing Role reversal	Social skill deficits Confrontations, conflict between adolescents and parents
19	Cognitive Change Methods (e.g. problem-solving skill training)	Crisis interventions — problematic situations including separation, death, and other upheavals Addictive behaviours Conflict situations Interpersonal functioning (conflict) Inhibitions Fears General coping situations Aggression
20	Self-control/Self-management/ Self-instruction	Interpersonal conflict Impulsivity Fear Academic performance deficits Hyperactivity
20/5	Self-management/Respondent/ Operant Training (Bell and pad method)	Enuresis
21	Agreements and contracts	Disruptive behaviour Stealing Interpersonal conflict School refusal
22	Self-confrontation (video feedback)	Obesity Interpersonal conflict Inappropriate parental behaviour

Social skills training

The majority of studies evaluating the effectiveness of SST has been conducted on children with *behavioural problems* such as unassertiveness, excessive aggression and social withdrawal. The results are highly encouraging (see Beck and Forehand, 1984, for an invaluable critical review: also Combs and Slaby, 1978).

There have been few, but promising studies of developmentally *delayed or retarded* children, whilst other work has focused specifically on skills training in school (e.g. McPhail *et al.*, 1978).

Helping unpopular, rejected children to improve the quality and quantity of relationships with peers has also been a matter of concern (Ladd and Mize, 1983).

Here again we find an increase in positive peer interactions and 'social standing' in the experimental situation, although the generalization (situational and temporal) issue remains problematic (see Herbert, 1986).

APPENDIX II

An Interview Guide

The initial behavioural interview (and other early interviews) have the purpose (see Haynes and Wilson, 1979) of
(a) gathering information about client concerns and goals;
(b) identifying factors that maintain and elicit the behavioural problem/s;
(c) obtaining relevant historical information;
(d) identifying significant reinforcers;
(e) assessing the caregiver's potential as an agent of behavioural change;
(f) providing an opportunity to educate, and discuss matters with, the client;
(g) obtaining informed consent; and
(h) formulating a statement on the goals and procedures of assessment and information.

The reader may find it helpful to have a summary of the steps covered by the Manual, plus other important information, which can be conveniently attached to a clipboard during the initial and early interviews. A guide to other potentially useful information is provided in Fig. 20.

INTERVIEW SCHEDULE

Client Names: Parent(s) _____   Child _____

Interviewer _____   Date _____

Interview Number _____   Location _____

1. INTRODUCTION   (a) Put client(s) at ease
                             (b) Explain who you are, how you work
                             (c) Seek permission to take notes; emphasize confidentiality

2. GENERAL   (a) Discuss the purpose of the interview
                         (b) Ask the client(s) to describe their concerns (their perception of the problem(s))
                         (c) Promise to return to this discussion after obtaining some background information

3. BACKGROUND INFORMATION

Biographical Data:
- (i)   Name of child
- (ii)   Date of birth
- (iii) Age
- (iv)   Address
- (v)   Details of household/family members

Educational Background:
- (i)   School
- (ii)   Academic progress
- (iii) Teacher's name
- (iv)   Attendance record
- (v)   Relationship with teacher/s
- (vi)   Relationship with peers

Medical Background: (Note anything out-of-the-ordinary under these headings.)
- (i)   State of present health
- (ii)   Medication, if any
- (iii) Childhood illnesses

Developmental History:
- Pregnancy
- Birth
- Developmental milestones
- Emerging patterns and routines of behaviour
  - feeding
  - sleeping
  - motor
  - toileting
  - language

4. DETAILED DESCRIPTION OF PROBLEM/S

- (a) Ask for a precise specification of the problem
- (b) Explore the desired outcomes
- (c) Construct a problem profile
- (d) Find out about the extent and severity of the problem(s)
- (e) Tease out the antecedents and consequences of the problem(s)
- (f) Find out what efforts have been made so far to remedy these difficulties
- (g) Establish problem priorities for further assessment

5. SETTING HOMEWORK TASKS

- (a) Explain the importance of parents being fully involved in the assessment and treatment, as exemplified by
- (b) Keeping records for the next week or two, and possibly beyond that

(c) Provide the client(s) with appropriate material (e.g. charts, tally sheets, ABC proforma) to record problem behaviours and interactions

6. MAKING AN APPOINTMENT TO VISIT THE HOME IN ORDER TO REVIEW BASELINE RECORDS AND TO MAKE DIRECT OBSERVATIONS

(a) You may have carried out your initial assessment interview in the home.

(b) Discuss the pattern of visits you are likely to make (or require of the family).

7. TERMINATING THE SESSION

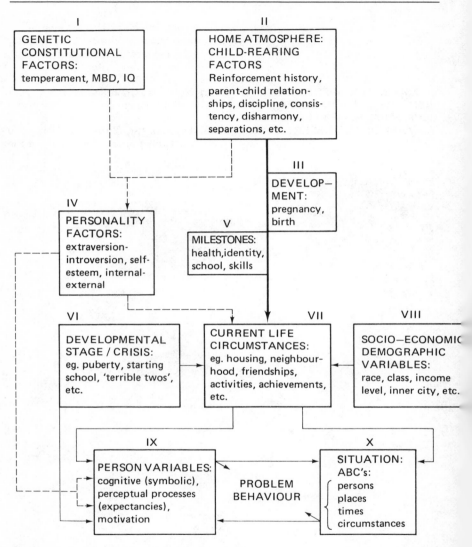

FIG. 20 The ten-factor clinical formulation, i.e. factors contributing to incidents of problem behaviour. (Adapted from Clarke, 1977.)

APPENDIX III

Handouts for Parents attending the Centre

Handout 1: An introduction to behavioural work

Ways to help you change your child's behaviour

You have decided that you need help in coping with your child whose behaviour you find a problem. This leaflet I hope will give you information which you can use to help you understand your child's behaviour yourself.

The nature of children's emotional and behaviour problems

Children are usually a source of great pleasure and endless wonder to their parents. These joys are sometimes tempered by the concern and heavy sense of responsibility that also accompany parenthood: the pleasure may be transformed into anxiety and the wonder into puzzlement when the child begins to behave in a peculiar or erratic manner. The youngster who has *not*, at some stage of his development, been the cause of quite serious worry to his mother and father is unique.

Emotional upsets and behaviour disturbances can best be thought of as problems which arise — as by-products — from coping with the difficulties of life. The point about these emotions and behaviours is that they have unfavourable consequences for the child (and those around him). They are harmful, inappropriate, or in some other way self-defeating.

How does a child develop problems?

Psychologists define learning as *any enduring change in behaviour which results from experience*. Memorizing a formula, recognizing a face and reading music are all examples of learning. So are habits — good and bad. The vast majority of the child's behaviours are learned, and this includes his problem behaviours.

Many of the problems of childhood are due to the child learning *inappropriate* responses; they are also the consequence of the child's *failure* to learn the *appropriate* behaviour.

Learning to be problematic*
How, precisely then does a child come to acquire those actions which his parents and teachers might call his 'incapabilities'. 'Danny is quite incapable of listening to what I tell him!' 'Janine is incapable of telling the truth!'

Children have to be taught how to behave normally, that is, in a socially appropriate manner. To do anything well demands good training; two persons are involved: a learner and a teacher. Fortunately it is not necessary for children to discover their way around their world entirely by trial-and error. We can save them a lot of time, and circumvent some distressing mistakes, if we prove to be — as parents — wise guides and mentors. To this end we need first to know the basic principles of learning, as aids to teaching children and bringing about change when necessary.

This knowledge will indicate how (and when) to teach children desirable behaviour and the means to help him 'unlearn' undesirable behaviour that they have picked up along the way. We also need to know how, once the desired behaviour shows itself in the child's repertoire, we can get them to maintain it. Good habits are so easily lost.

It must be emphasized that learning theory only tells us *how* to teach, not what to teach! Deciding what is desirable for your youngster is a question for your values as a citizen, individual and parent.

The ABC of behaviour
This is where the ABC of behaviour will provide useful.
A stands for *Antecedents* or what set the stage for (what led up to) the
B which stands for *Behaviour* (or what the child actually does); while
C refers to the *Consequences* (or what occurred immediately after the behaviour).

What we have is a rough and ready rule of thumb:
Acceptable behaviour + reinforcement (reward) = more acceptable behaviour
Acceptable behaviour + no reinforcement = less acceptable behaviour
Unacceptable behaviour + reinforcement (reward) = more unacceptable behaviour
Unacceptable behaviour + no reinforcement = less unacceptable behaviour

---

*Parents are encouraged to read (and discuss with the therapist) chosen selections from Martin Herbert's *Caring For Your Children: A Practical Guide* or *Living With Teenagers*.

The C term
All these examples illustrate how B *depends* upon C; consequences help to mould or shape behaviour. Parents (and teachers) influence behaviour by manipulating the consequences of behaviour. The technical term for this learning principle is instrumental conditioning; the person's action is instrumental in producing a favourable outcome.

It seems paradoxical to begin with the C term of the ABC equation, but instrumental conditioning is crucial to learning; it is the form of learning most essential to our understanding of the effects of children's *own* behaviour on their learning and subsequent actions.

First principle
We have said that if the consequences of a behaviour is rewarding (that is, favourable) to a child, that behaviour is likely to increase in strength. For example, it may become more frequent! Put another way: if Pat does something, and as a result of his action something pleasant happens to him, then he is more likely to do the same thing in similar circumstances in the future. When psychologists refer to this pleasant outcome as the *positive reinforcement* of behaviour, they have in mind several kinds of reinforcers: *tangible* rewards (e.g. sweets, treats, pocket money); *social* rewards (e.g. attention, a smile, a pat on the back, a word of encouragement); and *self-reinforcers* (e.g. the ones that come from within and which are non-tangible: self-praise, self-approval, a sense of pleasure). For instance, if you say 'Pat, that was nice of you to let Sally have a turn on your bike. I am very pleased with you', Pat is more likely to lend his bicycle again. (Note: we are dealing in probabilities not certainties.)

We know that it can be very helpful to look at difficult behaviour by analysing very *precisely* the behaviour itself, what led up to it and what happened immediately before *and* after (in other words, in ABC terms).

Making behaviour worthwhile
Some parents remember to reward (or in psychologist's jargon 'reinforce') desirable behaviour as below:

Antecedents	*Behaviour*	*Consequences*
Marjorie was asked to put away her toys.	She did so.	Her mum gave her a big hug and said thank you.

Marjorie is likely to tidy up her toys when asked again.

Some parents persistently overlook or ignore their children's desirable actions:

Antecedents	*Behaviour*	*Consequences*
James asked Dennis, his brother, for a turn on his new bike.	Dennis got off and helped James on to the bike.	Nil! Mother made no comment. James rode off without a word of thanks.

It won't be surprising if Dennis doesn't share his things next time around. Some parents unwittingly make undesirable behaviour worthwhile:

Antecedents	*Behaviour*	*Consequences*
David was told to leave the television off.	He kept putting it on.	It was eventually left on — to give people a bit of peace.
Anna was having breakfast.	She kept getting down from her place.	Mum followed her round with a bowl of cereal, feeding her with a spoonful whenever she could.

In both of these instances, the child's unacceptable actions were rewarded — by getting his or her own way. In other words, the child received positive reinforcement for behaving in an undesirable manner, which made it even more likely to occur again.

Some parents make undesirable behaviour unworthwhile:

Antecedents	*Behaviour*	*Consequences*
Johnnie wanted to go to the park; Dad said there wasn't time before tea.	Johnnie kicked and shouted, lay on the floor and screamed.	Dad ignored his tantrum; eventually Johnnie calmed down and began to play.

Second principle

Behaving in a manner that *avoids* an unpleasant outcome leads to the reinforcement of behaviour, thus making it more likely to recur in similar circumstances. If your child does something you do not like, such as losing her temper too easily, you may *increase* her ability to think first and hold her temper, by penalizing her consistently for failing to do so; in this way you are providing what is called *negative reinforcement* for her efforts to 'keep her cool'. You may not have to apply the penalty if she believes your threat because of your record of keeping your word. For instance, if you say, 'Donna, if you do not think first, but lash out at your sister, I will not allow you to watch the television', then her resolve to think first and desist from hitting out will be strengthened.

The 'A' term

The reason why we look at A (Antecedents) after C, so to speak, is that it seems that the antecedents of a behaviour, its cues or triggers are of rather less central significance than its consequences. Nonetheless, these antecedents are very important, and if you think about and watch the settings of your child's behaviour, it may be that he or she behaves in a non-compliant way, or has a tantrum on some occasions but not on others; that is, some situations seem to act as cues to him to behave in a particular way.

People tend to tailor their behaviour to the particular places and the different persons, in, and with whom, they find themselves; and in the case of children, this chameleon capacity often leads to misunderstandings between home and school—each blaming the other when (more often than not) they are difficult in the one setting but not the other. A child tends to look around him, consider the rules, the firmness of the adult, how other children behave, and what is expected of him. Then he adopts his behaviour accordingly. If your child displays awful behaviour with you, ask yourself: 'Is there anyone to whom she shows her better side?' If so, there may be something worth learning from him or her.

Handout 2: How we view the problem

The *'here-and-now'* is critically important for getting to grips with whatever it is that is troubling your son or daughter. Throughout the work we have carried out together we have asked the questions 'what', 'why' and 'how'. We asked these questions in order to *describe* what form the problems take; to *explain* why they have come about and persist (despite all previous efforts to change them); and to work out how to *intervene* so as to bring about a reduction or elimination of the difficulties. With the *What Question* we have endeavoured to be precise when describing the problem(s).

The why question

Some parents dwell on the past when they look for the why's and wherefore's of their offspring's difficulties. It is important to maintain a balance between past and present when trying to find reasons or causes for current behaviour. Prolonged and guilt-ridden 'post-mortems' going back to the child's (or teenager's) earliest years where you 'should' have done X or 'should not' have done Y, are not very constructive. You cannot change the past and, in any event, it is only in rare instances that current problems can be traced to specific past experiences with any degree of confidence.

Among all the allegedly harmful factors blamed in the psychological literature for this or that problem (be they adverse parental characteristics, family conflicts etc.) it is possible to identify significant numbers of children who developed without serious problems, despite being subjected to these influences. Certainly, we can point to some general influences that predispose young people to certain areas of difficulty. They set the stage in the broadest of terms, and we call these *indirect* contributory causes.

Human actions — whether simple or elaborate, normal or abnormal — are brought about by many influences rather than a single factor. Whatever the influence of personality traits, attitudes and ideas, shaped over years of learning and development, the child's or adolescent's day-to-day actions are powerfully controlled by present (current) events, such as opportunities and temptations to transgress the accessibility of forbidden substances (e.g. alcohol and drugs), their proximity to bad influences, would be 'tempters'.

Important too and critical because of their *direct* influence on behaviour are the circumstances whereby individuals *learn* to behave in acceptable or unacceptable ways, and the events which precede and follow particular actions making them more or less likely to be *performed*.

Knowledge of these factors allow parents to play a part in shaping events, rather than trailing helplessly after them, and to look optimistically to the present and future, rather than regretfully to the past.

Handout 3: Reducing stress*

1. Keep a running check on stresses in your life. Even the apparently trivial ones, when they accumulate, can become an excessive burden.
2. Positive self-talk helps us to keep the stresses and strains in our life in more reasonable proportion. (We return to this point.)
3. Don't try too hard to solve all your problems and expect to erase them altogether. This is usually a vain hope. Concentrate, instead, on *reducing* stress. Even a small reduction in each stress can lead to a big difference in our ability to cope.
4. Don't try to be all things to all people all the time. Ration yourself by taking a sensible view of your commitments, not forgetting to leave time for yourself and for some privacy.
5. Don't be at the mercy of your environment. You really *can* do quite a lot to re-arrange your world — if the will is there — to fit in with what you would like to happen.

*Adapted with permission from Beech, 1985.

6. Learn to say 'no'. You don't have to say 'yes' to the unreasonable (and even some of the reasonable) tasks that are foisted on you. Examine your needs and priorities in what is being dished out and feel able to refuse sometimes.

7. Cut down on the 'have to'. Question what you tend to take for granted, don't just go ahead and do it because you have always done so.

8. Don't set out to win everything. When it really doesn't matter then take a philosophical, relaxed approach. Many so-called confrontations aren't worth a candle.

9. Delegate. It doesn't always have to be *your* job. Spread the load more.

10. Slow down. Don't set impossible tiring or tedious schedules for yourself. Introduce rest pauses, moments of reflection and pleasure, into your day.

11. Get some balance into your day. Find time for leisure, hobbies, social life, family life, yourself and your work/studies.

12. Curb aggression. Try to plan your way through problems (we will come to problem-solving strategies). You'll end up by feeling better.

13. Learn to relax. Practice makes perfect and Appendix IV provides you (or your youngster) with some relaxation exercises to practise. For emergencies the following rules of thumb should prove helpful in controlling rising anger, tension or panic.

14. Concentrate on staying calm.

In an emergency take a deep breath rapidly but quietly; clasp your hands and press them hard against each other. If sitting brace your leg muscles, pull in your stomach muscles, clench your jaw and hold the muscular tension for 5 seconds. Now exhale slowly, feel the tension go out of you, saying the word 'relax' to yourself.

If you happen to be standing take a deep breath, clasp your hands behind you, pressing them hard together; force your knees back to create leg muscle tension — pull in your stomach muscles and clench your jaws. Maintain the tension for 5 seconds, then let it go slowly, exhaling and saying the word 'relax' to yourself.

Don't exaggerate the muscular tension but make sure you can feel it. Fix your gaze on something so that you appear to be preoccupied or deep in thought for a few moments, so as to conceal the stress you are controlling. Repeat the exercise if necessary.

Handout 4: Discipline and child management

Themes for individual/group discussions of discipline and child/adolescent behaviour management:

Guideline

1. Be clear about your priorities.
2. Foster bonds of respect and affection.

3. Set limits.
4. Be consistent.
5. Attend to 'good' behaviour.
6. Explain discipline by giving reasons.
7. Listen carefully to what your child says.
8. Tell her what she *should* do, not only what she can't do.
9. Use praise and encouragement.
10. Prepare your child for life by developing family routines.
11. Teach the child to discipline herself.
12. Give responsibility.

Accompanying texts (when required):

Herbert, M. (1985) *Caring For Your Children*. Basil Blackwell, Oxford.
Herbert, M. (1987a). *Living With Teenagers*. Basil Blackwell, Oxford.

Handout 5: An explanation of treatment principles for enuresis

A very high level of skill is needed before the bladder can be properly controlled during sleep. Some children find this is a difficult skill to learn, just as some children find it difficult to learn to swim or to ride a bicycle. It is perhaps not surprising that some children do not learn bladder control as infants, or easily lose their ability to control the bladder at night — we should perhaps be more surprised that so many do manage to learn such a complicated skill.

Some children who wet the bed have other problems, while others have few difficulties apart from their bedwetting. In either case it is usually possible to help the child to overcome the bedwetting problem.

It is likely that unpleasant experiences make the learning of bladder control more difficult, and often a child who has already become dry may begin to wet again after some disturbing event. Whether a child has been wet all his life, or has more recently lost control over his bladder, he needs special help in the difficult task of learning bladder control. The child will usually be examined first by a doctor in case there is a physical cause for his bedwetting, although this is rare. A sample of his urine will also be taken for examination.

When a child wets the bed, it seems that his brain is not properly aware of the amount of urine in his bladder, allowing it to empty automatically while he is asleep. The child cannot help this.

A device known as the 'enuresis alarm' has been developed to help children to overcome the problem of bedwetting. Basically, the alarm is made up of a pair of detector mats on the bed, connected to a buzzer next to the child's bed. As soon as the child begins to wet in his sleep, the buzzer sounds. The sound of the buzzer normally has two effects. First, the muscles that have relaxed to allow urine to pass contract once more, stopping the stream of urine that has already started (it may have been noticed that loud noises will often interrupt the stream of urine). Secondly, the sound of the buzzer awakes the child.

The use of the alarm produces these two actions — stopping the stream and waking — whenever the child's bladder begins to empty automatically during sleep. Gradually the child's brain learns to connect these two actions with the feeling of a full bladder. After a time, the brain becomes more aware of the amount of urine in the child's bladder, and itself begins to take the two actions of contracting the muscles and waking the child when the bladder is full. As the brain's control over the bladder becomes stronger, one can see how the actions learned from the alarm are used; the wet patches become smaller as the child's muscles are contracted more quickly, and when the bladder is really full he begins to awaken on his own before passing any urine at all. Eventually, the child is able to sleep without wetting, waking up on his own if he needs to use the toilet at night.

APPENDIX IV

Relaxation Training

A relaxation training script for children*

Hands and arms
Make a fist with your left hand. Squeeze it hard. Feel the tightness in your hand and arm as you squeeze. Now let your hand go and relax. See how much better your hand and arm feel when they are relaxed. Once again, make a fist with your left hand and squeeze hard. Good. Now relax and let your hand go. (Repeat the process for the right hand and arm.)

Arms and shoulders
Stretch you arms out in front of you. Raise them high up over your head. Way back. Feel the pull in your shoulders. Stretch higher. Now just let your arms drop back to your side. Okay, let's stretch again. Stretch your arms out in front of you. Raise them over your head. Pull them back, way back. Pull hard. Now let them drop quickly. Good. Notice how your shoulders feel more relaxed. This time let's have a great big stretch. Try to touch the ceiling. Stretch your arms way out in front of you. Raise them way up high over your head. Push them way, way back. Notice the tension and pull in your arms and shoulders. Hold tight, now. Great. Let them drop very quickly and feel how good it is to be relaxed. It feels good and warm and lazy.

Shoulder and neck
Try to pull your shoulders up to your ears and push your head down into your shoulders. Hold in tight. Okay, now relax and feel the warmth. Again, pull your shoulders up to your ears and push your head down into your shoulders. Do it tightly. Okay, you can relax now. Bring your head out and let your shoulders relax. Notice how much better it feels to be relaxed than to be all tight. One more time now. Push your head down and your shoulders way up to your ears. Hold it. Feel the tenseness in your neck and shoulders. Okay. You can relax now and feel comfortable. You feel good.

*From Ollendick and Cerny, 1982.

252

Jaw

Put your teeth together real hard. Let your neck muscles help you. Now relax. Just let your jaw hang loose. Notice how good it feels just to let your jaw drop. Okay, bite down again hard. That's good. Now relax again. Just let your jaw drop. It feels so good just to let go. Okay, one more time. Bite down. Hard as you can. Harder. Oh, you're really working hard. Good. Now relax. Try to relax your whole body. Let yourself go as loose as you can.

Face and nose

Wrinkle up your nose. Make as many wrinkles in your nose as you can. Scrunch your nose up real hard. Good. Now you can relax your nose. Now wrinkle up your nose again. Wrinkle it up hard. Hold it just as tight as you can. Okay. You can relax your face. Notice that when you scrunch up your nose that your cheeks and your mouth and your forehead all help you and they get tight, too. So when you relax your nose, your whole face relaxes too, and that feels good. Now make lots of wrinkles on your forehead. Hold it tight, now. Okay, you can let go. Now you can just relax. Let your face go smooth. No wrinkles anywhere. Your face feels nice and smooth and relaxed.

Stomach

Now tighten up your stomach muscles real tight. Make your stomach real hard. Don't move. Hold it. You can relax now. Let your stomach go soft. Let it be as relaxed as you can. That feels so much better. Okay, again. Tighten your stomach real hard. Good. You can relax now. Kind of settle down, get comfortable, and relax. Notice the difference between a tight stomach and a relaxed one. That's how we want it to feel. Nice and loose and relaxed. Okay. Once more. Tighten up. Tighten hard. Good. Now you can relax completely. You can feel nice and relaxed.

This time, try to pull your stomach in. Try to squeeze it against your backbone. Try to be as skinny as you can. Now relax. You don't have to be skinny now. Just relax and feel your stomach being warm and loose. Okay, squeeze in your stomach again. Make it touch your backbone. Get it real small and tight. Get as skinny as you can. Hold tight now. You can relax now. Settle back and let your stomach come back out where it belongs. You can really feel good now. You've done fine.

Legs and feet

Push your toes down on the floor real hard. You'll probably need your legs to help you push. Push down, spread your toes apart. Now relax your feet. Let your toes go loose and feel how nice that is. It feels good to be relaxed. Okay. Now push your toes down. Let your leg muscles help you push your feet down. Push your feet. Hard. Okay. Relax your feet, relax your legs, relax your toes. It feels so good to be relaxed. No tenseness anywhere. You feel kind of warm and tingly.

Conclusion
Stay as relaxed as you can. Let your whole body go limp and feel all your muscles relaxed. In a few minutes I will ask you to open your eyes and that will be the end of the session. Today is a good day, and you are ready to go back to class feeling very relaxed. You've worked hard in here and it feels good to work hard. Shake your arms. Now shake your legs. Move your head around. Slowly open your eyes. Very good. You've done a good job. You're going to be a super relaxer.

A relaxation training script for parents

The following exercises are suggested by Beech (1985). The exercises all involve the following general steps:
1. Lightly tense a given group of muscles (as listed below) and hold this tension for a slow count of 5 while holding your breath.
2. During (1) above, focus your attention on the sensations in the part of your body that has been brought under tension.
3. At the end of 5 seconds, breathe out, relax the tense muscles *as much as possible*, focusing your mind on the new relaxed sensations in that part of your body.
4. While letting go (as in (3) above), think of the words 'calm yourself' and 'relax'.
5. Allow your muscles to relax completely and, in your mind, compare the feelings of tension just experienced with the relaxation you now feel.

The particular exercises are as follows:

Arms: Clench the fists and tighten the muscles of both arms, holding your arms stiff and straight out in front of you.
Legs: Raise both legs (or one, if preferred) about 12–18 inches from their resting position, point the toes and stiffen the legs so that thigh and calf muscles are brought under tension. Repeat with other leg if necessary.
General torso: Pull the shoulders back, bringing the shoulder blades together, push the chest forward and out and, at the same time, use appropriate muscles to *pull in* the stomach, making a hollow in that part of your body.
Neck: Press the head firmly against the support of the chair back or mattress.
Face: There are three separate exercises here:
(a) Raise the eyebrows, forcing them up as far as you can as if trying to make them meet your hair line.

(b) Screw up your eyes tightly and, at the same time, wrinkle your nose and compress lips hard.

(c) Clench the jaws, as if chewing hard, while pushing your tongue hard against the roof of your mouth.

Remember, each of the above exercises is immediately preceded by taking a deep breath, creating tension, and holding it for five seconds, then exhaling while letting go the tension and saying the word 'relax' to yourself. In each case try to focus your mind on that part of your body that has been made tense and relaxed, in turn.

Don't try to hurry the programme of exercises, which should take about 20 minutes or so. After each separate exercise allow a minute or so for fuller relaxation to take place and for you to concentrate on the pleasant sensations that relaxation brings.

Most people need about three weeks of daily training to achieve a useful level of skill, but don't stop at that point.

APPENDIX V

Monitoring and Analysing Behaviour and Knowledge

No one method of recording is suitable for all problems or situations. The dimensions (frequency, intensity, etc.) along which you quantify the behaviour depend upon the nature of the problem. There are many ways of monitoring behaviour — from the molar to the molecular — some of which (and the sheer amount of time given to which) are more suitable to clinical research than to the work of a busy clinician.

Remember: What you are particularly interested in is behaviour variability, i.e the correlation or covariance between the rate of a target behaviour as displayed during one observation session, and the rate of the behaviour during previous or subsequent sessions (high correlation = low variability). Variability in observational data may be due to (i) variations in environmental influences (including your intervention), (ii) natural characteristics of the behaviour, or (iii) reactivity to the observation methods being employed. You have to take this variability into account when attributing change to your therapy.

The following list gives an idea of the range of measures available.

Physiological measures
Electroencephalographs are used to measure brain waves (i.e. electrical activity).

A galvanic skin response apparatus is used to measure the electrical resistance of the skin.

Various apparatuses measure blood pressure, heart rate, muscular tension and so on.

Polygraphs are used to record several physiological measures simultaneously.

Behavioural measures
High speed cameras, tape-recorders, videotapes, event-recorders, stop-watches, etc. are used to record, measure, collate and time large segments or sequences of behaviour (molar behaviour).

Diary description
This, the oldest method used in the study of child development, employs the parent's (or therapist's) diary to draw up an account of the sequences and changes in the child's (and parents') behaviours and interactions.

Situational tests
These tests place the client in a situation closely resembling or simulating a 'real-life' situation. An adolescent applicant for a position may be required to play a role as an interviewee or employer. There is particular value in structuring situations in which parent–child interactions of a problematic kind are likely to occur. The use of a one-way screen and a communication system with the parent allows the therapist to see certain confrontations and management sequences for himself. These situational techniques can be utilized for treatment as well as assessment purposes.

Measuring knowledge of behavioural principles as applied to children

O'Dell *et al.* (1979) designed a 50-item multiple-choice instrument which assesses verbal understanding of basic behavioural principles as applied to children. This is a 30–60 minute test which avoids behavioural jargon and presents a series of practical problem situations. The questions were derived from a series of principles enunciated in four parent training manuals. The authors caution that verbal knowledge of behavioural principles may not relate to actual skills with children.

Furtkamp *et al.* (1982) have produced a revision of the test, produced in two 10-item tests. The shortened tests exhibit some of the characteristics of parallel forms (equal means and variances and respectable intercorrelation, $r = 0.87$). The internal consistencies of the tests are 0.73 and 0.76 as compared with the original 0.86. The tests are suitable for research and evaluation.

Here are some examples of the multiple choice questions put to parents:

If you want your child to develop proper study habits, you should:
□ Encourage him to do his homework.

If you want your child to say 'please' and 'thank you' at the table, it is probably most important to:
□ Reprimand him when he forgets to say them.

☐ Help him to see school as pleasant.

☐ Reward him whenever he studies.

☐ Give him good reasons why he will need school.

☐ Explain why good manners are important.

☐ Remember to compliment him when he remembers to say them.

☐ Praise other members of the family when they use these words.

A child often cries over any small matter that bothers her. How should her parents react to best reduce her crying?

A father tells a child she cannot go to the shop with him because she didn't clean her room like she promised. She reacts by shouting, crying and promising she will clean the room when she gets home. What should the father do?

☐ Reward when she reacts without crying.

☐ Use a mild punishment when she cries.

☐ Try to find out what is really troubling the child and deal with that.

☐ Provide her with something interesting so she will stop crying.

☐ Ignore her and go to the shop.

☐ Take her to the shop but make her clean her room when they return.

☐ Calm her down and go help her clean her room together.

☐ Talk to her and find out why she doesn't take responsibility.

Reliability

There is little point in training caregivers to observe (itself a skill with a therapeutic pay-off) if the observations are not reliable. Methods for checking on observer reliability can be studied in Gelfand and Hartmann (1975); the more elaborate methods for calculating reliability will not be feasible for the busy therapist (although it may be a useful occasional team exercise — as a refresher or training task). However, it is a good idea (if you are an experienced observer) to record simultaneously with a parent, a sequence of behavioural events. Reliability for event recording can be calculated as follows:

$$\frac{\text{Number of agreed events}}{\text{Number of agreed events} + \text{number of disagreed events}} \times 100 = \% \text{agreement}$$

A rather more precise assessment of agreement between observers can be obtained by use of an interaction matrix. You assess agreements and disagreements for each sampling interval rather than overall observer agreement on event totals over an observation session (as above). Both observers mark 1 for the first interval observation; 2 for the second; and so on—in the appropriate interactional cells (see Fig. 4). Agreement is defined as both observers marking the same cell during the same sampling interval. Percentage agreement is worked out as above (80% or above is generally considered a satisfactory level).

For measuring agreement between two observers, product moment correlation coefficients can also be calculated, although the most favoured method at present is 'Cohen's Kappa' (Conger, 1985).

The issues of reliability, internal consistency and interobserver agreement are important aspects of behavioural observation but are too complex to deal with in depth in a pragmatic guide like the present one. The question of validity—the degree to which measured differences represent true differences—cannot be taken for granted, simply because you have carried out direct observations of behaviour. As a busy therapist you may not be able to implement all the 'niceties' of quantification and checking used by the researcher, but this is no excuse for not being aware of the problems and pitfalls of attaining reliable and valid data.

Complete sample coverage

To determine whether an observation is valid and has adequately sampled all the items in a behaviour catalogue, a *Coverage Indicator* can be established. Complete sample coverage is defined (Fagen and Goldman, 1977) as the probability of an independent act, observed at a random point in the recording, being of a type already represented within the total sample of behaviour. Hence to measure incompleteness, the number of behaviour types represented once or not at all (N) is found for each recording, and this figure divided by the total number of acts observed (I). This calculation is then taken away from one, to determine the probability of a rare act occurring within an observation.

Thus a useful behaviour catalogue 'coverage indicator' (g) is established with the application of the following formula:

$$g = 1 - \frac{N}{I}$$

Analysis and treatment of observational data

This subsection is drawn (with permission) from Kevin Browne's chapter *Methods and Approaches to the Study of Parenting*, (Browne, 1986). Several types of analysis can be applied to observational data based on a behavioural catalogue of items.

1. Frequency analysis

(a) *Proportional frequency scores* are necessary to take account of varying lengths of observation sample time. To compare every parent, each behaviour item can be calculated as a proportion of the total number of time interval units per episode e.g. 'Scolding Offspring' might total 18 units of a total of 36 observed units, and would receive a score of .50 for that sample.

(b) *Interaction frequencies*: for every parent and offspring the total number of time units spent on interaction can also be calculated as a proportion of the total number of observed time units in the sample. The number of (say) initiating and responsive interactive behaviours should then be determined and calculated as a proportion of the interaction score for the observation time.

Types of interaction may be identified in the following manner. If a general interactive initiative is shown (i.e. behaviour directed toward another person) it can have one of three possible outcomes; firstly, it may result in the respondent reacting with another interactive initiative (MUTUAL INTERACTION). Secondly, it may result in the respondent reacting with a non-interactive behaviour (CAUSAL INTERACTION). Thirdly, it may receive no reaction (FAILED INTERACTION).

For example, the parent is eating and the offspring reaches for the food (Interactive Initiative), the parent may give the offspring some food (Mutual Interaction), stop eating and attend to the offspring (Causal Interaction) or continue to eat (Failed Interaction).

The interaction frequencies may be calculated globally and in relation to specific items of behaviour:

e.g. VOCAL — VISUAL
     TACTILE — VISUAL
     TACTILE — VOCAL

2. Bout analysis

The duration of an 'interaction bout' can be established by summing the number of time-interval units that occur in sequence, containing an on-going interactive behaviour between parent and offspring. The start and finish of such a sequence can be determined by periods of non-interactive behaviour. It is usually best to choose bout criteria which lead to few within and between bout intervals being assigned to the wrong category (Slater and Lester, 1982).

Evidence shows that infants play an important role in initiating, monitoring, differentiating and terminating bouts of interaction. Indeed, few significant exchanges between mammalian caregivers and their young will fail to involve reciprocal stimulation. Furthermore, analysis of mother–infant interaction data by 'Time-series analysis' (Gottman *et al.*, 1982) has demonstrated that the interaction becomes more complex with age by adding faster cycles of reciprocal behaviour as the infant becomes more responsive.

The analysis of interaction can also indicate pathology, for example in humans, abusing mothers have significantly fewer mutual interactions with their infants compared to non-abusing mothers who show less failed interactions (Hyman *et al.*, 1979). In addition abusing mothers show shorter sequences of uninterrupted interaction (interaction bout) with their infants than non-abusers.

3. Sequential analysis

Recent studies on human parent–child relationships (e.g. Martin *et al.*, 1981; Cohn and Tronick, 1982; Dowdney *et al.*, 1984; Phelps and Slater, 1985) can be distinguished by the emphasis on temporal relationships and contingencies of behaviour, in interactive situations. Dyadic interactions are based on the interweaving of the participants' behavioural flow as time passes, and sequential analysis is a powerful method for analysing this behavioural flow.

Slater (1973) states that the simplest type of sequencing of events is a 'deterministic sequence' where events always follow each other in a fixed order, so that the nature of the preceding act defines precisely the nature of that which will follow. But most behavioural sequences are 'probabilistic' rather than 'deterministic' in form, meaning that while the probability of a given act depends on the sequence of those preceding it, it is not possible to predict at a particular point exactly which behaviour will follow. If the sequences are highly ordered they are usually referred to as 'chained responses'. In these cases, the probability of a particular event is markedly altered by the event immediately before it. If the sequences are not so highly ordered, some transitions may be observed between almost every behaviour and every other, and only those transitions which have a high probability of occurrence are then useful.

In the parent–offspring case, sequential analysis can be applied initially by determining sequences within the individual. For example, if a parent shows act A it could be interpreted as an indication that activity B may follow, if the parent shows B after A more frequently than any other behaviour. However, the sequences within the parent may also depend on what the infant does, and activity B might follow A, only if the infant shows activity C. Therefore, the determination of interindividual sequences is important.

Thus sequential analysis can yield three types of data:
(a) Sequential flow of behaviour for parent
(b) Sequential flow of behaviour for infant
(c) Sequential flow in interactive behaviour between parent and child (see Castellan, 1979).

References

Abramson, L. Y., Garber, J. and Seligman, M. E. P. (1980). Learned helplessness in humans: An attributional analysis. *In* J. Garber and M. E. P. Seligman (Eds), *Human Helplessness: Theory and Applications.* Academic Press, New York.

Argyle M. (1986). Social behaviour. *In* M. Herbert (Ed.), *Psychology for Social Workers* (2nd edn). B.P.S./Methuen.

Ayllon, T. and Azrin, N. H. (1968). *The Token Economy: A Motivational System for Therapy and Rehabilitation.* Appleton-Century-Crofts, New York.

Backeland, F. and Lundwall, L. (1975). Dropping out of treatment: a critical review. *Psychological Bulletin*, **82**, 738–783.

Bandura, A. (1969). *Principles of Behaviour Modification.* Holt, Rinehart and Winston, New York.

Bandura, A. (1973). *Aggression: A Social Learning Analysis.* Prentice-Hall, Englewood Cliffs, New Jersey.

Bandura, A. (1977a). *Social Learning Theory.* Prentice-Hall, Englewood Cliffs, New Jersey.

Bandura, A. (1977b). Self-efficacy: Towards a unifying theory of behavioural change? *Psychological Review*, **84**, 191–215.

Barlow, D. H. and Hayes, S. C. (1979). Alternating treatments design. *Journal of Applied Behaviour Analysis*, **12**, 199–210.

Becker, W. (1971). *Parents are Teachers. A Child Management Program.* Research Press, Champaign, Illinois.

Beech, R. (1985). *Staying Together*, John Wiley, Chichester.

Bekoff, M. (1979). Behavioural acts: description, classification, ethogram analysis and measurement. *In* R. B. Cairns (Ed.), *The Analysis of Social Interactions.* Lawrence Erlbaum Associates, New Jersey.

Bell, R. Q. and Harper, L. (1977). *Child Effects on Adults.* Lawrence Erlbaum Associates, New Jersey.

Berry, B. (1986). Unpublished Case Study, University of Leicester/Student Unit.

Berger, M. M. (1978). *Videotape Techniques in Psychiatric Treatment* (2nd edn). Brunner/Mazel, New York.

Bernard, M. E. and Joyce, M. (1984). *Rational Emotive Therapy with Children and Adolescents: Theory, Treatment Strategies, Preventative Methods.* John Wiley, New York.

Birnbrauer, J. S. (1985). When social reinforcement fails. Unpublished manuscript.

Bloom, M. (1975). *The Paradox of Helping.* John Wiley, New York.

Bornstein, M. R., Bellack, A. S. and Hersen, M. (1977). Social skills training for unassertive children. *Journal of Applied Behaviour Analysis*, **10**, 183–195.

Bornstein, P. H. and Quevillon, R. P. (1976). The effects of a self-instructional package on overactive preschool boys. *Journal of Applied Behaviour Analysis*, **9**, 179–188.

Brackbill, Y. (1958). Extinction of the smiling response in infants as a function of reinforcement. *Child Development*, **29**, 115–124.

Brewer, W. F. (1974). There is no convincing evidence for operant or classical conditioning in adult humans. *In* W. B. Wilken and D. S. Palermo (Eds), *Cognition and the Symbolic Processes*. Lawrence Erlbaum Associates, Hillsdale, New Jersey.

Bromley, D. G. (1977). *Personality Description in Ordinary Language*. John Wiley, Chichester.

Browne, K. D. (1986). Methods and approaches to the study of parenting. *In* W. Sluckin and M. Herbert (Eds), *Parental Behaviour*, pp. 343–373. Basil Blackwell, Oxford.

Browne, K. D. and Madaley, R. (1985). Ethogram — an event recorder software package. *Journal of Child Psychology and Psychiatry*, **26**, No. 6, Software Survey Section, p. 111.

Burns, E. and Cavallaro, C. (1982). A computer program to determine inter-observer reliability statistics. *Behavioural Research Methods and Instruments*, **14**(1), 42.

Castellan, N. J. (1979). The analysis of behaviour sequences. *In* R. B. Cairns (Ed.), *The Analysis of Social Interactions*, pp. 81–116. Lawrence Erlbaum Associates, New Jersey.

Christensen, A., Johnson, S. M. and Glasgow, R. E. (1980). Cost effectiveness in behavioural family therapy. *Behaviour Therapy*, **11**, 208–226.

Clarke, R. G. V. (1977). Psychology and crime. *Bulletin of the British Psychological Society*, **30**, 280–283.

Cohn, J. F. and Tronick, E. Z. (1982). Communicate rule and the sequential structure of infant behaviour during normal and depressed interaction. *In* E. Z. Tronick (Ed.), *Social Interchange in Infancy*, pp. 59–79. University Park Press, Baltimore.

Combs, M. L. and Slaby, D. A. (1978). Social skills training with children. *In* B. Lahey and A. Kazdin (Eds), *Advances in Child Clinical Psychology*, Vol. 1. Plenum, New York.

Conger, A. J. (1985). Kappa reliabilities for continuous behaviours and events. *Educational and Psychological Measurement*, **45**, 861–868.

Coopersmith, S. (1967). *The Antecedents of Self-Esteem*. W. H. Freeman, London.

De Risi, W. J. and Butz, G. (1975). *Writing Behavioural Contracts*. Research Press, Champaign, Illinois.

Dowdney, L., Mrazek, D., Quinton, D. and Rutter, M. (1984). Observation of parent–child interactions with two to three year olds. *Journal of Child Psychology and Psychiatry*, **25**, 379–407.

Dowrick, P. W. and Biggs, S. J. (1983). *Using Video: Psychological and Social Applications*. John Wiley, Chichester.

Durlak, J. A. (1979). Comparative effectiveness of paraprofessional and professional helpers. *Psychological Bulletin*, **86**(1), 80–92.

D'Zurilla, T. J. and Goldfried, M. R. (1971). Problem solving and behaviour modification. *Journal of Abnormal Psychology*, **78**, 107–126.

Eelen, P. (1982). Conditioning and attribution. *In* J. Boulougouris, (Ed.), *Learning Theory Approaches to Psychiatry*, pp. 3–18. John Wiley, Chichester.

Egan, G. (1986). *The Skilled Helper*. Brooks/Cole, Monterey.

Ellis, A. and Grieger, R. (Eds) (1977). Handbook of Rational-Emotive Therapy. Springer, New York.

Erwin, E. (1979). *Behaviour Therapy: Scientific, Philosophical and Moral Foundations*, Cambridge University Press, Cambridge.

Estes, W. K. (1971). Reward in human learning: theoretical issues and strategic choice points. *In* R. Glaser (Ed.), *The Nature of Reinforcement*. Academic Press, New York and London.

Eyberg, S. M. and Johnson, S. M. (1974). Multiple assessment of behaviour modification with families. *Journal of Consulting and Clinical Psychology*, **42**, 594–606.

Fagen, R. M. and Goldman, R. N. (1977). Behavioural catalogue analysis methods. *Animal Behaviour*, **25**, 261–274.

Fiedler, D. and Beach, L. R. (1978). On the decision to be assertive. *Journal of Consulting and Clinical Psychology*, **46**, 537–546.

Flanagan, S., Adams, H. E. and Forehand, R. A. (1979). A comparison of four instructional techniques for teaching parents to use time-out. *Behaviour Therapy*, **10**, 94–102.

Fleischmann, M. J. (1979). Using parenting salaries to control attrition and cooperation in therapy. *Behaviour Therapy*, **10**, 111–116.

Flowers, J. H. (1982). Some simple Apple II Software for the collection and analysis of observational data. *Behavioural Research Methods and Instruments*, **14**, 241–249.

Forehand, R. and McMahon, R. J. (1981). *Helping the Noncompliant Child: A Clinician's Guide to Effective Parent Training*. Guildford Press, New York.

Furtkamp, E., Giffort, D. and Schiers, W. (1982). In-class evaluation of behaviour modification knowledge: parallel tests for use in applied settings. *Journal of Behaviour Therapy and Experimental Psychiatry*, **13**, 131–134.

Gelfand, D. M. and Hartmann, D. P. (1975). *Child Behaviour: Analysis and Therapy*. Pergamon Press, Oxford.

Glass, G. V., Willson, V. L. and Gottman, J. M. (1973). *Design and Analysis of Time-Series Experiments*. Laboratory of Educational Research Press, Boulder, Colorado.

Goldfried, M. R. and Davison, G. C. (1976). *Clinical Behaviour Therapy*. Holt, Rinehart and Winston, London.

Gordon, R. L. (1969). *Interviewing: Strategy, Techniques and Tactics*. Dorsey Press, New York.

Gordon, S. B. (1975). Multiple assessment of behaviour modification with families. *Consulting and Clinical Psychology*, **43**, 6, 917.

Gordon, S. B. and Davidson, N. (1981). Behavioral parent training. *In* A. S. Gurman and D. Kniskern (Eds), *Handbook of Family Therapy*. Brunner/Mazell, New York.

Gottman, J. M. and Leiblum, S. R. (1974). *How to Do Psychotherapy and How to Evaluate it: A Manual for Beginners*. Holt, Rinehart and Winston, New York.

Gottman, J. M., McFall, R. M. and Barnett, J. T. (1969). Design and analysis of research using time series. *Psychological Bulletin*, **72**, No. 4, 299–306.

Gottman, J. M., Rose, F. T. and Mettelal, G. (1982). Time series analysis of social interaction data. *In* T. Field and A. Fogel (Eds), *Emotion and Early Interaction*. Lawrence Erlbaum Associates, New Jersey.

Griffiths, A. (1985). Unpublished case study, Psychology Department, University of Leicester.

Guthrie, E. R. (1935). *The Psychology of Learning*. Harper, New York.

Hall, R. V., Axelrod, S., Tyler, L., Grief, E., Janes, F. C. and Robertson, R. (1972). Modification of behaviour problems in the home with a parent as observer and experimenter. *Journal of Applied Behaviour and Analysis*, **5**, 53–64.

Hall, R. V. and Fox, R. G. (1977). Changing-criterion Designs: An alternative applied analysis procedure. *In* B. C. Etzel, J. M. LeBlanc and D. M. Baer (Eds), *New Developments in Behavioural Research Theory, Methods and Applications*. Lawrence Erlbaum Associates, New Jersey.

Hansen, E. W. (1966). The development of maternal and infant behaviour in the rhesus monkey. *Animal Behaviour*, **27**, 104–119.

Hargrove, D. S. and Martin, T. A. (1982). Development of a microcomputer system for verbal interaction analysis. *Behaviour Research Methods and Instruments*, **14**, 236–239.

Harper, V. (1977). Effects of the young on bouts of interaction. *In* R. Bell and V. Harper (Eds), *Child Effects on Adults*. L.E.A., New York.

Hartley, R. (1986). Imagine you're clever. *Journal of Child Psychology and Psychiatry*, **27**, 383–398.

Hatzenbuehler, L. C. and Schroeder, R. (1978). Desensitization procedures in the treatment of childhood disorders. *Psychological Bulletin*, **85** (No. 4), 831–844.

Haynes, S. N. (1978). *Principles of Behavioural Assessment*. Gardner Press, New York.

Haynes, S. N. and Horn, W. F. (1982). Reactivity in behavioural observation: a review. *Behavioural Assessment*, **4**, 369–385.

Haynes, S. N. and Wilson, C. C. (1979). *Behavioral Assessment*. San Francisco, Jossey-Bass.

Herbert, M. (1974). *Emotional Problems of Development in Children*. Academic Press, London.

Herbert, M. (1980). Socialization for problem resistance. *In* P. Feldman and J. Orford (Eds), *The Social Psychology of Psychological Problems*. John Wiley, Chichester.

Herbert, M. (1985). *Caring for your Children: A Practical Guide*. Basil Blackwell, Oxford.

Herbert, M. (1986). Social skills training with children. *In* C. R. Hollin and P. Trower (Eds), *Handbook of Social Skills Training. Vol. 1: Applications Across the Life-Span*. Pergamon Press, Oxford.

Herbert, M. (1987a). *Living with Teenagers*. Basil Blackwell, Oxford.

Herbert, M. (1987b). *Conduct Disorders of Childhood and Adolescence: A Social-Learning Perspective* (revised edn). John Wiley, Chichester.

Herbert, M. and Iwaniec, D. (1977). Children who are hard to love. *New Society*, **40**(759), 111–112.

Herbert, M. and Iwaniec D. (1981). Behavioural psychotherapy in natural home-settings: An empirical study applied to conduct disordered and incontinent children. *Behavioural Psychotherapy*, **9**, 55–76.

Hops, H. and Greenwood, C. R. (1981). Social skills deficits. *In* E. Mash and L. Terdal (Eds), *Behavioural Assessment of Childhood*. Guildford Press, New York.

Horne, A. M. and Patterson, G. R. (1979). Working with parents of aggressive children. *In* R. R. Abidin (Ed.), *Parent Education Handbook*. Charles E. Thomas, Springfield, Illinois.

Horton, L. (1982). Comparison of instructional components in behavioural parent training: a review. *Behavioural Counselling Quarterly*, **2**, 131–147.

Hotchkiss, I. (1976). A case analysis of a hyperactive child. Unpublished paper. Child Treatment Research Unit, University of Leicester.

Hudson, B. L. and Macdonald, G. M. (1986). *Behavioural Social Work*. Macmillan, London.

Hutt, S. J. and Hutt, C. (1970). *Direct Observation and Measurement of Behaviour*. Charles E. Thomas, Springfield, Illinois.

Hyman, C. A., Parr, R. and Browne, K. D. (1979). An observational study of mother–infant interaction in abusive families. *Child Abuse and Neglect*, **3**, 241–246.

Iwaniec, D., Herbert, M. and McNeish, S. (1985). Social work with failure-to-thrive children and their families. Part I: Psychosocial factors. Part II: Behavioural Casework. *British Journal of Social Work*, **15**, Nos 3 (June) and 4 (August) respectively.

Jones, R. T. and Kazdin, A. E. (1975). Programming response maintenance after withdrawing token reinforcement. *Behaviour Therapy*, **6**, 153–164.

Jones, R., Weincott, M. R. and Vaught, R. S. (1975). Visual *vs*. statistical inference in operant research. Paper presented at the A.P.R. Convention. *Symposium on the Use of Statistics in K-1 Research*. Chicago, Illinois, September, 1975.

Kanfer, F. H. and Goldstein, A. P. (Eds) (1986). *Helping People Change* (3rd edn). Pergamon, Oxford.

Kanfer, F. H. and Grimm, L. G. (1980). Managing clinical change: A process model of therapy. *Behaviour Modification*, **4**, 419–444.

Karoly, P. (1977). Behavioural self-management in children: concepts, methods, issues and directions. *In* M. Hersen, R. M. Eisler and P. M. Miller (Eds), *Progress in Behaviour Modification*, pp. 197–213. Academic Press, New York and London.

Kazdin, A. E. (1980). *Behaviour Modification in Applied Settings* (revised edn). The Dorsey Press, Homewood, Illinois.

Kazdin, A. E. (1982). *Single-Case Research Design: Methods for Clinical and Applied Settings*. Oxford University Press, New York.

Kazdin, A. E. and Bootzin, R. R. (1972). The token economy: an evaluation review. *Journal of Applied Behaviour Analysis*, **5**, 343–372.

Kazdin, A. E., Esveldt-Dawson, K. and Matson, J. L. (1982). Changes in children's social skills performance as a function of pre-assessment experiences. *Journal of Clinical Child Psychology*, **11**(3), 243–248.

Kelly, G. A. (1955). *The Psychology of Personal Constructs*. Norton, New York.

Kendall, P. C. (1981). Cognitive-behavioural interventions with children. *In* B. Labey and A. E. Kazdin (Eds), *Advances in Child Clinical Psychology*, Vol. 4, Plenum Press, New York.

Kent, R. N. and Foster, S. L. (1977). Direct observational procedures; methodological issues in naturalistic settings. *In* A. R. Cimenero, K. S. Calhoun and H. E. Adams (Eds), *Handbook of Behavioural Assessment*, pp. 279–328. John Wiley, London.

Kovitz, K. E. (1976). Comparing group and individual methods for training parents in child management techniques. *In* E. J. Mash, L. C. Handy, and L. A. Hammerlynk (Eds), *Behaviour Modification Approaches to Parenting*. Brunner/Mazel, New York.

Kuypers, D. S., Becker, W. C. and O'Leary, K. D. (1968). How to make a token system fail. *Exceptional Children*, **35**, 101–109.

Ladd, G. W. and Mize, J. (1983). A cognitive-social learning model of social skill training. *Psychological Review*, **90**, 127–157.

Lange, A. J. and Jakubowski, P. (1976). *Responsible Assertive Behaviour: Cognitive Behavioural Procedures for Trainers*. Research Press, Champaign, Illinois.

Lehrer, P. M., Gordon, S. and Leiblum, S. (1973). Parent groups in behaviour modification: training or therapy. American Psychological Association convention paper. Montreal, August.

McFall, R. M. (1982). A review of and reformulation of the concept of social skills. *Behavioural Assessment*, **4**, 1–33.

McIntyre, R. W., Jensen, J. and Davis, G. (1968). *Control of Disruptive Behaviour with a Token Economy*. Paper presented to Eastern Psychological Assoc., Philadelphia.

McLaughlin, T. and Malaby, J. (1972). Reducing and Measuring inappropriate verbalizations in a token classroom. *Journal of Applied Behavior Analysis*, **5**, 329–333.

Macfarlane, J. W., Allen, L. and Honzik, M. (1954). *A Developmental Study of the Behaviour Problems of Normal Children*. University of California Press, Berkeley.

Mackintosh, N. J. (1978). Cognitive or associative theories of conditioning: Implications of an analysis of blocking. *In* S. Hulse, H. Fowles and W. K. Honig (Eds), *Cognitive Processes in Animal Behaviour*, pp. 155–175. Lawrence Erlbaum Associates, New Jersey.

MacNamara, J. R. and MacDonough, T. S. (1972). Some methodological considerations in the design and implementation of behaviour therapy research. *Behaviour Therapy*, **3**, 361–378.

Martin, J. A., Maccoby, E., Baron, K. and Jacklin, C. N. (1981). Sequential analysis of mother–child interaction at 18 months. A comparison of macroanalytic techniques. *Developmental psychology*, **17**, 146–157.

Meichelbaum, D. H. (1977). *Cognitive Behaviour Modification: An Integrative Approach*. Plenum, New York.

Melamed, B. G. and Siegel, L. J. (1975). Reduction of anxiety in children facing surgery by modelling. *Journal of Consulting and Clinical Psychology*, **43**, 511–521.

Morgan, R. T. T. (1984). *Behavioural Treatments with Children*. Heinemann Medical Books, London.

Morris, E. K. (1986). The Molloy–Birnbrauer exchange. How many factors do a psychology make? *Behavioural Change*, **3**, 1–8.

Mussen, R. H. (Ed.) (1970). *Carmichael's Manual of Child Psychology*. John Wiley, Chichester.

Novaco, R. W. (1975). *Anger Control: The Development and Evaluation of an Experimental Treatment*. D. C. Heath & Co., Lexington Books, Lexington, Mass.

O'Dell, S. L., Flynn, J. M. and Belolo, L. A. (1977). A comparison of parent training techniques in child behaviour modification. *Journal of Behaviour Therapy and Experimental Psychiatry*, **8**, 261–268.

O'Dell, S. L., Tarter-Benlolo, L. and Flynn, J. M. (1979). An instrument to measure knowledge of behavioural principles as applied to children. *Journal of Behaviour Therapy and Experimental Psychiatry*, **10**, 29–34.

Oden, S. and Asher, S. R. (1977). Coaching children in social skills for friendship making. *Child Development*, **48**, 495–506.

Ollendick, T. H. (1979). Fear reduction techniques with children. *In* M. Hersen, R. M. Eisler and P. M. Miller (Eds), *Progress in Behaviour Modification*, Vol. 8. Academic Press, New York.

Ollendick, T. H. and Cerny, J. A. (1982). *Clinical Behaviour Therapy With Children*. Plenum, New York.

Parsons, B. V. and Alexander, J. F. (1973). Short-term family intervention: A therapy outcome study. *Journal of Consulting and Clinical Psychology*, **41**, 195–201.

Patterson, G. R. (1975). *A Social Learning Approach to Family Intervention. Volume 1 Families with Aggressive Children*. Castalia, Eugene, Oregon.

Patterson, G. R. (1982). *Coercive Family Process*. Castalia, Eugene, Oregon.

Pavlov, I. P. (1927). *Conditioned Reflexes* (translated G. V. Anrep). Clarendon Press, Oxford.

Phelps, R. E. and Slater, M. A. (1985). Sequential interactions that discriminate high and low problem single mother–son dyads. *Journal of Consulting and Clinical Psychology*, **53**, 684–692.

Phillips, L. W. (1981). Roots and branches of behavioural and cognitive practice. *Journal of Behaviour Therapy and Experimental Psychiatry*, **12**(1), 5–17.

Ray, R. S., Shaw, D. A. and Cobb, J. A. (1970). The workbox: an innovation in teaching attentional behavior. *The School Counselor*, **18**, 15–35.

Rinn, R. C., Vernon, J. C. and Wise, M. J. (1975). Training parents of behaviourally disordered children in groups. *Behaviour Therapy*, **6**, 378–387.

Risley, T. R. and Wolf, M. M. (1967). Strategies for analysing change over time. *In* J. Nesselroade and H. Reese (Eds), *Life-Span Developmental Psychology Methodological Issues*. Academic Press, New York.

Rose, S. D. (1972). *Training Children in Groups: A Behavioral Approach*. Jossey-Bass, San Francisco.

Ross, D., Ross, S. and Evans, T. A. (1971). The modification of extreme social withdrawal by modification with guided practice. *Journal of Behaviour Therapy and Experimental Psychiatry*, **2**, 273–279.

Rutter, M., Tizard, J. and Whitmore, K. (Eds) (1970). *Education, Health and Behaviour*. Longmans, Green, London.

Sadler, O. W. and Seyden, T. (1976). Groups for Parents: A Guide for Teaching Self-Management to Parents. Special Monograph Supplement: *Journal of Community Psychology*. Clinical Psychology Publishing Co. Inc., 4 Conant Square, Brandon, VT 05733.

Sandler, J. (1980). Aversion methods. *In* F. H. Kanfer and A. P. Goldstein (Eds). *Helping People Change* (2nd edn). pp. 294–333. Pergamon, Oxford.

Schaffer, R. (1977). *Mothering*. Penguin Books, Harmondsworth.

Schneider, M. and Robin, A. (1976). The turtle technique: a method for the self-control of impulsive behaviour. *In* J. D. Krumboltz and C. E. Thoreson (Eds), *Counselling Methods*, pp. 157–163. Holt, New York.

Seligman, M. E. P. (1975). *Helplessness*. Freeman, San Francisco.

Senn, M. J. E. (1959). Conduct Disorders. *In* W. E. Nelson (Ed.) *Textbook of Pediatrics*. W. B. Saunders, Philadelphia.

Shepherd, M., Oppenheim, B. and Mitchell, S. (1971). *Childhood Behaviour and Mental Health*. University of London Press, London.

Sidman, M. (1960). *Tactics of Scientific Research: Evaluating Experimental Data in Psychology*. Basic Books, New York.

Sidman, M. and Stoddard, L. T. (1967). The effectiveness of fading in programming a simultaneous form discrimination for retarded children. *Journal of Experimental Analysis of Behaviour*, **10**, 3–15.

Slater, P. J. (1973). Describing sequences of behaviour. *In* P. P. G. Bateson and P. H. Klopper (Eds), *Perspectives in Ethology*. Plenum Press, New York.

Slater, P. J. (1978). Data collection. *In* P. W. Colgan (ed.) *Quantitative Ethiology.* John Wiley, New York.

Slater, P. J. and Lester, N. P. (1982). Minimising errors in splitting behaviour into bouts. *Behaviour*, **79**, 153–161.

Sluckin, W., Herbert, M. and Sluckin, A. (1983). *Maternal Bonding.* Basil Blackwell, Oxford.

Spivack, G., Platt, J. J. and Shure, M. B. (1976). *The Problem-Solving Approach to Adjustment.* Jossey-Bass, San Francisco.

Stolz, S. B., Wienckowski, L. A. and Brown, B. S. (1975). Behaviour modification: A perspective on critical issues. *American Psychologist*, **30**, 1027–1048.

Sutton, C. (1987). Behavioural parent training: A comparison of strategies for teaching parents to manage their difficult young children. Unpublished PhD thesis, University of Leicester.

Tarler-Benlolo, L. and Flynn, J. M. (1979). An instrument to measure knowledge of behavioural principles as applied to children. *Journal of Behaviour Therapy and Experimental Psychiatry*, **10**, 29–34.

Thomas, A., Chess, S. and Birch, H. G. (1968). *Temperament and Behaviour Disorders in Children.* University of London Press, London.

Tyler, B. (1979). Time sampling: a matter of convention. *Animal Behaviour*, **27** 801–810.

Vila, J. and Beech, H. R. (1978). Vulnerability and defensive reactions in relation to the human menstrual cycle. *British Journal of Social and Clinical Psychology*, **17**, 93–100.

Walker, H. M. and Buckley, N. K. (1974). *Token Reinforcement Techniques.* Engelmann-Becker, Oregon.

Walter, H. I. and Gilmore, S. K. (1973). Placebo versus social learning effects in parent training procedures designed to alter the behaviour of aggressive boys. *Behaviour Therapy*, **4**, 361–377.

Ward, M. H. and Baker, B. L. (1968). Reinforcement therapy in the classroom. *Journal of Applied Behaviour Analysis*, **1**, 323–328.

Watson, J. B. and Rayner, R. (1920). Conditioned emotional reactions. *Journal of Experimental Psychology*, **3**, 1–14.

Watson, J. E., Singh, N. and Winton, A. S. W. (1985). Comparing interventions using the alternating treatments design. *Behaviour Change*, **2**, 13–20.

Weathers, L. R. and Liberman, R. P. (1978). Modification of family behaviour. *in* D. Marholin (Ed.), *Child Behaviour Therapy.* Gardner Press, New York.

Webster-Stratton, C. (1981). Modification of mother's behaviors and attitudes through a videotape modeling group discussion program. *Behavior Therapy*, **12**, 634–642.

Webster-Stratton, C. (1981). Videotape modeling: A method of parent education. *Journal of Clinical Child Psychology*, **10**, 93–98.

White, R. W. (1959). Motivation Reconsidered—The Concept of Competence. *Psychological Review*, **66**, 297–333.

Wildman, R. W., II, and Wildman, R. W. (1975). The generalization of behaviour modification procedures: a review—with special emphasis on classroom applications. *Psychology in the Schools*, **12**, 432–448.

Yelloly, M. (1972). The Concept of Insight. *In* D. Jehu (Ed.). *Behaviour Modification in Social Work.* John Wiley, Chichester.

Zeilberger, J., Sampen, S. and Sloane, H. (1968). Modification of a child's problem behaviours in the home with the mother as therapist. *Journal of Applied Behaviour Analysis*, **1**, 47–53.

Further Reading

Assessment and Measurement

Barlow, D. H. and Hersen, M. (1984). *Single Case Experimental Design Strategies for Studying Behaviour Change* (2nd edn). Pergamon Press, New York.

Boyle, M. H. and Jones, S. C. (1985). Selecting measures of emotional and behavioural disorders of childhood for use in general populations. *Journal of Child Psychology and Psychiatry*, **26**, 137–159.

O'Dell, S. L., Benlolo, L. T. and Flynn, J. M. (1979). An instrument to measure knowledge of behavioural principles as applied to children. *Journal of Behaviour Therapy and Experimental Psychiatry*, **10**, 29–34.

Parsonson, B. and Baer, D. (1978). The analysis and presentation of graphic data. *In* T. R. Kratochwill (Ed.), *Single Subject Research*. Academic Press, New York.

Thorley, G. and Yule, W. (1982). A role-play test of parent–child interaction. *Behavioural Psychotherapy*, **10**, 146–161.

Wilson, F. and Evans, I. (1983). The reliability of target-behaviour selection in behavioural assessment. *Behavioural Assessment*, **5**, 15–32.

Failure and Resistance

Foa, E. B. and Emmelkamp, D. M. G. (1983). *Failures in Behaviour Therapy*. John Wiley, Chichester.

Strean, H. S. (1985). *Resolving Resistances in Psychotherapy*. John Wiley, Chichester.

Interpersonal Skills and Counselling

Nelson-Jones, R. (1986). *Human Relationship Skills: Training and Self-Help*. Holt, Rinehart and Winston, London.

Egan, G. (1986). *The Skilled Helper: A Systematic Approach to Effective Helping*. Brooks/Cole, Monterey, California.

Interview Schedules/Methods

Gross, A. M. (1984). Behavioural interviewing. *In* T. H. Ollendick and M. Hersen (Eds), *Child Behavioural Assessment: Principles and Procedures*. Pergamon, New York.

Murphy, G. C., Hudson, A. M., King, N. J. and Remenyi, A. (1985). An interview schedule for use in the behavioural assessment of children's problems. *Behaviour Change*, **2**, 6–12.

Maintenance

Patterson, G. R. and Fleishman, M. J. (1979). Maintenance of treatment effects: some consideration concerning family systems and follow-up data. *Behaviour Therapy*, **10**, 168–185.

Manuals/Bibliotherapy

Dardig, J. C. and Heward, W. L. (1976). *Sign Here: A Contracting Book for Children and Their Parents*. Behaviordelia, Kalamazoo, Michigan.
Greene, B. F., Clark, H. B. and Risley, T. R. (1977). *Shopping With Children: Advice for Parents*. Academic Therapy, San Rafael, California.
Herbert, M. (1985). *Caring For Your Children: A Practical Guide*. Basil Blackwell, Oxford.
Herbert, M. (1987). *Living With Teenagers*. Basil Blackwell, Oxford.
Krumboltz, J. D., and Krumboltz, H. B. (1972). *Changing Children's Behaviour*. Prentice-Hall, New York.
Miller, W. (1973). *Systematic Parent Training*. Research Press, Champaign, Illinois.
Patterson, G. R. (1977). *Families: Application of Social Learning to Family Life*. Research Press, Champaign, Illinois.
Patterson, G. R. and Gullion, M. E. (1968). *Living With Children: New Methods for Parents and Teachers*. Research Press, Champaign, Illinois.
Sloane, H. N. (1976). *Behaviour Guide Series*; e.g., *Stop that fighting*. Telesis, Fountain Valley, California.
Wagonseller, B. R., Burnett, M., Salzberg, B. and Burnett, J. (1977). *The Art of Parenting*. Research Press, Champaign, Illinois.

Observation

Reid, J. (1981). *Observation in Home Settings*. Castalia, Eugene, Oregon.
Wood, J. R. A. (1986). Observation in training parents of handicapped children: A review. *Behavioural Psychotherapy*, **14**, 99–114.

Parental Behaviour

Sluckin, W. and Herbert, M. (Eds) (1986). *Parental Behaviour*. Basil Blackwell, Oxford.

Research/Treatment/Evaluation Designs
Kazdin, A. E. (1982). *Single-case Research Designs: Methods for Clinical and Applied Settings*. Oxford University Press, New York.

Index

ABC analysis (*see also* Problem behaviour), 17, 19–20, 31, 33, 50–54, 58, 78, 126, 244–247
    example, 53–54
    identification of, 31, 50–53
Abnormality of behaviour, 1, 2, 16
Achievement, 70, 141, 158
Age/sex appropriate-behaviour, 21
Aggression, 125, 172, 174, 201, 208
Antecedent stimulus control, 77, 176, 189, 224
Anxiety (*see also* Fear), 57, 64, 84, 148, 209, 216
Assertion training, 174–176
Assessment (*see also* ABC analysis, Diagnosis, Screening), 5, 9, 11–16, 26, 126
    of contingencies, 50–53, 126
    of extent of problem, 29
    initial steps in, 8–24
    of organismic variables, 61–65
Assets, 14
Attribution, 115, 116, 157–158
Autonomic response patterns, 64–66
Attention, 154, 179
Aversive (interfering) conditions, 176
Avoidance training, 159, 206

Balance sheets, 14, 67, 89, 90
Baseline (*see also* Assessment), 10, 25–26, 31
    definition of, 25, 26, 102
    in evaluation, 102, 103, 104
    length of, 102
Bedtime problems, 138
Behaviour (*see also* Problem behaviour)
    analysis of observational data, 259–261
    contingencies of, 3, 50–53
    contrast effects, 201

deficiencies, 4, 15, 42, 79, 92, 93, 167, 179
definition of, 2
developmental origin of, 57, 67–70, 79, 115, 153, 172, 243–247
excesses of, 15, 92, 93, 184
intensity of, 42
measurement of, 37–43, 103, 256–259
Behaviour modification (*see also* Behavioural casework, Psychotherapy), 4–7, 83
    criticisms made of, 23–24, 73–75
    definition of, 3, 83
Behaviour rehearsal, 20, 169–170
Bibliotherapy, 120, 123
Bout analysis, 260
Brain damage as a factor in problem behaviour, 21–22
    consequences of, 22
    effect on the nervous system, 22
Brainstorming, 218

Case reports, compilation of, 71
Case studies, 125–150
    Andrew, 76
    Jimmy and Wayne, 144–150
    John, 53–54
    Lorna, 18
    Ted, 124–141
    Tessa, 141–144
Causes, 75–79, 84
Centre for behavioural work with families (*see* CTRU)
Chaining, 178
Change, indices of in evaluation, 98–104, 108
    practical criteria, 108–109
    statistical analysis, 108

Child development, 57
  importance in making assessment, 67, 70
  'normal' behavioural patterns, 68–69
Classical conditioning (*see also* Learning theory), 2, 5, 84
Clinical formulation, 130, 135
  10 factors, 242
Coding system of recording, 37, 38
Coercion process, 20, 131, 155
Cognitive development, theories of, 60, 62
Cognitive learning (*see also* Learning), 2, 61, 85–86
  self-variables, 86–88
Cognitive restructuring, 116, 212–215
Congenital factors in problem behaviour, 21
Conditioned responses (*see also* Learning), 84
Conditioned stimulus (*see also* Learning, Stimulus control), 176
Conduct disorder (example), 125–141
Conflict resolution, 217
Consultation model, 120
Contingencies (rules) in treatment (*see also* Contracts), 153, 184
  contingency management, 159, 160–161
  identification, 50–53, 74
Contracts, 123, 229–232, 230, 231
Control group, 109
Cost-benefit analysis, 67, 89
Counselling, 89
Counter-conditioning, 200, 202
Counting chart, as system of recording, 30, 31, 32
Coverage indicator, 259
Covert self-control, 223–228
CTRU (Child Treatment Research Unit) (*see also* Case studies)
  parent training at, 117, 136–144, 147–150
Cueing, 177–183
Cue strengthening, 224

Data collection, 34–37, 256–259
Dentistry, fear of, 208
Depression (learned helplessness), 61, 64, 125, 147
Deprivation, 156

Desensitization, 84, 202, 203
  active participation, 203–204
  covert, 206–207
  symbolic, 141
  systematic–passive association, 204, 204–205
Developmental factors, 67
Diagnosis of problem behaviour, 65–67, 70, 209
  criteria in, 9, 65–67
  ethics in, 65, 89
Diary record, 28–29, 55, 257
Differential reinforcement, 165–167
  of other behaviours (DRO), 201
Direct observation techniques (*see also* Objective observation), 8, 31, 33, 34–36
  automation of, 36–37
Discipline, 249–250
Disruptive behaviour, 187, 198, 201
Distal antecedents, 9, 56
Distal outcomes, 9, 66
DRO, 201
Duration of problem behaviour (*see also* Problem behaviour), 29, 42, 49–50

Eating problems, 144, 224
Ego (self), concept of, 118
Emotion (dysfunctional), 202–206
Empathy, in self-control, 173, 228
Enuresis (bed-wetting), treatment format for, 250–251
Errorless learning, 180
Escape training, 159
Ethics
  of behavioural modification, 6, 23–24, 89
  in diagnosis, 65, 89
  in evaluation, 23
Evaluation
  designs, 104–108
  of treatment, 98, 103–104, 108–109
  of treatment programme, 98–109
Event sampling, 36
Exchange theory, 67
Expectancy, 62, 157, 158
Experimental designs, 104–109
Exposure training, 202, 203
Extinction, 184–189
  and reinforcement, 184, 185, 186, 188

Extinction *(Continued)*
  and satiation, 189
  and time-out, 188, 192
  as treatment method, 95, 184, 186

Fading procedures, 113–115, 179, 180
Failure of programmes, 13, 111, 112
'Failure to thrive', treatment of, 144–150
Family, involvement in behavioural treatment, 3, 4, 5, 12, 116
Fear (*see also* Anxiety), 202, 203, 207
  hierarchy, 202–204
  reduction by modelling, 169, 202, 207, 208, 210, 220
Feedback in treatment, 98, 170, 174, 197
  in school, 177, 182, 198
FINDS (parameters of problem behaviour), 29–33, 30, 126
  duration, 29
  frequency, 29
  intensity, 29
  number, 29
  sense (meaning), 29
Fixed role therapy, 211–212
Flooding (implosion), 206
Frequency of problem behaviour, 29, 33, 37–41, 260
Friendships, 172–174
Frustration, 225
Functional analysis, 18, 73, 173

Goal-setting, 16, 88, 172
Graphic rating scale, 43, 44
Graphs (*see also* Recording methods), 40, 41, 101, 106, 107, 108
Group processes, 120
  parent groups, 121
Guide to interviewing, 239
Guided participation, 203

Handicap (various), 178–180
Handouts, for parents, 243–251
Headbanging, 191
Hyperactivity, 63, 201, 226–227
Hypotheses, formulation of, 28, 71, 75

Ignoring, 154, 184–189
Implosion (flooding), 206
Insight, use of in behaviour modification, 116–117

Instantaneous sampling method, 35
Instrumental conditioning (operant conditioning), 2, 84
  in learning theory, 84
Intensity of problem behaviour, 29, 42–43
Interaction chart, 40, 258
Interval method, 34–35
Intervention, 83
Interview, 8, 11–12, 28, 239
  schedule, 239–241

Knowledge of behaviour principles, 257

Labelling, 13, 73
Learning, 70, 92, 209
  basic tasks, 4–5
  as diagnostic criterion, 70
  principles of, 152, 244–247, 257
Learning disability, 64, 70, 72
Little turtle technique, 224
Locus of control (external vs internal), 157, 196, 215

Manuals, 120
Meaning of problem behaviour, 60–61
Modelling as treatment method, 84–85, 117, 123, 167–169, 168, 203, 207–209, 210
Motivation, 119
Multiple baseline design, 107

Negative reinforcement, 159, 246
Normality of behaviour, 1, 2, 15, 16, 46
Norms, 1, 16, 46, 68–69, 153
  in diagnosis formation, 68
Number of problem behaviours, 29, 44
Numerical rating scales, 43

Objective observation (*see also* Recording methods), 31, 33, 256–261
  behaviour variability and, 37
  reactive effects of, 49
  reliability, 48–49, 258
Objectives in treatment (*see also* Baseline, Treatment goals)
  formulation of, 16, 88–91, 172
Observation reactivity, 28, 49, 256
Observational learning, 5, 84–85
Observer reliability, 258–259

Operant conditioning (Instrumental conditioning), 2, 5, 84
in learning theory, 84
Organismic variables, 9, 20–22, 61, 79
cognitive factors, 61–62
congenital factors, 21
physical factors, 64
temperament, 62–63
Outcome, 15, 52, 94, 118
Overcorrection, 199–200
Overlearning, 114

Parent training, 120–125
groups, 117, 120, 121
videotape modelling programmes, 233–234
Parental factors, 3, 4, 5
self-help parents' group, 141
Perceived self-efficacy, 87, 117–118
Personal concept tests, 44
Perspective-taking, 211
Physiological measures, 256
Phobia, treatment of, 141–144
Planned ignoring, 184–189
Positive reinforcement (see also Reinforcers), 96, 152–158, 245
definition, 93, 152
self-reinforcement, 75, 77, 159
time-out, 97
Premack's principle, 59
Problem behaviour
age-related behaviours, 46, 47
assessment of, 12–13, 15, 25–43, 50–53
checklist, 45
formulation/definition of, 1, 2, 12–13, 70–81
levels of influence, 74, 75, 76
parameters of, 22–23
priorities of, 22
transitory nature of, 50, 70
Problem priorities, 22–23
Problem profile (see also Case studies), 17, 18
Problem severity, 29, 42
Problem-solving skills, 209, 216–221, 225
Procedures, application of, 91, 123, 235–238
Prompting, 179
Prosocial behaviour, 14
Punishment, 190–192

Rating methods, 43–44
trait rating, 36
Rational Emotive Therapy, 215
Rationale for therapy, 24, 83–84
Recording methods (see also Record-keeping), 31–37, 54
Record-keeping, 8, 31, 32, 33, 38, 38–39, 40, 41, 42–43, 43, 51, 54, 103
Reinforcement
contingent, 74–75
differential, 165–167, 182, 201
history, 56, 157, 158
of incompatible behaviour (RIB), 200–201
intermittent, 113, 156
and learning theory, 57, 74–75, 77
motivational function, 60, 61
and negative reinforcement, 159
and positive reinforcement, 152
and response cost, 197, 198
schedules, 113, 156–157
and self-reinforcement, 75, 77, 159
timing of, 57, 155–156
Reinforcers of behaviour, 56, 96, 152, 164
charts, 142
definition, 56–57
examples, 58
identification of, 56–60
and positive reinforcement, 96, 152
timing, 155
Relaxation, 149, 202, 205, 225, 252–255
training scripts, 252–255
Reliability, 48, 258
Resources in treatment, 94–95
Response-cost, 197–199
and time-out, 198
Reversal design, 105
Rewards (see Reinforcers)
Role play, 123, 170, 209–210
in behavioural rehearsal, 170
in social skills training, 173
Role reversal, 209
Rules, 122, 153, 182, 222

Satiation, 189
Scan sampling method, 35
Screening (see also Assessment), 7, 8–24, 10
Self-confrontation, 232–234

Self-control training, 86, 115, 212, 222–228
  antecedent conditions control, 224–226
  and outcome conditions, 228
  and relaxation techniques, 225
Self-direction, 115
Self-efficacy expectations, 117, 122, 140, 203–204, 215, 222
Self-esteem, 70, 77, 118
Self-instruction, 226
Self-injurious behaviour, 187, 191, 201
Self-management, 198, 222–228
Self-monitoring, 223–224
Self-reinforcement, 75, 77, 115, 159
Self-talk, 212, 227
Sense (meaning) of problem behaviour, 29
Sensitization (covert), 206
Sequential analysis, 261
Shaping as treatment method, 166–167
Situation specificity, 27–29
Skills training (see also Behaviour rehearsal), 169–176
  assertion training, 174–176
  social skills, 171–175, 237–238
Social learning theory, 1–7
Sociometry, 36, 171
Social isolation, 173
Socialization, 115
Spontaneous remission, 50, 202
Stimulus change, 189–190
Stimulus control, 54, 56, 176–183, 224
  classroom use, 78, 177–178, 182–183
  cueing and, 177–178, 181
  defective/faulty, 77, 78, 181
  definition, 176
  fading, 179, 180
  generalization, 178
  inappropriate, 77
  prompting, 178–179
  shaping, 188
Stress, 248–249
  inoculation, 216
  management, 148, 215, 219, 225, 248
Surgery, fear reduction, 207
Systematic desensitization, 203

Tally chart, 39
Target behaviours (see Problem behaviour), 17

Teaching, 116, 120, 173
Temperament, as variable of behaviour, 62–63, 133
Termination of treatment, 110–115
  fading procedures in, 113–115
  failure, 111, 112
Therapist, 119
  personality of, 119–120
Thought stopping, 215–216
'Three-term contingency' (see ABC analysis)
Time budgets, 34
Time-out, 95, 97, 192–196, 199
  in the classroom, 195–196
  method of, 192, 194–195
  timing of, 194
Time sampling, 34–35, 39
Token economies, 162–165, 163, 164, 165
  group setting, 164–165
  methods of increasing behaviour, 151
  methods of reducing behaviour, 183
  planning, 94
Trait rating, 36
Treatment
  initiation, 109–110
  procedures, selection of, 91–93
  self-direction, 115
  side-effects, 103
  systematic variation in design, 104–109
Treatment design
  AB and ABC, 104–105
  control group, 109
  multiple-baseline, 107–109
  reversal, 105–107
Treatment goals, 15–16, 24, 88, 89, 90–91
  social skills, 172–173
Treatment, methods of, 91–110, 151–234
  methods of increasing behaviour, 151, 152–176
  methods of producing stimulus control, 176–183
  methods of reducing behaviour, 183, 183–221
  planning, 94–95
Triadic model, 3, 4
Typical day, 28

Verbal/non-verbal communication, 171, 172
Video-feedback, 170, 233